Beyond Alterity

Postcolonialism across the Disciplines 29

Postcolonialism across the Disciplines

Series Editors
Graham Huggan, University of Leeds
Andrew Thompson, University of Exeter

Postcolonialism across the Disciplines showcases alternative directions for postcolonial studies. It is in part an attempt to counteract the dominance in colonial and postcolonial studies of one particular discipline – English literary/cultural studies – and to make the case for a combination of disciplinary knowledges as the basis for contemporary postcolonial critique. Edited by leading scholars, the series aims to be a seminal contribution to the field, spanning the traditional range of disciplines represented in postcolonial studies but also those less acknowledged. It will also embrace new critical paradigms and examine the relationship between the transnational/cultural, the global and the postcolonial.

Beyond Alterity

Contemporary Indian Fiction
and the Neoliberal Script

Shakti Jaising

Liverpool University Press

First published 2023 by
Liverpool University Press
4 Cambridge Street
Liverpool L69 7ZU

Copyright © 2023 Shakti Jaising

Shakti Jaising has asserted the right to be identified as the author of this book in accordance with the Copyright, Design and Patents Act 1988.

All rights reserved. No part of this book may be reproduced, stored in a retrieval system, or transmitted, in any form or by any means, electronic, mechanical, photocopying, recording, or otherwise, without the prior written permission of the publisher.

British Library Cataloguing-in-Publication data
A British Library CIP record is available

ISBN 978-1-83764-512-1 cased

Typeset in Amerigo by Carnegie Book Production, Lancaster
Printed and bound by CPI Group (UK) Ltd, Croydon CR0 4YY

Contents

Preface vii

Acknowledgments ix

Introduction 1

1 Neoliberal Subjectivity and the Alterity Paradigm 19

2 The Neoliberal Script 39

3 The Maturing Entrepreneur of Popular Indian Fiction 67

4 Undercity Fiction and the Crisis of Urbanization 89

5 Fixity Amid Flux: Literary Fiction and Rural Dispossession 109

6 Contesting the Script 133

Notes 157

Index 189

Preface

I came of age in India during the 1990s, in the midst of massive cultural transformation triggered by the turn to neoliberal capitalism. Like many people living through the early years of this transformation, I understood its meaning primarily through some of the more readily apparent markers of change. In Bombay, where I grew up, a landmark bookstore for inexpensive, Soviet-published books was replaced overnight (or so it seemed at the time) by a showroom for new cars and luxury vehicles. In the college I attended, the subject "History of Economic Thought" was scrapped from the curriculum, leaving us to instead take "Maths-Stats" and Econometrics, which were deemed more critical for our careers. On television, there were now multiple, privately owned satellite channels, beyond the one state-run channel, and 24-hour TV was a reality for the first time. In the newspapers, the word "globalization" was suddenly everywhere. And as leaders in the West spoke of the dawn of a "new world order" following the collapse of the Soviet Union, leaders in India were declaring the nation's second independence and its emergence as a world power. This was a new India, we were told: we were to liberalize trade, deregulate capital, and privatize public services, just like in the West, and the benefits were bound to trickle down to the poorest of the poor.

Looking back, that was when I was personally inculcated into what I describe in this book as a neoliberal script—a sequence of ideas that has attained the status of dogma and that frames liberalized capital, as opposed to state-led redistribution, as the ideal means of engendering social progress. In India this script featured prominently in the speeches of politicians and big businessmen, who associated the process of what came to be referred to as "economic liberalization" with not just private gain but also freedom for the nation from poverty and underdevelopment. The rapidly expanding range of TV channels and business publications arose as a reliable platform for disseminating their message. In time, literature and film, too, were animating the neoliberal script in undeniable ways. Repeated enactments of this script have given the ideology of neoliberalism a solidity and stickiness in the collective imagination, which in turn has helped to justify further economic liberalization, even in the face of worsening inequality and growing precarity over the last three decades.

This book charts a cultural history of post-liberalization India by attending in particular to the role of imaginative literature and film in registering and processing the significant shifts in consciousness that have occurred during this time. While the book focuses on the Indian case, my hope is that it will serve to bring clarity to a universal phenomenon. For, as I point out, India and its cultural production are far from unique and in fact offer critical insight into the material and ideological impacts of contemporary capitalism across the North–South divide.

Acknowledgments

The ideas in this book have been germinating for several years and I have many to thank for their input. As a graduate student at Rutgers I was lucky to meet Josie Saldaña, who has remained a wonderful advisor and friend. I am indebted to her for her openness to my ideas, for her invaluable feedback, and for inspiring me with her brave and original scholarship. I am also grateful to John McClure for modeling energetic and eloquent engagement with politics, literature, and the world at large. It was in John's class on the cultures of globalization that I did some of my earliest thinking on the material in this book. Sonali Perera's and Brent Edwards's instruction and mentorship have also been vital to my process, and I thank them sincerely.

Many friendships have fed my thinking. For rich and generative conversations I thank Jen Sinton, Geeta Colaco, Priya Sen, Sonali Gulati, Huixia Lu, Malati Rao, Madhvi Zutshi, Nellickel Jacob, Sonali Barua, Anantha Sudhakar, Liz Reich, Carrie Malcom, Nimanthi Rajasingham, Candice Amich, Jill Campaiola, Johanna Rossi-Wagner, Jinee Lokaneeta, Sangay Mishra, and Audrey Evrard. In recent years, Kyle Goen, Lisa Hunt, Lourdes Follins, and Sherry Wolf have provided much-needed camaraderie and community.

Aruna Krishnamurthy, Bernadine Mellis, Nivedita Majumdar, Shivaani Selvaraj, and Sujatha Subramanian have listened to me talk at length about my ideas, and have done so with much patience and generosity. Nivedita's careful reading and incisive comments led me to recognize and clarify the book's underlying stakes. Bernadine's excellent editing skills, astute insights, and empathic attention helped me navigate some of the hardest parts of the writing process. Candice Amich and Liz Reich read and weighed in thoughtfully on portions of the text. And Andrea Lawlor, Auritro Majumder, Jordy Rosenberg, and Trevor Perri intervened at key moments with much-needed feedback and advice.

At Drew University, I am grateful to my colleagues in the English department for their fellowship, to my students for making me see the world with fresh

Acknowledgments

eyes, and to the Dean's office for a sabbatical that allowed me to do much of the research and writing for this book.

I am also grateful to the organizers and panelists of the various ACLA seminars where I have shared work in recent years. Special thanks to Tim Brennan for taking the time to offer rich and incredibly useful feedback at a critical point in the project's development.

Parts of the book have benefitted from reworking. A portion of chapter 5 was previously published as "Fixity Amid Flux: Aesthetics and Environmentalism in Amitav Ghosh's *The Hungry Tide*," *Ariel: A Review of International English Literature*, 46.4 (2015): 63–88. Sections from the Introduction appeared within "The Rich and Poor Don't All Suffer Under the Pandemic Equally," *Jacobin*, May 2020. At Liverpool University Press, many thanks are owed to Chloe Johnson, and to the editors of the Postcolonialism Across the Disciplines series for embracing my work. Thanks also to the anonymous readers for their excellent and generous comments and suggestions, and to Sarah Davison and Sarah Warren for their invaluable work coordinating copyediting and production.

I don't know what I would do without my nightly chats with my mother, Rajkumari Jaising, or without the love of my siblings, Rashmi and Hitesh. Sammer, my partner, has been with me through all the various twists and turns of this journey, helping me sort through conundrums, reading ideas in formation, reminding me of what matters, and anchoring me during waves of self-doubt. No words can fully convey my gratitude to him; so let me just say simply—but from the bottom of my heart—thank you, my love.

This work is dedicated to my father, Yogeshkumar Jaising, whose passion for movies, music, and ideas left a mark on me, and to my college professor, Eunice de Souza, whose singular lectures and arresting poetry set me on the path to writing this book.

Introduction

> The contradictions and costs of a minority's progress, long suppressed by historical revisionism, blustery denial and aggressive equivocation, have become visible on a planetary scale.
>
> —Pankaj Mishra, *Age of Anger*[1]

Since the rise of postcolonial studies in the 1980s, much discourse within literary and cultural studies has adhered to the notion of "alterity" or fundamental difference between the global North and South. When literary and cultural production from the South is turned to, it is often with the expectation that it will provide an opposing view, a "writing back" to power, a reflection of alternative modernities, or an antidote to capitalist and individualistic cultures of the North or West.[2] This alterity-based perspective has its roots in Orientalism but was solidified by critiques of Eurocentrism within postcolonial studies that cast cultural texts emerging out of the formerly colonized world as radically "other" and as emblems of resistance. Simultaneously, the commodification of postcolonial literatures as "exotic" furthered a fetishization of notions of absolute cultural difference and incommensurability between East and West and North and South.[3]

We see the continuing effects of this alterity-based worldview today—and not just in postcolonial studies but also in scholarship on neoliberalism, a four-decade capitalist project that has increased inequality, fueled the power of the far right, and drained societies of the capacities needed to address public emergencies of the kind we face today. In recent analyses of neoliberalism's impact on literature, the examples come overwhelmingly from Britain and America, reflecting an implicit understanding that the global South represents the atypical or exceptional. Similarly, in social theory on neoliberalism, differences between North and South are often privileged over

Introduction

continuities. For instance, in her influential account of neoliberalism's effects on subjectivity, political theorist Wendy Brown elides growing inequality in both Northern and Southern economies, while differentiating between a "soft power"-led, consent-driven, neoliberalism in the North and a coercively imposed or "hard power"-backed neoliberalism in the South.[4]

Beyond Alterity argues that neoliberal capitalism has produced significant continuities in political and economic reality, subjectivity, and cultural representation across the North–South divide—continuities that are at least as worthy of our consideration as differences arising from the history of colonialism. To begin with, the book contends that neoliberalism's characteristic policies of privatization and austerity have required coercive imposition everywhere, including in the North where they have—by defunding public services and weakening the working class—operated as a form of hard power, whose destructive impact is felt most acutely by precarious and downwardly mobile groups. Much of the book, though, is a study of the soft power of ideas and narrative, specifically in India, a quintessential Southern economy that marked 30 years of neoliberal reforms in 2021. The following chapters analyze a variety of contemporary Indian texts, especially bestselling and acclaimed English-language novels and their audiovisual adaptations, which lay bare the crucial role of soft power in normalizing neoliberalism in the South—much as in the North—particularly among the middle classes. Building primarily on Indian examples, I show how fictional works integrate into narrative form what I describe as a neoliberal "script"—an ideational sequence promulgated by global elites that hollows out possibilities for progressive state intervention, while lifting up free markets and private enterprise as the keys to radical economic and social transformation.

In India the neoliberal script circulated crucially via official narratives in the 1990s that framed privatization and deregulation as harbingers of a "new" entrepreneurial nation that has broken free from state-led development. Over the last three decades, such narratives have been used with some regularity to defend neoliberal policies and to justify the resulting crises of unemployment, underemployment, and poverty that afflict the vast majority of the population. More recently, this script has fed into the reigning rhetoric of Hindu nationalism and served to paper over the far-right government's steady abdication of responsibility to the private sector. But alongside its consistent, even compulsive, regurgitation in political and media discourse, the neoliberal script has also been repeatedly performed and animated within fiction. As *Beyond Alterity* tracks contemporary Indian fiction's interactions with this script, it affords insight into some of the subtler processes by which neoliberalism gains dominance and becomes incorporated into modes of subject production in one of the largest economies and cultures of the global South.

Yet, even as recent Indian novels and their cinematic and serialized adaptations illuminate dynamics that are specific to the South, they simultaneously bring into relief universal processes related to the structuring of consciousness and experience under neoliberalism. Furthermore, the increasing translation and movement of this fiction across languages and media indexes key transformations taking place in literary and cultural markets globally, and not merely within India. Hence, ultimately, this book treats contemporary Indian fiction as exemplary rather than as exceptional. In doing so, it traces a path out of alterity, to illuminate instead the trajectory of global capitalism as it shapes economies, cultures, and subjectivities in the North as well as the South. While political organizing across national lines is admittedly an enormous practical challenge, the *imagination* of solidarity across these lines is within reach, and this is what *Beyond Alterity* aims to enable—in the hopes of building an internationalist analysis and response to the crises of the present.

The Alterity Paradigm

In his influential 1986 essay on "Third-World Literature," Fredric Jameson framed literary works from the global South as especially attuned to the public realm and, therefore, as "radically different" from their First-World counterparts that invest in "recontain[ing] ... [collective] horror by transforming it into a rigorously private and subjective 'mood.'"[5] Jameson speaks often in this essay of radical difference—the "radical difference of non-canonical [third-world] texts," the "radical structural difference between the dynamics of third-world culture and those of the first-world cultural tradition"—and of how "in third-world texts ... the relationship between the libidinal and the political components of individual and social experience is radically different from what obtains in the west and what shapes our cultural forms."[6] Based on this understanding of radical structural difference, he then argues that Third-World literary texts are "national allegories," in that they present a "different ratio of the political to the personal" relative to First-World texts, and even "libidinal investment [in these texts] is to be read in primarily political and social terms."[7] In the most prominent contestation of Jameson's ideas, Aijaz Ahmad pushed back against his notion of Third-World literature. This reading of non-Euro-American texts, Ahmad pointed out, is based on a problematic binary between First- and Third-World literature that on the one hand ignores the position of minority writers in countries like the US and, on the other, casts writers from places like India as existing outside of, rather than also shaped by, the forces of global capitalism. Jameson's conception of Third-World literature, Ahmad noted, is less a reflection of reality than of the US Marxist critic's unacknowledged attachment to the fantasy of a cultural "other" that can provide an alternative to the "self."[8] But what is additionally problematic about Jameson's approach here is the implication that Third-World national allegories—with their different ratio of the political to the personal, and their framing of even libidinal investment in social terms—will inevitably supply a more *progressive* alternative to literature

Introduction

from the First World. Because Jameson's essay arises from the imperative to diversify literary studies curricula in the US by including "Third-World" literature, he tends to idealize this literature and frame it as necessarily supplying a counterforce to the "rigorously private and subjective 'mood'" expressed in cultural production from the global North.

In the late 1990s and early 2000s, Franco Moretti's and Pascale Casanova's accounts of "world literature" reproduced, though in different terms, the binaristic logic underlying Jameson's essay. Moretti and Casanova were invested not so much in radical difference between First- and Third-World cultures as in exposing the inequality structuring global literary markets. By identifying a world literary system, these authors inspired new methodologies with the potential to take literary criticism beyond mere celebration or critique of individual texts, authors, and aesthetic traditions. Nevertheless, like Jameson, they sidestepped unevenness *within* national contexts, while considering inequality primarily between Western and non-Western literatures circulating—or competing, as they emphasized—within the global sphere. In *The World Republic of Letters* (1999), Casanova characterized literary spaces of the formerly colonized world as "new" and "poor" relative to "the oldest—and, accordingly, the best endowed" national literary spaces, such as France.[9] This view, while appearing to simply describe an unequal "world republic of letters" produced by European colonialism, in fact advances an inadequately historicized and largely Eurocentric view of non-Euro-American literary spaces. Formerly colonized spaces like India are deemed uniformly "poor" because they are only considered in relation to the "best endowed" spaces of the West; their history, in other words, is reduced to that of the colonial encounter. Meanwhile, Moretti, in a roughly concurrent and widely debated essay, "Conjectures on World Literature" (2000), drew on world-systems theory to offer his new theory of inequality within the literary realm. Focusing primarily on the novel, he argued that, "in cultures that belong to the periphery of the literary system (which means: almost all cultures, inside and outside Europe), the modern novel first arises not as an autonomous development but as a compromise between a western formal influence (usually French or English) and local materials."[10] Moretti's model, like Casanova's, imagines a world and "world literature" determined ultimately by the lingering effects of European colonialism. It therefore overlooks the history of core–periphery dynamics internal to national contexts, as well as the possibility that—as in the case of the Latin American novel—new forms may have "developed in the periphery, not as a compromise with forms from the centre, but as [part of] a self-conscious literary project that addressed local imperatives, ... and in due course expanded them for world literature as a whole."[11] In the end, like Jameson's account, Moretti and Casanova's theories reinforce the vision of a fundamentally bifurcated world in which internally undifferentiated non-Euro-American literary spaces are locked into a dynamics of competition and compromise with the powerful, yet similarly undifferentiated, "core."

More recently, the Warwick Research Collective (WReC) has built on but also challenged the limitations of Moretti's framework. Invoking the Marxist understanding of "combined and uneven development" under capitalism, it highlights core–periphery dynamics not just between the global North and South but also within these regions and thereby identifies features of an "aesthetics of peripherality" that traverses the North–South divide.[12] *Beyond Alterity* is aligned with the WReC's work in *Combined and Uneven Development* (2015), as it attends to the internal differentiation that characterizes capitalist contexts of both the North and South. At the same time, I question the basis for some of the generalizations about literature from peripheral and semi-peripheral spaces that emerge out of this work. According to the WReC, the "(semi-) periphery" is where "the pressures of combined and uneven development find their most pronounced or profound registration—including in the sphere of culture, where new forms are likely to emerge, oriented (and uniquely responsive) to these pressures which constitute their final determinants."[13] To support this view of (semi-)peripheral literatures as "uniquely responsive" to the shocks of uneven development, the WReC privileges texts that go "beyond 'ideal-type' realism" and deploy an "irrealist aesthetics" marked by catechresis, superimposition, disjunction, and a mixing of imaginary and factual elements. These irrealist texts, it is argued, exemplify "new forms" produced in the (semi-)periphery in which both form and content register the contradictions of capitalism, and which show how "the work of literary representation in (semi) peripheral contexts seems to *require* a supplementation or heightening of … the 'ideal-type' of realism," leading to an "elective affinity … between the general situation(s) of peripherality and irrealist aesthetics."[14] But, in defining literature from semi-peripheral spaces primarily through irrealist aesthetics, much (indeed the majority of) cultural production from these spaces, which is commercial or non-"literary" fiction, written often in the realist mode, is glossed over. Furthermore, the privileging of works in which *both* form and content register the effects of uneven development leads to the overlooking of much literature from the (semi-)peripheral regions that is marked by *tension* between form and content, resulting from an attempt to simultaneously register and suture over the shocks produced by capitalist processes. Indeed, generalizations made by the WReC and others about "the work of literary representation" in the (semi-)periphery, or about "the semi-peripheral novel,"[15] are hard to sustain without a considerable flattening of the literature in question, as well as of what Pierre Bourdieu refers to as the "field" of literary production, commodification, and circulation.[16] To read literature from the South primarily for acts of resistance, or to assume that "the work of literary representation" in the periphery "requires" irrealist aesthetics, is to overlook the literary field's operation within a much broader "field of power or the social field,"[17] which increasingly links the Southern periphery to—as opposed to distinguishing it from—the Northern core.

The following chapters attend closely to a quintessential example of cultural production from the semi-periphery—the Indian English novel—by including

Introduction

both its formally experimental, globally circulating, "literary" varieties *and* its domestically circulating works of popular and genre fiction. Domestically oriented commercial fiction in particular complicates assumptions of the radical difference as well as unique aesthetic responsiveness of (semi-)peripheral literature to pressures imposed by uneven development. Much of this fiction is in the realist mode, and *contra* Jameson's implication that Third-World literature models a progressive form of national allegory, this commercial fiction highlights the ways in which plots of personal development can often channel an official (rather than progressive) nationalist discourse that reconciles middle-class readers and viewers with state-sanctioned capitalist mythologies. Increasingly, moreover, both commercial and literary varieties of the Indian English novel have been sought after by streaming services like Netflix, owing to their capacity to reach simultaneously domestic and international audiences. Indeed, this fiction illuminates not simply "the situation of peripherality" but also what Sarah Brouillette describes as the broader "turn to trying to save literature by diversifying access to its creation, dissemination, and readership."[18] Hence, even as this study centers the English novel from contemporary India, it also reads it for its relations and ties to commodified cultural production from other neoliberalizing contexts, including the United States, South Africa, and Brazil. Together, these texts and relations—which cut across the North–South divide—make sharply visible the dynamics underpinning what WReC scholars Sharae Deckard and Stephen Shapiro refer to as "neoliberal world-culture."[19]

"Emerging" India in the Neoliberal World-Culture

Whereas "neoliberalism" has been part of the critical vocabulary in Latin America since the 1970s, the term did not enjoy much currency in the Anglo-American academy until the 1990s. Since then, two major strands of theorizing have framed much of the scholarly discourse on the topic. For Marxist geographers and social scientists like David Harvey and Jamie Peck, neoliberalism is a political "project" for the restoration of class power that has shaped the latest phase of global capitalism;[20] while for Foucauldian cultural theorists like Aihwa Ong and Wendy Brown, the term denotes a reigning economic "rationality" that governs by producing highly individualistic and responsibilized subjects.[21] Sustained scholarly engagement with these theoretical perspectives has led to neoliberalism becoming a keyword—and not just in the social sciences but also across humanities disciplines such as anthropology, American studies, and media and cultural studies.[22] During the 2010s, prominent journals of literary and cultural theory began publishing special issues on topics such as "The Genres of Neoliberalism," "Neoliberal Culture," and "Neoliberalism and the Novel."[23] Simultaneously, debates about the so-called neoliberal novel,[24] and a number of book-length studies on neoliberalism and literature[25] also emerged. Following the election of Donald Trump in 2016, much of this scholarship turned to examining the relationship between neoliberalism and far-right authoritarianism, and, within this context, the role of cultural production in the production of new subjectivities.[26]

Although emerging scholarship on neoliberalism within literary and cultural studies has not excluded the global South, it has tended to emphasize the advanced capitalist world[27] and especially the production of a new kind of "self-enclosed individualism"[28] or "hyper-individualized neoliberal subject"[29] within this world. Referring primarily to the North, cultural theorist Jeremy Gilbert, for instance, argues that

> what defines the regularity of neoliberalism as a discursive formation is precisely the persistence of an individualistic conception of human selfhood and of the idea of the individual both as the ideal locus of sovereignty and the site of governmental intervention. In fact this observation may help us to explain the peculiar persistence and success of neoliberalism in recent decades.[30]

If Gilbert, writing in 2013, associated neoliberalism with "an individualistic conception of selfhood," then recent definitions by literary and cultural critics have associated the term also with a decline in liberal and democratic values. Nancy Armstrong, writing in the context of Donald Trump's election in the US, frames neoliberalism as a "culture marked by the collapse of the categories of liberalism (democracy/class hierarchy; democratic writing/literary genres; freedom/subjection)."[31] Such characterizations elide the significant force of class power—in shaping both neoliberal policies and the broader ethos. Gilbert's definition, by attributing the "persistence and success of neoliberalism" to its "idea of the individual," obscures how much this persistence and success have to do with the ongoing work of political and economic elites in mobilizing neoliberal ideology to serve their interests. Meanwhile, Armstrong's definition of neoliberalism as a "culture" erases the social agents responsible for shoring up "class hierarchy," which she mentions parenthetically and simply as a "category of liberalism."

Closely related to the sidestepping of class dynamics is the assumption that the character of neoliberalism in the advanced capitalist world is fundamentally unlike that which exists in the global South. When examining the South, literary and cultural theorists have tended to place emphasis on the externally mandated nature of neoliberal reforms in this part of the world. They have asserted, for instance, that "in regions 'underdeveloped' by colonial and imperial modernity, neoliberalism appears as debt-induced structural adjustment mandated by new international banking and commerce institutions such as the World Bank, the International Monetary Fund (IMF), and the World Trade Organization (WTO),"[32] or that a "US-mandated approach to economic development [was] forced on countries in the global South as a condition for IMF and World Bank loans." With neoliberalism in Southern nations understood as "an updated version of colonialism, a current import

Introduction

that represents the same old colonialist values in a new guise,"[33] domestic class interests, when attended to, are seen primarily as being in service to the neo-imperialism of the West. Consequently, specific kinds of Southern cultural texts—typically "literary" novels—are privileged as objects of study and examined for their critiques of and challenges to Northern dominance and Western ideologies of individualism. Whereas works from advanced capitalist nations are frequently perceived as enmeshed within the broader ethos—as "accept[ing] the ethic of unlimited individual responsibility,"[34] as displacing questions about the real economy by focusing instead on matters of individual identity,[35] and as "reiterat[ing] neoliberal capital's expanding investment in consumer affect and sentiment," given authors' "treat[ment] [of] formal literary innovation as a matter of competition, market assessment, and entrepreneurial risk taking"[36]—literature from the South tends to be turned to for modeling "resistance to neoliberal formations,"[37] for "contesting neoliberalism's market logic and ethos of entrepreneurial self-care," for offering "potential sites of antineoliberal agency,"[38] and for "open[ing] the possibility of another politics."[39] Alternatively, literary fiction with roots in the South is invoked as a means of countering certain habits of thinking in the US academy—for instance, the "default and often imprecise critical virtue of plurality"[40]—or of raising ethical questions about "the libidinal economy of the global North.'"[41]

In other words, with inadequate attention paid to class within nations of the global South, the longstanding tendency in postcolonial studies to frame the South as an undifferentiated site of alternative modernity and resistance to the West is reproduced within much of the emerging scholarship on neoliberalism within literary and cultural studies. Furthermore, whereas this scholarship is attuned to ways in which cultural production in places like Britain and the US might reflect and even be subsumed by the logic of capital, when it turns to the South it is often with the assumption that texts and cultural producers in this part of the world are in opposition to, or have greater distance from, capital and the demands of the cultural marketplace. This privileging of Southern texts that trouble neoliberal values produces a sense of the South as engaged first and foremost in opposition to neoliberalism, much as it was once embroiled in opposition to European colonialism.

Chapter 1 examines the problems with such an understanding of neoliberalism through a close analysis of Wendy Brown's *Undoing the Demos* and Aihwa Ong's *Neoliberalism as Exception*—influential accounts of neoliberal subjectivity that have informed a good deal of scholarship within literary and cultural studies. Countering the Marxist framing of neoliberalism as a class project, and building on Foucault, Brown and Ong define the term as a "governing rationality"[42] or "technology"[43] that is reshaping not just material life but also consciousness. I argue that while these theoretical interventions rightly call attention to the effects of neoliberal capitalism on our inner lives, they problematically obscure class dynamics internal to societies and hence end up emphasizing differences over continuities in how subjectivities are being forged across the

North–South divide. Referring primarily to how professionalized middle-class Americans have come to be hyper-individualistic, Brown claims that in the North—as opposed to the South—the neoliberal logic has proliferated less through overt political pressure and economic compulsion and more via the internalization of norms and values of individualism. Thus, Brown's analysis has little to say about economic violence and what David Harvey calls "accumulation by dispossession"[44] in advanced capitalist nations and their impacts on the poor and working classes. Meanwhile, Ong suggests that neoliberalism in East Asia is distinct—because East Asian nations have been compelled by the North to adopt neoliberal reforms and because professionalized groups in these nations have nevertheless found ways of resisting through cultural means the hyper-individualism demanded by a US-style corporate ethos. In making this culturalist argument and also privileging professionalized groups, Ong's analysis minimizes the role of economic compulsion in shaping subjectivities, especially of the poor, while simultaneously eliding the role of East Asian elites in embracing and promoting, rather than simply tolerating or resisting, neoliberal ideology in their national contexts. In other words, the dichotomy between North and South implied by both Brown and Ong overlooks, on the one hand, the role of material compulsion in the shaping of consciousness *everywhere*, including in the North, and, on the other hand, the ideological labor performed by narratives of entrepreneurial individualism in the South *as well*. I suggest that Brown's and Ong's characterizations of essential difference between a neo-imperialist North and a vulnerable South are misleading because although the ideational origins of neoliberalism may indeed lie in the global North, in practice it has been, as Jamie Peck puts it, a "constructed project"[45]—constructed, that is, by elites from *both* the North and the South, rather than simply a case of neo-imperialism imposed by Northern powers. Moreover, both overt pressure, and subtler forms of ideological interpellation have been necessary for constructing the neoliberal project and its subjects, whether in the North or the South.

If the first chapter establishes the need to attend to class dynamics internal to nations, then the second chapter illustrates these dynamics through the example of India, where economic stagnation enabled the ruling class to initiate the process of neoliberalization—or what is referred to simply as "liberalization" in the Indian public sphere. Although this process began in the mid-1980s, many industrialists, politicians, and intellectuals had for decades wanted to move away from the planned economy of the postcolonial developmental state and towards a deregulated form of capitalism. The so-called architect of neoliberal reforms, Manmohan Singh, described the 1991 balance-of-payments crisis that triggered large-scale liberalization in India as a "blessing in disguise" and a long-awaited opportunity to further push forward neoliberal policies.[46] Singh and others in the ruling class echoed the IMF's and the World Bank's calls for cuts to public spending, arguing that curbs on expenditure were unavoidable in order to counter the deficit and prevent future crises.[47] Then, as elsewhere in the world,

Introduction

"neoliberal economists, journalists, and politicians by sheer repetition created a widespread impression that all alternatives had 'failed' or were 'exhausted'"[48]—and that a deregulated private sector was India's best hope. After 1991, these segments of society began loudly proclaiming that India was a new nation, finally released from the shackles imposed by central planning and developmentalism. In subsequent years the nation was celebrated widely by Indian as well as foreign journalists and businessmen as a "hot zone," "fast culture," an emblem of the "flat world" created by globalization and an exceptional site of entrepreneurialism.[49] Such media and official narratives of a "new," "emerging" India and "enterprise culture" have played a vital role in justifying neoliberal economic reforms in the domestic as well as global spheres,[50] while masking the ways in which the burden of these reforms has been carried overwhelmingly by India's poor.[51]

With the government's abandonment of the peasantry, significant weakening of organized labor, and high rates of informal and precarious employment in urban areas, real wages for the vast majority of the population have remained stagnant over the last three decades, despite high national growth rates. Added to that, "a continued lack of essential social services (from schooling and health care to the provision of safe water and drainage)" has meant that, as Jean Dreze and Amartya Sen note, the "societal reach of economic progress in India has been remarkably limited."[52] In contrast to the first three decades following India's Independence in 1947—when the bottom half of the population increased their incomes and captured almost a third of total growth—between 1980 and 2014, the top 0.1 percent of earners received a higher share of total growth (i.e. 12%) than the bottom 50 percent (which earned 11%). Around 2014, "the share of national income accruing to the top 1% income earners ... [reached] its highest level since ... 1922."[53] Also, the wealth of Indian *billionaires* relative to national income "soared to the equivalent of more than 17 per cent of gross domestic product, one of the highest shares in the world."[54] India is now one of the most unequal societies in the world, with the bulk of the gains of liberalization accruing to the upper echelons of society, and the majority of the population existing in a state of heightened precarity.

But in this regard, India's story is not fundamentally unlike that of an advanced capitalist economy such as the United States, where neoliberal ideology has similarly been promoted by ruling elites, and where income and wealth inequality have also risen sharply since the 1980s as a result of massive cuts to social spending, coupled with policies that have destroyed labor rights, slashed wages, and triggered upward redistribution of wealth.[55] Although neither developmentalism nor Keynesianism yielded perfect societies in places like India and the US, their influence nonetheless helped to make dominant a necessary agenda of social redistribution and equity that has been steadily eroded in the neoliberal era. In 2020 billionaire wealth rose in *both* the US and India to about a fifth of these respective nations' GDPs.[56] Moreover, across these contexts, the pressure to self-manage amidst such growing inequality and insecurity has led to an overwhelming sense of alienation and provided fuel for the rise of far-right nationalisms. The onset of a global pandemic brought into stark relief the effects of gross inequality, massively depleted public health infrastructures, and toxic cultural nationalism across both of these emblematic nations of the North and South. So undeniable were the costs of neoliberalization that in the early days of the pandemic even pro-business institutions like the World Economic Forum and IMF, as well as publications like the *Financial Times*, began arguing that we need to "move on from neoliberalism"—that "there should be no return to austerity," and that governments ought instead to focus on "[popular] redistribution, basic incomes and wealth taxes."[57]

Thus, by observing the political-economic and cultural impact of neoliberalization on India, as well as its continuities with advanced capitalist economies like the US, the first two chapters contest the supposed opposition between a North in which neoliberalism has proliferated largely through ideological indoctrination and a South in which neoliberalism has been imposed primarily through acts of overt domination. Furthermore, by attending in particular to the role of national elites in actualizing India's neoliberal turn, these chapters push back against arguments that attribute this turn principally to pressures imposed by a neo-imperialist North.

The Neoliberal Script and Its Incarnations

The second chapter also introduces the concept of a neoliberal script. In contrast to dominant understandings within literary and cultural studies, my conception of the neoliberal script suggests that neoliberalism is much more than a species of extreme individualism.[58] In fact, were it merely a form of hyper-individualism, it is unlikely that it would have earned the kind of social legitimacy it enjoys in much of the world today. I argue that over the last four decades, a standardized script about how to produce not simply personal growth but also fundamental social change has been rendered into dogma by ideologues and elites across the North–South divide—as a way of undermining the currency of previously dominant approaches of state-led redistribution, including Keynesianism and developmentalism.

The neoliberal script popularizes the insidious argument that policies like deregulation, privatization, and austerity are *progressive* solutions—that these policies, as opposed to state remedies, are elixirs for treating all manner of social and collective problems, including poverty and underdevelopment. This claim to transforming the plight of the poor has enabled neoliberal ideology to resonate with populations across the North and South. I show the neoliberal script at work in *Free to Choose*, an influential book and documentary series that the Nobel Prize-winning Chicago School economist, Milton Friedman co-authored with his wife, Rose. Friedman is arguably the world's best-known neoliberal, and *Free to Choose* is one of his most widely

Introduction

consumed works—a result of the documentary being broadcast on US public television in 1980 and being made freely available on the Internet in recent years. Featuring Friedman's international travels—including to India—the televised documentary makes clear how the rise of neoliberalism to the status of ideological and cultural dominant has entailed not simply appeals to seductive notions of individual and market freedom. I show how Friedman draws crucially on images of India's abject poverty to construct a moral case against central planning, and to thereby frame government intervention as the ultimate cause of poverty. In the process, he reactivates colonial-era imagery of a backward civilizational Other and implies that India's postcolonial state has been far worse for its people than British colonial rule. Through India's example, together with portraits of working-class families in the US and Britain, the series then makes the counterintuitive argument that the poor everywhere are *damaged* by social welfare and are the ones with most to gain from the elimination of government subsidies, regulations, and assistance. Ultimately, Friedman's documentary insists that *collective* progress and national development depend upon—indeed necessitate—the privatization of public services, the deregulation of capital, and the encouragement of private wealth accumulation.

It is a version of this argument that India's political and economic elites amplify in the 1990s when they position the planned, developmental state as a dystopian Other, for the purposes of constructing a utopian imagination of market capitalism that transforms the nation's fate as well as the plight of the poor. Drawing on the speeches of Indian economist and former Prime Minister Manmohan Singh, I show how a Friedmanesque neoliberal script begins to be incorporated within nationalistic narratives of India's emergence as a new power that is going through a second independence movement. As in Friedman's account, postcolonial planning is framed as the ultimate antagonist and as yielding a corrupt "License Raj" that does a greater disservice to the population than the colonial regime or British Raj. In subsequent decades, the "national biography"—a category of nonfiction typically penned by India's professional and managerial elite—helps to popularize this script and sell neoliberal reforms as the catalyst for large-scale societal progress and long-awaited cultural revolution. Translated into a number of Indian languages, bestselling national biographies like Gurcharan Das's *India Unbound* (2000) and *India Grows at Night* (2013) contest a growing popular perception that neoliberal reforms are helping the rich at the expense of the poor. They do this largely by proliferating—both within and beyond India's borders— imagistic and anecdotal evidence to support the idea that rich and poor alike are finally actualizing their true potential in India. In recent years, the genre of the national biography has also borne across the ideology of the Hindu right and conveyed some of the "mutating forms"[59] by which neoliberalism continues to retain dominance as a policy paradigm, even in the aftermath of the global financial crisis of 2008, seen by some as marking the end of the neoliberal era.

Together with nonfiction genres like the television documentary and national biography, fictional narratives of entrepreneurial maturation have played a significant role in naturalizing a Friedmanesque neoliberal script in India over the last decades, as Chapter 3 shows. This chapter begins the book's exploration of the interactions between literature and the neoliberal script, by attending to recent English-language novels from India. The anglophone Indian novel—typically associated with authors such as Salman Rushdie, Amitav Ghosh, Vikram Seth, Arundhati Roy, and Aravind Adiga—has long been the most internationally mobile category of Indian literature, owing to the global dominance of English and the economic dominance and mobility of English-speaking sections of Indian society. Since especially the 1980s, it has been commodified in Europe and America by what Graham Huggan calls the "alterity industry," and it has been instrumentalized as part of the "exoticist production of otherness" of the formerly colonized world.[60] Within India, the audience for this fiction has until recently been confined to the English-educated middle classes and elites of major metropolitan centers like Delhi and Mumbai. However, following the liberalizing of India's book publishing industry, and the rise since the mid-1980s of both independent and international publishers, new kinds of Indian English novels began to enter the domestic market. Over the last 20 years in particular, *Bildungsromane* by authors like Chetan Bhagat—"the biggest-selling English-language novelist ever in India"[61]—have acquired increasing currency with the Indian middle class. Bestselling novels tracing the development of enterprising strivers have flooded India's domestic publishing market and—amidst deepening unemployment and poverty—shored up the image of a new, market-driven nation in which ordinary citizens are finally free to rise. Written in a linguistic idiom familiar to an Indian readership, sold at affordable prices, and circulating via translation into other Indian languages as well as adaptation to popular Hindi cinema, or Bollywood, this new English-language fiction has fueled a boom in domestic publishing that has made India one of the largest book markets in the world.[62] Although the authors of this new commercial Indian fiction arise mostly from the metropolitan middle and upper classes, their works often address the aspirations and anguish of middle- and lower middle-class Indians living in the nation's hinterlands. Additionally, novelists like Bhagat have, by marketing themselves as self-starters and guides, helped to normalize a neoliberal conception of the author as—in Mark McGurl's words—"a kind of entrepreneur and service provider" to "reader-customers."[63]

In many ways this domestically oriented Indian English fiction presents a refreshing departure from the "literary" novel with its stylistically complex narratives that translate the local for global and cosmopolitan audiences. But as refreshing as this new fiction is for its accessibility, its attunement to collective preoccupations, and its "attempt to take possession of English as an Indian language,"[64] it has also proven to be especially amenable to animating the neoliberal script—as I show through Bhagat's *The 3 Mistakes of My Life* (2008) and lesser-known novelist Parinda Joshi's *Made in China* (2019).

Introduction

Departing from the contestations of nationalism in literary fiction by Rushdie and Ghosh, the novels of Bhagat and Joshi channel official nationalism via narratives tracing the personal development of entrepreneurial subjects in present-day India. These novels also reject the postcolonial pessimism that marks some of the more internationally celebrated works of Indian English fiction. *The 3 Mistakes of My Life* and *Made in China* are both set in Gujarat, a key site of capitalist mythology; and by following the economic rise and emotional development of small businessmen, these novels offer hope that a mature, "free market" capitalism based on talent and ingenuity—rather than parochialism and corruption—will deliver profound social change in India. Their narratives of personal development also point to the growing interconnectedness of the imagination of a maturing Indian capitalism with the discourse of Hindu nationalism. Moreover, their adaptations into popular Hindi films point to a narrowing of the gap between the English novel and Hindi cinema—textual categories that, as Sangita Gopal observes, were once considered antithetical to one another and addressed to distinct rather than overlapping audiences.[65] Together, the novels and their filmic adaptations evince the ways in which the neoliberal script—and its fantasy of a capitalism that is not just personally beneficial but also socially progressive and beneficial for the collective—has traveled through the public sphere and gained legitimacy among large sections of India's middle class. If, as Joseph Slaughter argues, the *Bildungsroman*'s rise was tied to the function of reconciling national subjects with the anxieties of capitalist modernization,[66] then these contemporary Indian narratives of the entrepreneur's maturation perform a similar role—by exposing, yet ultimately expunging the contradictions of India's "enterprise culture."[67]

Following Chapter 3's fleshing out of the domestic context of new, commercial Indian fiction, Chapter 4 turns to some of its global implications. Here I take up Vikas Swarup's *Q&A* (2005), a relatively minor novel, along with its highly influential Oscar-winning adaptation, *Slumdog Millionaire* (dir. Danny Boyle, 2009), and read both of these texts as key examples of a genre of fiction about urban poverty that attains particular significance during the neoliberal period. As policies of economic liberalization erode government support for the agricultural sector, compelling large numbers of rural people to migrate to cities and join the vast informal labor force, we see the steady proliferation of texts like *Q&A* and *Slumdog Millionaire*, whose aesthetics and politics intersect with those of other globally bestselling representations of urban poverty. Notable among these is the acclaimed Brazilian film *City of God* (dir. Fernando Meirelles and Katia Lund, 2002), based on the homonymous 1997 novel by Paulo Lins. Like their Brazilian counterparts, *Q&A* and *Slumdog* trace the movement of exceptional strivers out of hellish and relatively static spaces of urban poverty. Building on journalist Katherine Boo's concept of an "undercity" (in Mumbai) that is separated from the "overcity," I refer to these representations as "undercity fiction"—specifically for their construction of arenas of poverty, blight, and criminality that appear disconnected from, rather than as products of, the depredations of corporate and finance capital. In the spectacularly violent films, which have enjoyed greater commercial success and notoriety than the novels, exceptional protagonists make their way out of apparently self-contained zones of squalor and misery. Because the systemic causes of urban poverty are obscured by the films' narrative and aesthetic strategies, the characters who do remain in the slums and *favelas* appear to be relics of a bygone age, or else as *fated* to being erased. I argue that these much-watched and internationally celebrated literary adaptations have not merely represented the segregation of urban spaces in the global South; they have also contributed to maintaining this segregation on an imaginative level. *Q&A*'s Oscar-winning adaptation brings into sharp relief the internal contradictions of undercity fiction. For, even as this film exposes the effects of capitalist accumulation by dispossession in Mumbai, its representational strategies risk reinforcing the notion that there is no alternative to capitalism, if we are to transcend deep-seated inequality and to propel modernization.

The global commercial success of representations like *City of God*, *Q&A*, and *Slumdog Millionaire* has also helped to service the illusion that the entrepreneurial energies unleashed by neoliberal capitalism are opening up new possibilities in the South, so that solutions can finally be found to longstanding problems of poverty and stagnation. As the neoliberal project comes under increasing scrutiny for its failure to improve material reality for the vast majority of people, these literary and cinematic works from the South perform a vital ideological function: to metropolitan audiences across the North–South divide, their stories of entrepreneurial development signal the potential of capitalism to transform the former Third World into "emerging" economies. The highly successful films in particular call attention to the flow from not just Euro-America to the rest of the world but also the global South to the North—and they exemplify ways in which cultural production from the South has contributed and given fuel to neoliberal framings of poverty and the poor.

From this popular fiction about the urban underbelly, Chapter 5 moves to "literary" representations of rural poverty. This chapter suggests that even the more aesthetically and politically sophisticated, or "serious," genre of literary fiction has not simply resisted the neoliberal script and its privileged model of entrepreneurial subjectivity. An exemplary case is Amitav Ghosh's *The Hungry Tide* (2004), which offers a nuanced history of rural dispossession and collective struggle in India's Sundarbans region, but one that is nonetheless informed by the structure and imagination of the neoliberal script. Moving between the 1970s and the present, the novel connects a network of rural and metropolitan characters—including an Indian-American marine biologist, a small businessman from Delhi, and a local fisherman. In its construction of a "network narrative," and also its investment in histories of popular resistance, *The Hungry Tide* bears striking affinities with another acclaimed work of literary fiction from the global South—South African novelist Zakes Mda's *Heart of Redness* (2000). As in *The Hungry Tide*,

Introduction

an America-returned protagonist anchors Mda's network narrative, which is set in a village of the impoverished Eastern Cape province of post-apartheid South Africa. Both of these literary works are engaged with critiquing the ways in which neoliberalization is causing the hollowing out of agriculture and village life in the contemporary South. However, the interactions between metropolitan and provincial characters that they stage result in a nostalgic "fixing" and idealizing of the peasant, whose function is reduced to that of catalyzing metropolitan characters' development into progressive, socially engaged entrepreneurial subjects. I argue that *The Hungry Tide* and *Heart of Redness* are pulled between the aesthetics of networks on the one hand and nostalgia on the other, or between energies of transformation and fixity. As a result of this tension in both texts, present-day grassroots struggles against rural dispossession—or "the environmentalism of the poor"[68]—are eclipsed, while the power to create social change is transferred to enterprising, transforming metropolitan subjects. In short, this literary fiction—much like the explicitly commercial undercity narrative—is internally contradictory: it at once exposes the plight of the rural poor and flattens rural characters into mere symbols, in order to mourn the losses resulting from neoliberalism's destruction of rural ecologies.

If, as I have shown, Indian English fiction is not merely a source of anti-capitalist critique, then, by the same token, nor is it *simply* a means of legitimating the pro-capitalist, neoliberal script, as the concluding chapter demonstrates. Since winning the Booker Prize for *The God of Small Things* (1997), Arundhati Roy has often been framed as an emblem of India's emergence as a world power. Chapter 6 reads the baggy and ponderous form of her latest novel as a reaction to literature's entanglements with the neoliberal script and as an attempt at constructing a capacious and unpredictable form of storytelling that is hard to reconcile with the streamlined and commodified narratives of personal and national emergence that dominate the present. Published in Narendra Modi's Hindu nationalist India, *The Ministry of Utmost Happiness* (2017) has as its protagonist not a middle-class entrepreneur, but rather an organically formed collective composed of those who have been variously dispossessed by processes of neoliberalization. To narrate the story of this collective, Roy's text fragments the developmental plot and its tracing of the rise of an ethical, entrepreneurial subjectivity. This narrative fragmentation then paradoxically enables a coalescing of strands that are typically disconnected within dominant accounts of "emerging" India—that is, the government's military occupation of Kashmir, routine displacement of rural populations, growing marketization of cultural expression, and the entrenchment of the Hindu right within popular culture and collective consciousness. By weaving the personal into a web of social and ecological relations, the novel confronts what Sujatha Fernandes describes as a global "shift in emphasis away from the collective and political modes of narration toward the personal mode," or what I describe as the "disciplining" of storytelling to conform to the compulsory privileging of the personal within the neoliberal era.[69] The second half of the chapter then turns to Aravind Adiga's *Selection Day* (2016), which similarly contests dominant accounts of personal and national emergence in contemporary India. Adiga's novel tracks the failure—rather than social integration—of two impoverished teenaged cricketers who are compelled to become an investment project for a rich financier. The novel is thus an inversion of generic cricket fiction (or "crick lit"), which includes Bhagat's *The 3 Mistakes of My Life*, described in Chapter 3. Much like Adiga's Booker Prize-winning debut novel *The White Tiger* (2008), *Selection Day* foregrounds the ways in which the entrepreneurial subject in India is coerced into being—and how there are costs to turning human beings into investments.

Ironically, though, the televisual adaptation of *Selection Day*, produced for a global audience by Netflix, upholds the possibility of an Indian capitalism that can triumph under ideal, free-market conditions and deliver change for all. Whereas the novel's satirical voice disarticulates the coming-of-age plot from the mythology of India's rise, the adaptation reinstates the discursive ties between personal and national emergence, thereby exposing the enduring currency of neoliberal India's progress narrative. I end the book with this adaptation, which also exemplifies a new phase in the commodification of anglophone Indian fiction in particular and world literature in general. Indian novels' global circulation via streaming platforms like Netflix means that they now exist in new relations of conversation with a whole host of cultural products, including a growing variety of international cinematic and televisual adaptations—thus compelling us to rethink assumptions about the radical difference and categorical separateness of non-Western literatures.

To challenge the notion of fundamental opposition between North and South, as I have done in this book, is in no way to disavow the power differential between richer and poorer nations; nor is it to deny the lingering effects of European and US imperialism on the global South. Indeed, as the vaccine nationalism of advanced capitalist nations in the midst of the pandemic has shown, the political and economic imbalance between North and South remains real and present. But the pandemic has *also* exposed how, across the North–South divide, governments' erosion of public health infrastructures over the last few decades has disproportionately affected poor and historically marginalized groups and left them particularly vulnerable during economic and health emergencies. Furthermore, the pandemic has highlighted the manner in which far-right regimes like Donald Trump's and Narendra Modi's have systematically exploited the collective misery brought on by neoliberal capitalism to further their interests and agendas, resulting in the deepening of inequality, together with cultural polarization. The misery exposed by the pandemic on a planetary scale suggests that in order to engage in a project of large-scale decolonization—the ultimate project of postcolonial studies—we need first and foremost to confront neoliberal capitalism. For this, rather than a belief in essential difference between North and South, what is needed is an internationalist

Introduction

perspective that is attuned both to deepening crisis and to emerging possibilities for solidarity across national boundaries. Such a perspective means not glossing over very real differences in the nature and extent of precarity experienced within nations of the North and South, but rather holding these differences in our minds together with an understanding of their shared origins and converging effects.

CHAPTER 1

Neoliberal Subjectivity and the Alterity Paradigm

> [T]he stake in all neoliberal analyses is the replacement every time of *homo œconomicus* as partner of exchange with a *homo œconomicus* as entrepreneur of himself, being for himself his own capital, being for himself his own producer, being for himself the source of [his] earnings.
>
> —Michel Foucault[1]

Although neoliberalism is far from monolithic as a political-economic philosophy, recent scholarship has shown how a coherent neoliberal identity was developed in the postwar period through the efforts of intellectuals like Austrian School economist Friedrich Hayek, who organized the first meeting of the Mont Pèlerin "thought collective" in 1947.[2] Annual meetings of this collective in Switzerland provided a crucial forum for forging a community of *laissez-faire* intellectuals which included other Austrian economists like Ludwig von Mises, German Ordoliberals like Wilhelm Ropke, and Chicago School economists like Milton Friedman, who perceived themselves marginalized by the then-reigning model of Keynesian economics. Dieter Plehwe notes that many of these intellectuals had formerly been part of the Colloque Walter Lippman, an organization that promoted "the superiority of the market economy over state intervention."[3] In the postwar years, these intellectuals coalesced as a collective that ultimately came to coordinate the efforts of foundations, think tanks, academics, media professionals, and businessmen engaged in the proliferation of pro-market ideas.[4] Their efforts, in conjunction with the proselytizing work carried out by the Chicago School of Economics, contributed to why neoliberal solutions such as deregulation, privatization, and state withdrawal from welfare were, as Friedman put it, the ideas found "lying around"[5] when leaders and policymakers experimented with responses to the economic crises of the early 1970s.

By the time Michel Foucault delivered his 1978–1979 Collège de France lectures, neoliberalism had emerged as the dominant economic approach in the advanced capitalist world, taking the place of Keynesian approaches. Foucault drew mainly on the work of the German Ordoliberals and the Chicago School in order to define neoliberalism as the reigning "rationality," a "general art of government,"[6] and a "technology of government"[7] that aimed to produce a self-regulating, hence governable, subject. If classical liberalism had understood *homo economicus* or economic man as a "partner of exchange," then, Foucault argued, neoliberalism was committed to replacing this figure with "a *homo economicus* as entrepreneur of himself." Neoliberalism had constructed a new subject, he suggested—a subject that was responsibilized and ready to ride the waves of economic instability.

Foucault's Collège de France lectures were first published as *The Birth of Biopolitics* in 2008. Since then, they have shaped significantly much of the scholarship on neoliberalism emerging out of the humanities and social sciences. Crucially, Foucault's lectures have supplied a theoretical alternative to Marxist accounts that define neoliberalism primarily as an economic project spearheaded by elites in order to shore up class power in the midst of a crisis in capital accumulation.[8] In recent years, cultural theorists like Aihwa Ong and Wendy Brown have critiqued the limits of Marxist perspectives on neoliberalism. Building on Foucault, they have emphasized that neoliberalism is more than a mode of economics; it is, rather, a rationality that governs by compelling individuals through norms and values to become autonomous market actors. Ong's 2006 ethnographic work, *Neoliberalism as Exception*, was particularly influential for a first wave of cultural studies scholars exploring the nature of subjectivity and consciousness under neoliberalism. Through examples from East Asian economies like China, Hong Kong, Malaysia, and Singapore, Ong's book contests Marxist characterizations of a singular neoliberal state. Neoliberalism is an adaptable rationality, Ong argues, that has been taken up by diverse political formations, including both authoritarian and democratic regimes. As a result, people in East Asia increasingly find themselves compelled to "self-govern," even though they remain in many cases "skeptical about market criteria and its assault on collective values and community interest."[9]

Brown's 2015 publication, *Undoing the Demos*, makes similar claims about neoliberal subjectivity, though with reference to the advanced capitalist world. This widely read work has informed much of the recent scholarship on neoliberalism coming out of literary and cultural studies. Brown describes the ways in which "neoliberal rationality saturates political life" in the global North and "configures human beings exhaustively as market actors." In the US, for instance, "neoliberal reason configures both soul and city as contemporary firms rather than as polities."[10] The result is that "one might approach one's dating life in the mode of an entrepreneur or investor." Or, "a parent might choose a primary school for a child based on its placement rates in secondary schools" and "elite colleges."[11] As subjects increasingly internalize a compulsion to "self-invest"—or, as they come to relate to the self as something to be constantly pruned, perfected, and measured against market standards—democracy and a collectivist ethos become seriously undermined.

By attending to not simply political economy but also felt experience, Brown and Ong have provided much-needed interventions and analyses of neoliberalism's impacts on North America and East Asia, respectively. However, there are problems with how these accounts define the qualities of experience and consciousness under neoliberalism—problems that stem from their overwhelming focus on the middle classes. *Undoing the Demos* tends to privilege the positionality of professionalized groups in the United States, as Annie McClanahan suggests.[12] As a result, Brown's general claims about the "self-managing" or "self-investing" *homo economicus* entail an elision of the experience of intensified forms of exploitation and dispossession, to which economically and racially marginalized groups are particularly vulnerable. *Neoliberalism as Exception* is more explicit in its attentiveness to the plight of the poor and dispossessed; however, Ong's account, too, invests primarily in the internality of white-collar employees, leaving at best opaque the experiences of East Asian migrant workers whose exploitation she references. In both accounts, the positioning of the professionalized middle classes as emblematic subjects of neoliberalism leaves the reader with the impression that impingements on subjectivity in the contemporary moment arise ultimately from internalized norms, values, and *ideas* of self-management rather than also from material pressures imposed by mounting unemployment, underemployment, and inequality within neoliberalizing nations across the North–South divide.

Because they overlook the important role of material pressures and class tension in shaping consciousness, Brown and Ong are led to overemphasize difference and under-appreciate continuities in subject formation across the neoliberalizing North and South. In *Undoing the Demos* Brown proposes that, whereas "'soft power' drawing on consensus and buy-in" has been crucial in disseminating neoliberalism in the North, "hard power" and violent imposition have been more significant to neoliberalism's proliferation in the South.[13] This opposition minimizes the "hard power" of economic violence in Northern contexts like the United States, and its effects especially on poor and downwardly mobile groups. Meanwhile, Ong highlights how the turn to neoliberalism in East Asia is the product of governments being pressured by US-dominated global capital to make adjustments to their economies. With neoliberalism framed as Northern imposition, Ong then describes ways in which East Asian elites and executives push back against what Pierre Bourdieu and Loic Wacquant refer to as the "symbolic violence" and "imperialism of neoliberal reason."[14] As these privileged groups emerge as resistant to West-imposed corporatism, their role in championing and pushing forward programs and narratives of deregulation and privatization in their respective national contexts is minimized. Thus, a misleading opposition between neoliberalism in the North and South emerges in Ong's work as well, even though it is better attuned than Brown's to class and to growing inequality within nations.

This chapter closely analyzes Ong's and Brown's influential theories and questions some of their assumptions about the nature of experience and consciousness under neoliberalism. Moreover, it suggests that if we attend more carefully to domestic class dynamics, then it becomes possible to see that continuities across Northern and Southern contexts might be at least as significant as contrasts between these contexts arising from histories of colonial domination and subjugation. Drawing on examples primarily from India and the United States, and questioning Brown's theory, I propose that soft and hard power, and consent and coercion, work in tandem in shaping material realities as well as consciousness—whether in the North or the South. Across nations like India and the United States, economic coercion has been key to disciplining vast sections of the labor force over the last four decades; simultaneously, soft power—including domestic elites' promotion of narratives of competitive individualism and cultural nationalism—has played a crucial role in enabling and legitimizing coercive economic policies. Indeed, *contra* Ong and Brown, governments of Southern, formerly colonized nations have not simply been pressured by the West to adopt neoliberal policies. In India, for instance, government technocrats in conjunction with local elites and sections of the middle class have actively pushed forward neoliberal policies since the 1990s, often through narratives of self-reliance steeped in the logic of cultural nationalism. As in the global North, the soft power of such storytelling has had a profound impact on collective consciousness. In recent years this soft power has also been deployed to console and manage overwhelming alienation, which, as Pankaj Mishra argues, is a universal condition, as more and more people experience the ever-growing gap between the ideals and realities of neoliberalism.[15]

The South as Exception

In "Neoliberalism as a Mobile Technology," Aihwa Ong challenges universalizing, Marxist formulations—or "Neoliberalism with a big 'N'"—which assume that "a determining set of economic relationships ... in all domains produce an all-encompassing condition under the hegemony of unfettered markets." These Marxist formulations include David Harvey's conception of the "neoliberal state," Stuart Hall's view of neoliberalism as a "class-based ideology," and the arguments of "Structural Marxists" including Stephen Gill and Jean Comaroff and John Comaroff, which produce "cultural remappings in epochal terms ... [and] seem to ignore how particular political environments are also being reconfigured by neoliberal policies." Ong argues that such formulations obscure the "dynamism" that neoliberalism "encounters in particular environments."[16] Contesting these formulations and drawing on Foucault and Foucauldians like Nikolas Rose, Ong asserts that neoliberalism should be seen not in universal terms but rather as an adaptable rationality, or "mobile technology" and "migratory set of practices" that "co-exists with other political rationalities." Instead of a Marxist "analytics of structure," she therefore presents an "analytics of assemblage."[17] Ong also suggests that the impact of migratory neoliberal practices differ between "advanced liberal nations" and "emerging non-Western contexts." Invoking Nikolas Rose's analysis of neoliberalism in Britain, she notes that "neoliberal practices pervade all areas of contemporary British society." By contrast, "in emerging non-Western contexts, the strategy of governing and self-governing is not uniformly applied to all groups and domains within a nation." This is because non-Western governments make "calculations" that privilege certain citizens while excluding others.[18]

In *Neoliberalism as Exception*, Ong draws on Foucault to complicate the widely held perception of neoliberalism as US imperialism "that uses intermediaries such as the International Monetary Fund (IMF) to pry open small economies and expose them to trade policies that play havoc with these nations' present and future economic welfare." In contrast to this view, Ong notes that "Asian governments have selectively adopted neoliberal forms in creating economic zones and imposing market criteria on citizenship,"[19] and that "since the 1970s, 'American neoliberalism' has become a global phenomenon that has been variously received and critiqued overseas."[20] But while she begins the book in this manner—by challenging "the framework of a neoliberal North versus a South under siege"[21]—the rest of her account only reinforces this framework by portraying neoliberalism in East Asia as largely a response to, and "critique" of, North-dominated "global markets" and "global capital." A core opposition between Euro-American and Asian states emerges, as Ong suggests that the latter have essentially been pressured to neoliberalize by the former. She argues that Asian economies are "compelled to be flexible in their conceptions of sovereignty and citizenship if they are to be relevant to global markets." They have also been prompted to "adjust political space to the dictates of global capital"; and if they have risen, then this is by "subordinating themselves to the demands of major corporations and global regulatory agencies."[22] Similarly, when describing transformations taking place in Malaysia and Indonesia, Ong speaks of how "Asian tiger states, which combine authoritarian and economic liberal features, are *not* neoliberal formations, but their insertion into the global economy has entailed the adoption of neoliberal calculations for managing populations to suit corporate requirements."[23] The implication here is that governments like those of the United States and Britain *are* neoliberal formations, whereas their more overtly authoritarian counterparts in East Asia are merely adopting selective neoliberal "calculations" in order to adjust and adapt to global markets.

Reinforcing this opposition between neoliberal governments of East Asia and their counterparts in Britain and the US, Ong notes that

Such neoliberal calculations, from the perspective of small or emerging countries seeking to be competitive, sometimes come into conflict with the neoliberal logic at a higher scale, as when international financial imperatives of disciplinary neoliberalism force small and medium-sized countries to exercise spatial controls in a different way.[24]

She then goes on to describe how the IMF tried to discipline East Asian economies after the Asian financial crisis of the late 1990s: "The IMF represents the strategic aspect of 'disciplinary neoliberalism,' whereby emerging states are subjected to rules that intensify their subordination to global market forces."[25] On the whole, East Asian economies are seen as primarily "vulnerable to neoliberal demands at the global level" and to being "reconstituted and disciplined through the 'structural adjustments' imposed by global agencies" like the IMF.[26] Thus, although Ong initially contests the "the framework of a neoliberal North versus a South under siege," her subsequent analysis reinforces this framework through the image of a South that has ultimately been compelled to surrender to the demands of North-dominated global capital.

This imagination of the "vulnerability" of East Asian nations forms the basis for Ong's subsequent focus on occasional acts of resistance displayed by these nations' elites and professionalized middle classes. She argues, "The pervasive demands of globalized economic systems act very strongly on the elites, the executives, and those who wield power at the intermediate level."[27] Therefore, it is the managerial classes that dominate her account, even though her analysis of "emerging sites of globality"[28] also introduces the reader to sweatshop workers in special economic zones and migrant domestic workers who work under conditions that she describes as "neo-slavery." Although Ong details the horrific abuse of migrant domestic workers from the Philippines, she ultimately treats these workers' *employers* in places like Singapore as the emblematic subjects of neoliberalism. For the employers are "subjected to neoliberal norms," whereas the migrant workers on whose labor they depend are deemed "outside the preview [sic] of these norms."[29] By the end of the book, Chinese corporate professionals, and their apparently non-"obsequious" response to the demands placed on them, enable Ong to shore up her claim about a distinct, non-Western alternative to neoliberal subject production:

As selective recipients and transformers of global business concepts and practices, urban Chinese show that they can operate effectively in a transnational, transcultural milieu without becoming truly "controllable" or "denationalized" by global capital ... Professionals and managers in Shanghai internalize managerial norms and yet deflect global corporate norms, display an ironic sense of cultural commercialization as well as nationalist capitalism, and are market savvy without giving up the claims of *guanxi* ethics [related to social networks and obligations]. Will Shanghai soon reexport global business practices that rewire the Western business mentality for engaging Chinese markets?[30]

Through Shanghai's corporate professionals and their ability to not simply "internalize" but also "deflect global corporate norms," Ong asserts a form of Southern or postcolonial difference, as well as *resistance* to "the Western business mentality." Based in part on her interviews with these professionals, Ong notes that "Chinese men especially are driven by a logic of entrepreneurial self-fashioning that seeks to control markets and forge a different kind of Chinese capitalism."[31] It is the example of these men, then, that helps Ong prove that "global capital claims will [not] be received compliantly by the host city and its population" and that "neoliberal rationality and managerial knowledge makes an exception for situated ethics."[32]

Similarly, when describing the effects of neoliberalism on India, Ong focuses on Indian computer engineers in the US, who exemplify "Asian knowledge workers" who "have arisen to challenge Western monopoly over knowledge and skills required in contemporary circuits of capitalism."[33] As opposed to the cosmopolitan discourse that celebrates these migrant workers and glosses over their vulnerabilities in the workplace, Ong highlights how the labor-contracting agencies or body shops that hired them during the 1990s dotcom boom "controlled where they worked and when they were paid." Within this context, "some [Indian] technomigrants [were] reduced to a kind of indentured high-tech servitude" and paid "much less than long-term employees."[34] Simultaneously, she attends also to the constraints placed on their counterparts in India—mainly call-center workers employed by US corporations—as the Indian government's move "systematically to dismantle tariff and export controls" in 1991 results in companies like General Electric using outsourcing to displace "jobs but also ... American middle-class values and entitlements overseas." In other words, India's neoliberalization emerges in Ong's book largely through the lens of migrant "knowledge workers"—and through "India's emergence as a site for high-tech jobs" and call centers.[35] In the process, the Indian knowledge worker is framed as a *challenge* to the United States' economic dominance. If in the Chinese case it is the corporate male that poses a potential challenge to "Western business mentality," then in the Indian case it is the knowledge worker that, for Ong, exemplifies "emerging" Asia's challenge to "Western monopoly over knowledge and skills."

But by arguing that "elites, ... executives, and those who wield power at the intermediate level"[36] are especially pressured by, yet also potentially resistant to, the corporate norms that dominate the neoliberal order, the role of these groups in shaping and influencing their governments' "neoliberal calculations" remains obscure. From the outset, Ong rules out the universality of the notion of a "neoliberal state"—where, as David Harvey notes, "Businesses and corporations not only collaborate intimately with state actors but even acquire a strong role in writing legislation, determining public policies, and setting regulatory frameworks (which are mainly advantageous to themselves)."[37] Although *Neoliberalism as Exception* mentions the ways in which East Asian governments give special benefits to corporations, the latter in turn do not appear to wield much power over governments. Domestic

Beyond Alterity

capital does not seem to have much of a role in shaping political economy in the Indian context either. In other words, the obfuscation in Ong's account of how national elites and upper echelons of the middle class have driven—and not simply been vulnerable to—the neoliberal project leads to a conception of Asian states as essentially subjected, and occasionally resistant, to impositions from the West. Ong's replacement of an "analytics of structure" with an "analytics of assemblage" therefore leads to a sense of categorical difference between the neoliberalizing North and South.

A Classless North

Almost a decade after the publication of *Neoliberalism as Exception*, Wendy Brown's *Undoing the Demos* provides new grounds for supporting categorical opposition between the neoliberalizing North and South, even though the North–South relationship is not as central to Brown's account as it is to Ong's. If Ong frames Northern states as neoliberal "formations" in contrast to Southern states that selectively adopt neoliberal "calculations" to respond to the demands of North-dominated capital, then Brown's book differentiates between a soft power-led, insidious, and widespread neoliberalization in the North and a hard power-imposed neoliberalism in the South.

In order to identify the basis for Brown's oppositional framework, it is important to first understand the ways in which she builds on Foucault's interpretation of Chicago School economist Gary Becker's concept of human capital. In his Collège de France lectures Foucault pays close attention to Becker's work, which he frames as an attempt at constructing a labor-centered economic theory that can effectively counter the view of labor offered by the left. Foucault observes that in contrast to mainstream economic theory's marginalization of the worker, in Becker's theory the worker "is not present in the economic analysis as an object—the object of supply and demand in the form of labor power—but [rather] as an active economic subject."[38] But this worker who is an active economic subject is then framed as simply another kind of capitalist. Foucault paraphrases Becker's strange cause-and-effect logic as follows: if, when seen from the point of view of the worker, "wages" are simply a form of "income," and if "income" *also* refers to returns on capital, then it is possible to "call 'capital' everything that in one way or another can be a source of future income." Work, for Becker, then becomes the product not of expenditure of labor but rather of *investment* in "human capital"; and the worker, by consequence, is not someone whose interests are antithetical to that of the capitalist but rather is *homo œconomicus*, or "economic man"—a free and active agent who is, in Foucault's words, "entrepreneur of himself."[39] Foucault observes that this notion of the worker as "active economic subject" and "entrepreneur of himself" is part of Becker's and other Chicago School neoliberals' construction of a market subject whose interests appear to "converge spontaneously with the interest of others."

This is a subject "who accepts reality or who responds systematically to modifications in the variables of the environment"—someone who, therefore, "appears precisely as … manageable" and "eminently governable."[40]

It is this notion of the "eminently governable" political subject that lies at the heart of Wendy Brown's interest in extending Foucault's ideas to the twenty-first century. However, Brown proposes that Foucault's insights need some modification if they are to capture the present character of political subjectivity. Specifically, she argues that the *homo œconomicus* of today is *not* driven by interest, but rather is motivated "by (human) capital appreciation,"[41] or by the need to "strengthen its competitive positioning and appreciate its value"[42] due to being "integrated into and hence subordinated to the supervening goal of macroeconomic growth."[43] She refers to this new neoliberal subject *not* as "entrepreneur of himself" who is "source of [his] earnings," but rather as "human capital" driven by the need to constantly increase returns on self-investment:

> Human capital is not driven by its interests, as was *homo oeconomicus* of yore … Rather, human capital is constrained to self-invest in ways that contribute to its appreciation or at least prevent its depreciation; this includes titrating inputs such as education, predicting and adjusting to changing markets in vocations, housing, health, and retirement, and organizing its dating, mating, creative, and leisure practices in value-enhancing ways.[44]

In other words, Brown sees the contemporary subject as propelled by the need to make all parts of his or her life—from education and health to dating and mating—"value-enhancing." Brown elsewhere refers to this subject as "responsibilized" and, therefore, declares, "I do not think 'interest' adequately captures the ethos or subjectivity of the contemporary neoliberal subject."[45]

To make the case that the contemporary, responsibilized subject is "not driven by its interests" but is instead propelled by the need to "strengthen its competitive positioning and appreciate its value," Brown draws overwhelmingly on the example of the professionalized sections of the US middle class. As McClanahan points out, Brown's descriptions of subjectivity seem to be based on her observations of the plight of "white, educated, professionally employed citizens of the developed world."[46] It is these citizens' apparent experience that shapes Brown's conception of what she posits as the typical, self-investing neoliberal subject, what she calls "human capital."

However, in erasing the role of material interests, Brown risks reproducing Becker's disavowal of class and of the fundamental, interest-based conflict between capital and labor. For Becker, the worker is not someone in an antagonistic relationship with capital, but simply a "rational actor" motivated by the need to invest in and amass human capital through a variety of activities including "schooling, on-the-job training, medical care, migration, and searching for information about prices and incomes … [that] improve skills, knowledge, or health, and thereby raise money or psychic incomes."[47]

Beyond Alterity

Moreover, Becker imagines the workplace as based on mutually beneficial relations. This is a space where "Workers and their employers get bonded together in large part because of the on-the-job learning and training."[48] This workplace resembles the self-regulating marketplace imagined by Friedrich Hayek—an arena and set of relations that naturally, and without coercion or domination, work in the interest of all "players" in a market "game."[49] What Becker's theory obscures is the fact that, as Harvey notes, it is "capital and not the worker that reaps the benefit" of investments in the worker's human capital.[50] Indeed, by erasing the power differential structuring the workplace, Becker "bur[ies] the significance of the class relation between capital and labour."[51] We are all capitalists, according to Becker—charged with the responsibility to invest in our human capital in order to compete successfully in the market game. Failure by some to take on this responsibility is what produces inequality—rather than structures premised on the power differential between workers and owners of capital.

Unlike Becker, Brown neither disavows power nor ignores structural inequality in the United States. However, by claiming that the contemporary neoliberal subject or "human capital" is driven *not* by the need to satisfy interests but rather by the internalized impulse to appreciate value and be autonomous, Brown, much like Becker, obscures the ways in which material necessity—the need to secure food, shelter, healthcare, and so on—continues to compel the choices of the vast majority of workers everywhere. By focusing primarily on how middle-class individuals become self-investors,[52] Brown's theory privileges *self*-imposed constraints (i.e. those emanating from an internalized impulse towards self "management")[53] rather than constraints imposed on workers by economic necessity and by exploitation occurring in the workplace. As a result, Americans in Brown's analysis appear more vulnerable to the imposition of norms of self-management than to powerful and pervasive material pressures resulting from economic insecurity, powerlessness, and deprivation.

Even if Brown does not totally deny structural inequality, her analysis downplays the growing economic divide within the contemporary United States. When she mentions inequality in *Undoing the Demos*, it is only to say that inequality is normalized "in legislation, jurisprudence, and the popular imaginary."[54] This framing of inequality glosses over the expanding power differential between financially secure and insecure, which creates vulnerable workforces and furthers exploitation.[55] On one of the few occasions when the notion of class appears in *Undoing the Demos*, Brown simply notes its "disappearance," alongside the disappearance of "labor" in the US: "labor disappears as a category," she notes, "as does its collective form, class, taking with it the analytic basis for alienation, exploitation, and association among laborers." By treating class as a disappearing "category," Brown invisibilizes the existing force of class power—exerted by capital in conjunction with the state—as well as ongoing class struggle, thereby rendering class an abstraction rather than a reality.

Brown does note that labor laws, protections, as well as benefits are being chipped away at in the Euro-Atlantic world.[56] However, she implies that such dismantling of worker protections are part of neoliberalism's slow, "termitelike" violence in this part of the world. As she puts it, "neoliberalization is generally more termitelike than lionlike ... its mode of reason boring in capillary fashion into the trunks and branches of workplaces, schools, public agencies, social and political discourse and, above all, the subject."[57] This characterization of the process of neoliberalization glosses over aggressive (or "lionlike") processes perpetrated by capitalist elites—for instance, the stripping away of worker rights as well as benefits in places like the United States. In addition, the neoliberal state in the US appears in Brown's analysis to be far less involved in overt domination and in securing the interests of the capitalist class than is actually the case. As Jodi Dean points out, Brown's account of US neoliberalism glosses over "the militarization of the police, intensification of surveillance, harsh sentencing, and practices of raced harassment and murder that accompany the emergence of the strong neoliberal state."[58] In other words, Brown's claim about the disappearance of categories of labor and class can lead to the impression that class power and class conflict have been rendered defunct. However, given its elision of the particularities of the working class's repression, as well as of ongoing labor struggle in the US, it is Brown's theory that might, even if unwittingly, be the one to "disappear" class from analysis.

Based, then, on an understanding of the experiences of largely middle-class, professionalized Americans, and building on Jamie Peck's conception of "the unruly historical geographies of [the] evolving interconnected project" of neoliberalism,[59] Brown goes on to differentiate between neoliberalism in the North and South:

> While neoliberalism in the South was and continues to be violently imposed through coups d'etat and juntas, occupations, structural adjustments (now jumping across the Strait of Gibraltar), and militarized disciplining of populations, its dissemination in the Euro-Atlantic world came about more subtly, through transformations of discourse, law, and the subject that comport more closely with Foucault's notion of governmentality. In the North, while policing and security are certainly both the subject and the object of neoliberal transformations, its main instruments of implementation have been soft, rather than hard power. As a consequence, neoliberalism has taken deeper root in subjects and in language, in ordinary practices and in consciousness.[60]

Here Brown puts forward key claims about neoliberalism in the North and South—and, relatedly, about how neoliberal ideas "take root" in subjectivity. First, she claims that "neoliberal transformations" of societies in the North have been implemented mainly through instruments of soft rather than hard power, which is what sets them apart from the neoliberal transformations of Southern societies. Second, Brown suggests that neoliberal transformations carried out through soft power ensure that neoliberal ideas take "deeper root in subjects and in language, in ordinary practices and in consciousness" than they might if they were imposed by hard power. Soft power prompts subjects to internalize neoliberal values and ideas that circulate through discourse as well as the law; hard power imposes those values from above, which prevents their *deep* rooting in subjectivity. Brown's statements imply that subjects coerced by hard power into following neoliberal ideas might not believe in these ideas as fully as those who have internalized them through soft power.

Brown's opposition between violently imposed neoliberalism in the South and soft power-led neoliberalization in the North is problematic for at least a couple of reasons. To begin with, this opposition reinforces Brown's elision of class politics, including the economic violence imposed by the ruling classes of advanced capitalist nations like the US. The many ways in which US workers are effectively being "coerced," as Erin Hutton puts it, are thus glossed over. Labor coercion, Hutton notes, is not "only a thing of the past, an import from the global South, or a common characteristic of 'bad' jobs,"[61] but rather a reality faced by the vast majority. Specifically, "economic coercion"—or the fear of losing one's job, and the threat of poverty, hunger, and homelessness—is "particularly acute in this era of resurgent labor precarity … [when US workers] face rising employment insecurity and welfare retrenchment along with intense social stigmatization of unemployment and welfare."[62] In addition to economic coercion, physical coercion continues to be exercised, especially towards racialized and other vulnerable populations, via the punitive power that employers might wield within the workplace. And, finally, "status coercion" is exercised by employers' "power to discharge [workers] from a particular status [including immigration status] … and thereby deprive them of rights, privileges, and future opportunities that such status confers."[63] Hutton notes that "status coercion helps *create* the vulnerable and compliant workers on whom neoliberal precarity relies. Whether priming workers for undervalued and insecure positions as adjuncts and postdocs (as does graduate school) or as day laborers and fast-food workers (as do prison labor and workfare), … coercive labor regimes … actively produce the 'precariat,'"[64] the highly insecure labor force that has been growing within as well as outside the United States.

Along with labor coercion, predatory forms of accumulation by dispossession—visible especially in the subprime loans and home foreclosures that led to a transfer of assets away from poor and racial minorities[65]—are particularly hard to reconcile with Brown's characterization of neoliberalization in the North as essentially "termitelike," rather than "lionlike." Following the 2008–2009 housing crisis, triggered in part by higher rates of predatory lending to African Americans, wealth levels among white families began to recover, but "the typical black family lost an additional 13 percent of its wealth," and it is anticipated that "disparities in wealth and home equity between white and black households [will remain] for generations to come."[66] These forms of capitalist predation have been key to increasing inequality in the US in recent decades.

Furthermore, when Brown opposes a hard power-driven neoliberalism in the South to a soft power-led neoliberalism in the North, this obscures the fact that "fiat and force," rarely operates in isolation, or without interaction with "consensus and buy-in."[67] For instance, the ideological pressure on Americans to become self-managing homeowners played an important role in *enabling* the encroachments of predatory finance capital. The termite-like infiltration of consciousness also served to justify lionlike depredation, once it had occurred, by shifting the blame onto responsibilized individuals—and by priming them to tolerate future exploitation and depredation. In other words, "consensus and buy-in" both justifies and facilitates the operation of "fiat and force."

This is true in the global South as well, where the hard power of economic coercion has been enabled in part by the infiltration of consciousness with norms of entrepreneurial individualism. For a few decades now Southern elites have promoted "the idea that the poor are inherently entrepreneurial"[68] and that obtaining cheap and easy access to credit will enable them to transform their lives on their own terms, without state intervention. In the 1980s and 1990s the poor became a "'frontier market'—with microfinance opening up new horizons of capital accumulation"[69] for profit-driven corporate banks. These banks often used coercive loan collection strategies that involved abusing, harassing, and humiliating poor, distressed women who were unable to pay back loans.[70] But, as Ananya Roy argues, "Ways of understanding and explaining the world of microfinance, … [or] poverty knowledge, go hand in hand with poverty capital."[71] In other words, *ideas* about the entrepreneurial poor work in conjunction with the violent business of making the poor into a new "frontier" for finance capital. Roy therefore suggests that in addition to being a purely economic practice, "financialization must be understood as 'a subjectivity and moral code,' 'a way to develop the self,' 'an invitation to live by finance.'"[72] As in the US, in India, too, lending practices that promise greater agency to impoverished and marginalized sections of the population have fueled "coercive redistribution"[73] of wealth and facilitated the "ongoing plunder of subaltern populations specific to the latest phase of neoliberal capitalism."[74] Furthermore, microfinance-based "self-help groups"[75] have shifted the burden of overcoming poverty from the developmental state onto the poor. As in the rest of South Asia, the co-operation of "poverty capital" and "poverty knowledge" has, in addition to shaping subjectivity, "accelerated privatization, weakened the powers of the state, and diminished government investments in the public sector."[76]

But while the promotion of values of entrepreneurialism, self-government, and self-investment has enabled coercive redistribution of wealth, this does not mean that these values have been *internalized* to the same extent by all sections of the population. And this might well be the case across the North–South divide. Whether in the global North or the South, it is quite likely that the degree of internalization of these values varies depending on the extent to which individuals perceive their material interests to be served from engagement in market competition and entrepreneurial activity.

Consider, for instance, Lamia Karim's study of rural Bangladeshi women, in which she points to how middle-class borrowers of microcredit loans often became moneylenders and lent to needier sections of their communities, displaying in the process the "competitive aspects of the neoliberal subject."[77] These petty moneylenders—typically members of the rural middle class— benefited materially from microcredit "at the expense of the poor."[78] As a result, they seemed to display the entrepreneurial traits that Brown and Ong treat as emblematic of neoliberal subjectivity. Meanwhile, impoverished groups, and those most acutely subjected to the hard power of lending institutions were less likely to willingly embrace values of competitive individualism. Karim found that those dispossessed by microcredit instead used a discourse of "social justice based on moral obligations … [in which] the relationship between the borrower and lender lay outside of a financial relationship."[79] Karim's interesting observations suggest that the entrepreneurial subjectivity that Ong and Brown privilege might be more readily observable among groups that materially benefit from the processes of market competition.[80]

In short, it is not merely their "grooming" by a "market sector," as Ong suggests, nor simply their indoctrination into normative values of entrepreneurial individualism, as Brown implies, but also their ability to benefit economically from competitive processes that makes them into market "players" who might also then internalize norms of entrepreneurialism. In the North, too, norms and values of entrepreneurial individualism may not have been uniformly internalized by all sections of the population. The significant recent attempts at collective organizing in the US by diverse segments—from fast-food workers to public school teachers and gig economy employees— testify to the enduring potency of notions of collectivity and social justice, however much organized labor and the welfare state may have been weakened by neoliberalization. Indeed, across the North–South divide, the impact and internalization of neoliberal norms of self-management may well depend on the extent to which one's material interests are served by conforming to these norms. On the one hand, then, there may be class-based differences in subject constitution *within* national contexts and, on the other, continuities *across* the North–South divide, in terms of how and how much these values are absorbed and internalized by various classes.

Rethinking the Alterity Paradigm: The Case of Neoliberal India

The case of neoliberal India helps to complicate and reframe the categorical opposition between North and South that emerges in Brown's and Ong's accounts. To begin with, it is important to note that although the "ideational origins of the [neoliberal] project … [are] transatlantic,"[81] the neoliberal turn in the South did not result simply from the coercive influence of US-dominated transnational organizations like the IMF and World Bank and their mandate of structural adjustment. Even in Chile—where economists trained at the

Chicago School played a vital role in transforming the economy after the 1973 CIA-backed military coup—the neoliberal state was shaped by a confluence of forces, chief among which are the maneuverings of the domestic ruling class. The government of General Pinochet instrumentalized Chicago School-promoted strategies of deregulation and export-led growth as a means of weakening the industrial working class, privatizing state enterprises, and thereby satisfying the business elites who were key to shoring up his military regime.[82] Elsewhere in the South—including in India—neoliberalism has been dynamically "made and remade, as a constructed project,"[83] as Jamie Peck puts it, by a number of situated actors from the ruling classes.

Vijay Prashad argues that many Southern elites had long rallied for liberalization and privatization of their economies in the postwar period:

> The [Southern] ruling classes ... had, like their European and American cousins, long wanted to abandon the cultural strictures of old Nationalism: the requirements of the social-democratic Welfare State in the Atlantic sector; and the requirements of the anticolonial Third World State in the continents of Africa, Asia, and Latin America. Small pockets of elite opinion harbored resentment at the anticolonial heritage. Out of these pockets came new intellectual agendas, including the revival of the Hayek school of liberalism, holding that the state must be excluded from economic activity as much as possible. Cultural ideas of individualism and enterprise were celebrated in the corporate media, at the expense of the national liberation ideas of socialism and the collective good. The impatient elites wanted to set themselves apart from the obligations of the postcolonial state ... It was fitting for them that the new postcolonial states had failed in so many ways: the failures were used as a measure to push for their own agendas. These elites produced their own neoliberalism in response to the same debt crisis [of the 1980s] that had opened their countries up to the factories of the North.[84]

In the history that Prashad recounts, what emerges is not a simple story of Third-World nations being forced to comply with Northern dictates in the aftermath of capitalist crises in the 1970s and 1980s, but rather a more complex one in which "lack of agreement on the strategy for development in the South,"[85] combined with Southern elites' material and ideological alliances with their Northern counterparts, paved the way for what he calls "Neoliberalism with Southern Characteristics." Moreover, Prashad asserts, "The IMF did not force [elites of the global South] into [neoliberal] ideas; they came to them willingly. In some cases the elites took refuge behind the IMF, allowing it to take the blame for policies that would otherwise have been politically unappetizing if they had come from ... already weakened political parties."[86]

In India, structural adjustment was both an imposition by agents like the IMF and World Bank *and* an opportunity embraced by economic elites who had long wanted to counter state-imposed limits on capital. The post-independence mixed economy, which combined central planning and market-led strategies, had succeeded in generating industrial growth during the 1950s and early 1960s; however, by the mid-1960s, this growth had stalled. Economists Jayati Ghosh and C.P. Chandrashekhar attribute stagnation to the government's failure in the early postcolonial years to check the power of rural landowners and monopoly capitalists and thereby improve wages and strengthen the purchasing power of the vast majority of the population. In the mid-1980s, the government, while still sidestepping the root causes of stagnation, opted to boost the weak domestic market through debt-financed public spending and partial liberalizing of the economy. In adopting this strategy, India followed many developed and developing nations at the time who were taking advantage of "access to foreign exchange that was afforded by the rise to dominance of finance internationally." But this growing reliance on commercial borrowing from abroad, including from the IMF and the World Bank, precipitated a balance of payments crisis in 1991, which was then used by pro-liberalization advocates—including technocrats in the government as well as leaders and managers of big corporations—to justify "an accelerated process of liberalization."[87]

As in the global North, in India, too, the capitalist state has relied heavily on soft power to justify neoliberal policies in the name of national progress. Since the early 1990s the name "New India" has been marshaled by political and economic elites to, in Ravinder Kaur's words, brand a "postreform, technofriendly, high-consumption entrepreneurial nation." The term was actively deployed within spectacular, state-led nation branding efforts to "perform hope and promise for global capital" and to suggest that its postcolonial "nationalist dreams [were] fully harnessed to the ever-enchanting project of capitalism."[88] In this aspect, India joined other "third world turned emerging markets" like Brazil, Mexico, Egypt, and South Africa, where "the promise of the growth story ... [was being] affectively entangled with the collective dreamworlds visualized and illuminated in the great spectacle of mass-publicity campaigns."[89] These campaigns were designed to "boost the global image of the nation as an investment destination, to draw foreign capital, to garner favorable trade agreements, and to sell economic reforms to its own citizens as pathways to progress and prosperity."[90] While campaigns like Incredible India were used primarily to promote New India abroad, publicity efforts like India Shining enabled the government to sell neoliberal reforms domestically, amidst a crisis of rural poverty that had become acute and undeniable by the early twenty-first century. During the first decade of liberalization the urban middle classes were privileged within the government's imagination and discourse of the New India, but campaigns like India Shining in the early 2000s helped to popularize within the domestic public sphere the image of a liberalizing nation "that was enterprising and inclusive and that everyone could be part of provided they signed on to the project of economic reforms."[91]

The branding and promotion of India as a new, entrepreneurial nation has in recent years been picked up and reinforced by a number of journalists in the advanced capitalist world looking to justify policies of privatization and state withdrawal in their respective national contexts. Stories of "emerging India" figure often in publications like *The Economist*, and this formerly colonized nation appears as a symbol of collective liberation or as an index of the sort of progress that contemporary capitalism can make possible. Within India, stories of national emergence are daily repeated by the mostly private news media, and have contributed to popularizing not just the image of a new nation but also ideas of entrepreneurialism and self-help, which are deemed essential for its transformation. Nandini Gooptu describes the formation of an "enterprise culture" in India, and notes that there has been an "overwhelming emphasis on, and ubiquity of, the idea of enterprise and the enterprising self in Indian public discourse ... and in many emerging areas of everyday practice"[92]—even though "it is debatable whether enterprising value systems are being adopted wholesale."[93] In particular, a "fanciful essentialist notion that Indians are culturally and congenitally endowed with entrepreneurial acumen from time immemorial has had a meteoric ascendance in recent years, promoted and articulated by a vast range of actors and institutions."[94] Both state and non-state actors have deployed this culturally essentialist discourse of Indian entrepreneurship and the enterprising self for the justification of neoliberal policy. Moreover, there has been a mainstreaming of conceptions of "Sociopreneurs, or social entrepreneurs, ... as the agents of change who can find enterprising solutions to social and political problems and can deploy entrepreneurial skills to overcome social challenges, including those of poverty and deprivation" within India.[95] Simultaneously, "The poor too ... [have been] projected as entrepreneurial assets of the nation ... [and] depicted as historically experienced self-reliant and enterprising innovators."[96]

As in the US, class politics are frequently dismissed within recent government and media discourse in India, and poverty and inequality are discursively reframed as problems that can be solved through the enterprise of the poor and the social entrepreneurship, patriotism, and charity of the middle and upper classes. Simultaneously, the increasing embrace and celebration of powerful Indian conglomerates and their CEOs has led to normalizing corporate vocabulary within the public sphere. Kaur notes that the "informal practice of addressing political executives as CEOs gained currency with Prime Minister Manmohan Singh," and this is "a mantle that the current prime minister, Narendra Modi, has enthusiastically assumed."[97] In recent years the Modi-led right's promotion of nationalist maxims like "Make in India," and explicitly neoliberal ones like "Minimum Government, Maximum Governance," has also enabled the whitewashing of majoritarian Hindu nationalism by reframing it as essentially pro-business and pro-efficiency. This convergence of the discourses of business and cultural nationalism under Modi's government is only the most recent instantiation of the sustained ways in which political and economic elites have worked to influence collective consciousness in post-liberalization India.

In *Age of Anger*, Pankaj Mishra argues that neoliberal capitalism has created "global structures of feeling and thinking."[98] If Foucauldians like Brown attribute the rise of cultural nationalism in the present to "a neoliberal mode of reason" or "neoliberal rationality [which has] prepared the ground for the mobilization and legitimacy of ferocious antidemocratic forces in the second decade of the twenty-first century,"[99] then Mishra offers a more nuanced explanation that takes into account the collision between elites' constant promotion of fantasies of upward mobility and on-the-ground realities of increasing economic stagnation and downward mobility that have provoked widespread anger and resentment. Drawing on Nietzsche's observations about "men of ressentiment" in industrializing Europe, together with Hannah Arendt's comments on postwar globalization, Mishra characterizes the early twenty-first century as marked by a

> "tremendous increase in mutual hatred and a somewhat universal irritability of everybody against everybody else", or *ressentiment*. An existential resentment of other people's being, caused by an intense mix of envy and sense of humiliation and powerfulness, *ressentiment*, as it lingers and deepens, poisons civil society and undermines political liberty, and is presently making for a global turn to authoritarianism and toxic forms of chauvinism.[100]

Tracing the roots of this growing *ressentiment*, Mishra notes that "Beginning in the 1990s, a democratic revolution of aspiration—of the kind Tocqueville witnessed with many forebodings in early nineteenth-century America—swept across the world, sparking longings for wealth, status and power, in addition to ordinary desires for stability and contentment, in the most unpromising circumstances." Given that these longings and aspirations have remained unfulfilled for the vast majority, more and more people increasingly perceive a gap between experience and ideology—between lives of precarity on the one hand and the ever-present narratives of upward mobility on the other.

In other words, for Mishra, the problem lies not just with the internalization of neoliberal ideas of individual freedom, but rather with the persistent experience of a gap between these ideas and the harshness of daily precarity. The "particular experience of individual freedom in a void," Mishra points out, is "now endemic among populations in the 'developed' as well as the 'developing' and the 'underdeveloped' world."[101] In a variety of national and cultural contexts, educated middle classes' "fears of social redundancy … combined with the rage of the dispossessed … and the indifference, bordering on contempt, of the plutocracy" have created ideal conditions for the rise of far-right authoritarian regimes.[102] As "billions more people have been exposed to the promises of individual freedom in a global neo-liberal economy that imposes constant improvisation and adjustment—and just as rapid obsolescence … one moves quickly from unlimited freedom to a craving for unlimited despotism."[103]

The following pages are aligned with Mishra's insights, and they treat India as an emblematic site for understanding the "global structures of feeling and thinking" produced over the last three decades. Thus, I approach Indian authors and texts not simply as representatives of the particularities of the global South, but also as illustrations of broader transformations taking place within culture and subjectivity under neoliberal capitalism. The next chapter explores these broader transformations, by tracking the consolidation of a neoliberal "script" that has been actively promoted over the last three to four decades by ideologues, elites, and members of the professional and managerial class. The story of this script's development and circulation, especially in India, provides a potent illustration of the role of "soft power" within the rise of neoliberalism globally.

CHAPTER 2

The Neoliberal Script

A myth has grown up that free market capitalism increases ... inequalities, that the rich benefit at the expense of the poor. Nothing could be further from the truth. Wherever the free market has been permitted to operate, the ordinary man has been able to attain levels of living never dreamed of before.

—Milton Friedman[1]

[W]e must restore to the creation of wealth its proper place in the development process. For, without it, we cannot remove the stigma of abject poverty, ignorance and disease ... For the creation of wealth, we must encourage accumulation of capital.

—Manmohan Singh[2]

The critics of the [economic] reforms remind us ad nauseam that liberalization will only make the rich richer. This is not true ... By opening the economy, we seem to have opened the way for a new merit order, where talent, hard work, and managerial skills matter far more than inherited wealth.

—Gurcharan Das[3]

Pierre Bourdieu has argued that if neoliberal ideas are now seen as self-evident, then "this is as a result of a whole labour of symbolic inculcation in which journalists and ordinary citizens participate passively and, above all, a certain number of intellectuals participate actively. Against this permanent, insidious imposition ... researchers have a role to play ... [by] analys[ing] the production and circulation of this discourse."[4] Taking Bourdieu's cue, this chapter attends to the "labor of symbolic inculcation" that has produced neoliberalism as a cultural and ideological dominant, not just in the "most important homelands of the movement: France, Germany, the UK, and the United States"[5]—but also in emerging economies like India, which began the process of economic liberalization and privatization in the 1980s. Since the early 1990s, when the Indian government accepted a loan from the International Monetary Fund (IMF) and began promoting and justifying structural adjustment in the public sphere, Indian elites have played a crucial role in co-constructing with their Northern counterparts a much-repeated "neoliberal script." This is a script that—as the opening epigraphs illustrate—plots the resolution to problems like poverty and inequality by ascribing progressive agency to deregulated markets and private enterprise. The centrally planned state figures in this script as a shadow figure—a dystopian "other" to the free market ideal.

The above epigraphs also point to how notions of free markets, individual enterprise, and private gain are rarely promoted as ends in themselves within neoliberal discourse but rather are framed as delivering progress for all. If Chicago School economist Milton Friedman pronounces free-market capitalism morally sound, owing to its benefits for not just the rich but also "the ordinary man," then Manmohan Singh—the architect of India's neoliberal reforms—casts "wealth creation" from [private] "accumulation of capital" as necessary for fighting "poverty, ignorance, and disease" in the nation; and public intellectual Gurcharan Das, too, has the nation in mind in his positing of market liberalization as the ideal path to a "new merit order." Whereas many theorists of neoliberalism, including Bourdieu, speak of "a radical separation [in neoliberal discourse] between the economic and the social, ... [with the social] left to one side, abandoned to sociologists, as a kind of reject,"[6] in fact—as the above epigraphs suggest—far from abandoning the social, or "radically separating" the economic and social, neoliberal ideologues actively tap into social and collective concerns to defend their pro-market prescriptions. Their rescripting of collective welfare—such that it appears dependent on private wealth creation—has had a profound impact on consciousness and has made neoliberal ideology into the "insidious imposition" Bourdieu talks about.

My use of "script" derives in part from the world of theater and film, where the term refers to a source of sequentially organized information designed to elicit interpretation, performance, and repetition. Since roughly the 1970s, a number of scholars across disciplines like sociology, psychology, cognitive science, history, and literary studies have extended this theatrical conception of the term to think about the existence of "social scripts." Countering the sense that, for instance, racial, gender, or sexual identity arise entirely out of biological attributes and predispositions, social constructionists have described the force of social scripts that are learned through routine, interpersonal interactions, as well as texts inculcating normative behaviors and ways of seeing.[7] Invoking the theatrical provenance and building on the notion of norm-producing social scripts, I define the neoliberal script as an ideational sequence that has through imaginative acts of repetition-with-variation helped to normalize the view that deregulated business and private enterprise are the best engines for delivering both personal and societal growth. The constant repetition of this script—by intellectuals, technocrats, journalists, cultural producers,

The Neoliberal Script

and others—has contributed to legitimizing market-based solutions to problems such as poverty, while eroding the currency of strategies of popular redistribution.

Whereas later chapters of this book examine fictional texts' interactions with the neoliberal script, this chapter explores how influential *non*fiction works have shaped and proliferated this script. It begins with Friedman's *Free to Choose* television series and its companion volume that, since their initial appearance in 1980, remain "the most popular and widely disseminated introduction" to the celebrated, Nobel Prize-winning economist's neoliberal ideas.[8] The series stages Friedman's travels across Europe, Asia, and the United States, as well as his debates with a number of prominent intellectuals and advocates. Recent scholarship has brought to light Friedman's "exploitation" of white supremacist anxieties in his advocacy for the privatization of education in the United States.[9] My analysis of the *Free to Choose* series shows how related to Friedman's exploitation of racial ideology is his exploitation of a colonial imagination. In particular, by drawing on affecting images of India's abject poverty, *Free to Choose* attaches colonial constructions of "backwardness" to the idea of state intervention. India's poverty is attributed entirely to what Friedman describes as its "tyrannical" postcolonial developmental state; moreover, India's example is then used to bolster his case against the so-called welfare "trap" created by governments in the advanced capitalist world. In the process, the legacies of British colonialism in the Indian subcontinent are effectively erased.

Despite its problematic racial and imperial hubris, however, Friedman's rhetoric is ultimately not that singular. In fact, it anticipates in key ways arguments that were proliferated in the postcolonial world by prominent advocates of economic liberalization like Manmohan Singh, India's finance minister in the early 1990s and its prime minister from 2004 to 2014. Singh's public speeches have played a key role in popularizing the notion that market liberalization is India's liberation from the postcolonial developmental state, or "License Raj"—a derogatory term that echoes colonial rule or the "British Raj." The rhetorical framing of India's neoliberal turn as marking the nation's "second independence" was then reiterated by prominent public figures like Gurcharan Das, a former corporate executive who began an illustrious career as writer and proselytizer of economic reforms in the 1990s. I attend closely to storytelling patterns in *India Unbound* (2000), Das's widely acclaimed and bestselling "national biography" that—both in its original English-language form and in translation—helped to sell the project of economic liberalization to vast sections of India's middle class. Like Friedman, Das engages with the ideas of major intellectuals, including contemporary American philosophers like John Rawls and John Kenneth Galbraith, in order to give scholarly heft and ethical amplification to his arguments against what he describes as India's "rapacious" developmental state. In terms of both rhetorical strategy and argumentative logic, Das's work illustrates vividly some of the striking continuities in articulations of neoliberal ideology across the North–South divide.

Beyond Alterity

Considering together better- and lesser-known neoliberals, in conjunction with an array of their influential oral, written, and audiovisual works, affords insight into the variously scaled, multilingual, and multimedia platforms by which the neoliberal script has been repeatedly staged for popular consumption over the last decades. Because *Free to Choose* and *India Unbound* are explicit in their critiques of progressive redistribution and in their attempts to promote the logic of privatization, these works offer particularly clear insight into the process of staging neoliberal ideas for symbolic inculcation—and hence are the performances of the neoliberal script I analyze most closely in this chapter. Over the last decades, such performances have been used across the richer and poorer nations of the world to defend cuts to state spending, which have only further exposed the poor to the depredations of market competition. Moreover, the repeated presentation of such spending as *inherently* oppressive has contributed to erasing the gains made by the welfare and developmental states of the twentieth century, as well as to hindering the imagination of future forms of state-led redistribution that could be *more* just than those of the past and better in responding to the needs of the vast majority.

With the steady undermining of all forms of progressive state intervention, it is not surprising that a Hayekian notion of the "strong" state has gained ascendency globally. We see this clearly in Das's more recent writing, which abandons an earlier, Friedmanesque anti-statism and veers instead towards the notion that, to effectively back capital and ensure its transformation of the economy, India needs a state whose primary job is the enforcement of rule of law and private-sector contracts. In 2014, Das lent his support to Narendra Modi's government, which came to power by promising further liberalization and privatization carried out by a tough, Hindu nationalist state. Shifting articulations of the neoliberal script in Das's work point to a growing openness to cultural nationalism—the only ideology, as Radhika Desai argues, that is "capable of being a legitimising ideology under the prevailing global and national political economy."[10] These shifting articulations also point to the need to track the various incarnations of neoliberalism, which, far from being a "pure" and stable ideology is, as Jamie Peck points out, a contradictory and shape-shifting one, based on a "mix of prejudice, practice, and principle," and capable of cultural adaptation as well as mutation over time.[11]

Reframing Poverty in *Free to Choose*

The trajectory of Milton Friedman's career—including his engagements with India—index the evolving status of neoliberal thought in the advanced capitalist world during the mid-to-late twentieth century. In 1947 Friedman was one of those invited by Friedrich Hayek to join the first gathering of the Mont Pèlerin Society. By 1978, when production for *Free to Choose* began, he was an internationally recognized, Nobel Prize-winning economist

The Neoliberal Script

who was influencing policy decisions of the Nixon and Carter administrations.[12] Friedman had already begun offering his economic expertise to the US government in the 1950s, when he wrote a manifesto of sorts and prophesied that "neo-liberalism" could in time emerge as "the major current of opinion."[13] In 1955, at the behest of President Eisenhower's Council of Economic Advisers, Friedman traveled to India as an emissary of the free-market perspective and in order to "counter the influence of the [Soviet Union's] left-wing advice" on the Indian government's Second Five Year Plan.[14] While his visit did not have much impact on the Indian government's Plan, it nonetheless had a significant effect on his subsequent intellectual production. India's postcolonial state would come to play a crucial role in *Free to Choose*, an influential work of neoliberal propaganda released in the United States on the cusp of the Reagan revolution.

As Angus Burgin notes, *Free to Choose* emerged out of a moment "of unusually intense debate over economic policy, [when] the most prominent public exemplars of left- and right-wing economic views … found themselves engaged in competing demands to reach a mass audience through the maturing medium of television."[15] The idea for a documentary series came from US Public Broadcasting Service (PBS) executive Robert Chitester, who saw the need to counter the influence of the widely broadcast 1977 BBC series *The Age of Uncertainty*, featuring post-Keynesian economist John Kenneth Galbraith. Chitester—who had gone through an ideological transformation after reading Friedman's bestselling *Capitalism and Freedom* (1962)—approached Friedman with the idea of making a rival series that would be privately funded but produced and distributed via PBS. To finance the series Chitester raised, partly with Friedman's help, about three million dollars in donations from powerful private entities including the Pepsico Foundation, General Motors, General Mills, Bechtel, as well as the Readers Digest Association (which in 1944 had published another widely disseminated work of neoliberal ideology, Hayek's *Road to Serfdom*).[16]

Friedman had long believed in popularizing neoliberal ideas. During the first Mont Pèlerin Society meeting, he "assailed the tendency of liberals to represent their ideas as a 'defense of the status quo' and urged his colleagues to rely instead on rhetoric that was 'dynamic and progressive.' It was essential, he said, to relay the fact that their organization was 'concerned in the progress of man's welfare.'"[17] In the years following this meeting, Friedman remained committed to framing neoliberal perspectives as "dynamic and progressive"—and to doing so in simple language, so as to reach a broad audience. He therefore welcomed Chitester's proposal to produce a popular, televised defense of *laissez-faire* economics. The ten-part *Free to Choose* series appeared on US public television shortly after the 1979 release of a companion print volume that Friedman co-wrote with his wife, Rose. In the end, the series and companion volume proved to be far more commercially successful and influential than Galbraith's *Age of Uncertainty*. "The clarity and consistency of Friedman's message [in the documentary series]," Burgin writes, "convinced many viewers that there were clean solutions to problems that other opinion leaders continued to represent as messy."[18]

The preface to the Friedmans' companion volume to *Free to Choose* makes clear their aim to "persuade" and "convert" by making accessible the abstract ideas of *Capitalism and Freedom*.[19] This aim also comes through in the televised documentary's title sequence, where an image of Friedman with the US Capitol in the background is followed by stills of workers and families of different ethnicities. The series' full title, *Free to Choose: A Personal Statement*, unfolds amidst shots of the economist gazing intently, but also smiling affably, while seated in the US gold reserve. Underwritten by bracing orchestral music, this title sequence establishes Friedman as an influential intellectual who is nonetheless in tune with ordinary Americans. Moreover, as Friedman debates a small group gathered at the University of Chicago library at the end of each episode, he performs openness to diverse opinions and thereby demonstrates that neoliberalism is compatible with democracy and tolerance of difference. Ultimately, this careful construction of persona bolsters the credibility of Friedman's message—that the so-called free market is the best means of improving the plight of the "common man" and also of "foster[ing] harmony and peace among the peoples of the world."[20]

The episodes that follow entail layering and repetition of potent images of work, migration, and trade, which are made to function as metonyms for Friedman's conception of the free market and its logic of competition. The affective charge of these visuals allows the documentary to quickly gloss over historical complexity. For instance, in the opening episode, "The Power of the Market" Friedman narrates over evocative shots of the New York Harbor how the Canarsie Indians who once lived on the swampy island of New York traded it to the Dutch for "$24 of cloth and trinkets." "The newcomers founded a city, New Amsterdam, at the edge of an empty continent," he notes, simply—thereby at once acknowledging the presence of Native Americans, and promptly negating this presence by invoking the myth of North America as an "empty continent." US history is thus cleansed of the violence that constitutes its settler colonial past; and unequal power relations between colonizer and colonized are framed as fair economic exchange between freely trading parties.

Subsequent archival footage of European immigrants arriving at Ellis Island and populating the markets of Manhattan's Lower East Side are accompanied by Friedman's "voice of God" narration,[21] which describes New York's emergence as a magnet for those "driven by fear and poverty" who ended up building "a new nation, with their sweat, their enterprise, and their vision of a better future." In the "personal" voice promised by the series's subtitle, the economist recounts how his own parents emigrated from Hungary in the late nineteenth century, with few resources and no government programs to turn to but also fewer rules and regulations, licenses, and permits to restrict them. When the film cuts to the present, a cheery Friedman appears inside a poorly ventilated garment factory in New York's Chinatown, which he compares to

The Neoliberal Script

the factory where his own mother worked when she was a new immigrant. Women workers are visible in the foreground and background of shots taken inside this factory, but the viewer is not given access to their perspectives. Friedman acknowledges the poor working conditions at the factory but argues that it is nonetheless beneficial for the mostly female workers, who are bound to leave it, just as his mother eventually left the factory where she once worked. If in the opening moments Friedman's narration cleanses US history of settler colonial violence, then his direct address to the viewer from the Chinatown factory empties the workplace of all signs of conflict between employer and employee. Friedman's presence within the factory, coupled with the workers' silence, contributes to casting the workforce as compliant. This presentation is not simply problematic, it is also ironic, especially in light of the actual attempts at collective organizing in New York's Chinatown during the late 1970s. These attempts resulted only three years after the production of *Free to Choose* in a successful strike led by "more than 20,000 immigrant women garment workers"—the largest of its kind in the community's history.[22]

Eliding the workers' perspectives, the documentary series positions the Chinatown garment factory as an exemplary site of free-market capitalism— and then moves on to parallel sites in Hong Kong. Here Friedman's voice-of-God narration suggests that, if in the late nineteenth century European immigrants were fleeing persecution in their home countries by migrating to the US, then in the late twentieth century hundreds of thousands of Asians were migrating to Hong Kong to flee persecution in communist China and Vietnam. Shots of ships arriving at Hong Kong's harbor and of vendors selling their wares in open-air marketplaces all recall the earlier archival footage of late nineteenth-century America. Through an implied connection between scenes of harbors, borders, and markets in Hong Kong and the US, Friedman concretizes abstractions such as "impersonal market forces" and Adam Smith's "invisible hand." Instead of these abstractions, the visible movement of individuals at borders and in marketplaces helps establish for the viewer a vivid sense of the dynamic energy of the "free market." Thus, the ideological opposition between mobilizing and energizing markets on the one hand and stagnation-inducing governments on the other is given concrete shape.

When the viewer is shown a garment factory in Hong Kong—strongly reminiscent of its counterpart in New York—Friedman makes a point of specifying that Hong Kong's success is "*not* based on the exploitation of workers." However, once again, we are denied access to the workers' voices and points of view. Friedman speaks for them, asserting with his characteristic aplomb that the workers are "free," "free to work what hours they choose, free to move to other jobs if they wish. The market gives them that choice." When he walks through market-filled streets and speaks of "impersonal market forces," he notably does not communicate with the actual subjects engaged in transactions. Then, addressing the camera whilst standing against the backdrop of Hong Kong's harbor and skyline, an ebullient Friedman declares Hong Kong the "freest market in the world." "The free market," he proclaims,

45

Beyond Alterity

"enables people to go into any industry they want, to trade with whomever they want, to buy in the cheapest market around the world, to sell in the dearest market around the world. But, most important of all, if they fail, *they* bear the cost. If they succeed, *they* get the benefit. And it's that atmosphere of incentive that has induced them to work, to adjust, to save, to produce a miracle." Hong Kong's silent workers are thus, like their counterparts in New York's Chinatown, imagined as free and willing participants in an economy based on "incentive."

When he turns to the slums and houseboats where the poor live, Friedman admits that Hong Kong is no utopia, but he implies that its poverty results from migration from the un-free markets of communist China and Vietnam. His voice-of-God narration here reassures the viewer that despite being "desperately poor" these migrants into Hong Kong are still "free"—given that they now have the "freedom and opportunity to … improve their lot." Shots of children splashing merrily around the houseboats lead to Friedman's declaration that their "appalling poverty" is not what it might appear: rather, it is "a poverty to which [most people in the world] would aspire, a state of affairs they would like to achieve." Friedman admits that, "there is no system that is going to eliminate completely poverty." But, he asks, "Which system has the greatest chance? Which is the best arrangement for enabling poor people to improve their lives?" Friedman answers this question through Hong Kong's example: in Hong Kong, the "freest market in the world," even the "appalling poverty" is of a kind that is worth aspiring to.

The "Tyranny" of the Postcolonial Indian State

Friedman's defense of Hong Kong as a virtual utopia is reinforced in the next episode, "The Tyranny of Control," in which the centrally planned economy of postcolonial India comes to function as Hong Kong's dystopian "other."[23] India's poverty—Friedman makes clear—is *not* of a kind worth aspiring to. For India, he suggests, is marked by stagnation and dependence, stemming entirely from its government's misguided regulation of markets.

The motif of garment manufacturing persists in the sequences focused on India, though in sharp contrast to the urbanity of Hong Kong the focus here lies on textile production in *rural* India. Shots of village women drawing water from a well and using spinning wheels to make cloth, coupled with Friedman's lamentations about India's postcolonial economy, indicate to the viewer that Indians are not just poor but also set back in time. Over scenes of daily life in a South Indian village, Anakaputhur, Friedman explains the causes underlying its poverty: "The government decided that traditional weaving should be protected from twentieth-century competition … By subsidizing the cotton that the villagers spin and the cloth that they weave, [the government has] made it difficult for modern industry to develop." Moreover, he complains, the government-subsidized handloom sector produces "patterns that never

The Neoliberal Script

vary and methods that never change." Standing in a dingy handloom factory with rudimentary equipment, Friedman directly addresses the camera. "Other industries," he declares, "both textile industries and industries of a variety of kinds have been restricted, explicitly kept back, prevented from providing more productive employment, in order to make room for *this* industry. The effect has been to inhibit the development, to prevent the growth, to prevent the dynamic activity that could otherwise develop out of the energies and abilities of the people of India." The handloom workers, barely visible in the background, do not speak. Their invisibility and silence are crucial in enabling Friedman to draw on the ideological power of colonial notions of the formerly colonized world as inherently "backward" in order to reinforce the case against central planning.

With the dingy village factory as setting, Friedman launches his argument about the inherent backwardness of all governments: "Throughout the world, governments always profess to be forward-looking. In practice they are always backward-looking, either protecting the industries that exist or making sure that whatever ventures *they* have decided to undertake are encouraged and developed." In this manner, he identifies the postcolonial Indian government's *central planning* as the source of its failure to improve the plight of rural populations. He thereby advances a now-familiar reading of India's developmental state—that by deciding to plan the economy and make interventions in support of the poor, this state in fact sowed the seeds for corruption and stagnation. This framing erases the actual gains made by the developmental state, especially in the first decade and a half following India's independence, when the incomes and standard of living of the bottom half of the population increased substantially, and the economy grew by about 3.5 percent annually—a remarkable achievement, as Jean Dreze and Amartya Sen point out, especially "compared with the near-zero growth (and at times even economic decline) that occurred in the colonial days."[24]

Beyond Alterity

Scenes from life in Anakaputhur are later juxtaposed with images of desperate urban poverty, thereby casting even the active rural workers within Friedman's imagination of India as a "human tragedy": "The human tragedy," he notes, "is that in India ... [workers'] potential has been stifled by the straightjacket imposed by an all-wise and paternalistic government. Central planning in practice has condemned India's masses to poverty and misery." Whereas he celebrates Hong Kong workers for being dynamic, adaptive, enterprising, Friedman characterizes the active, rural Indian workers as tragic victims, with their entrepreneurial "potential" stifled by the "tyrannical" government. But without access to the villagers' perspectives, the role of the handloom industry in their lives remains unclear. Whereas it is quite conceivable that the handloom industry might serve as a welcome source of employment in the village, Friedman's commentary assures us that it—like the government subsidies that support it—is inherently "backward looking."

The stirring shots of urban poverty and homelessness that follow scenes in the village factory function as not merely representations of reality but also indexes where, as Mary Ann Doane notes, the "sole proposition [is] that of 'thereness,' irrefutable presence." "In the [indexical] trace," she observes "things speak themselves; they are not spoken."[25] Much like the index, the image of homelessness and abject poverty in urban India functions as an "empty sign"[26] that purports simply to point to reality, rather than to frame or explain it in any particular way. From what appear to be "empty signs" of India's poverty, the documentary then cuts jarringly to street life in a glittering, vehicle-dense, hypermodern Japanese city. In other words, the indexical force of photographic images of Indian poverty on the one hand and of Japan's glittering success on the other is used to present as natural and irrefutable the contrast Friedman constructs between "backward-looking" government and "forward-looking" markets.

The Neoliberal Script

Turning from this glittering urban landscape to a weaving factory in Japan, Friedman declares that by *any* standards its textiles are beautiful—thereby prompting the viewer to mentally contrast them with Indian handloom cloth he had previously criticized for its unvarying patterns. Friedman's voiceover is accompanied with visuals of a modern, electronically mechanized loom, and the movements performed by Indian handloom workers now appear emulated by high-end Japanese machines. The factories also look bigger and brighter than the workshops in which the Indian workers toiled; and Friedman pronounces the Japanese workers to be "highly skilled and well paid." This contrast between a low-tech handloom operation in India and a high-tech weaving factory in Japan is misleading, however, because it conflates India with industrial backwardness and gives the impression that the nation does not *also* possess modern, industrialized textile manufacturing of the kind seen in Japan. In fact, by focusing on the small-scale handloom sector, Friedman erases the centrally planned Indian state's support of large textile manufacturers who "use[d] state intervention as a device to consolidate and expand their monopolistic positions."[27] In making it appear as though the postcolonial Indian state subsidized the handloom sector at the expense of modern industry, Friedman obscures the fact that this state in fact secured domestic markets for large textile companies by protecting these companies from foreign competition. Relatedly, we lack context of the history of the Japanese textile industry and the extent to which it, too, may have been supported by government investment. Instead, the stark visual contrast between poverty and affluence, and between traditional weaving practices in rural India and technologically advanced practices in hypermodern Japan, fuels Friedman's drama of opposition between centrally planned dystopia and free-market utopia.

In their print volume to the television documentary, the Friedmans elaborate on the "especially illuminating example" that is the "contrast between the experiences of India and Japan."[28] Both India and Japan had

49

ancient civilizations and feudal societies, they note. In Japan, it was the Meiji Restoration that propelled change, while in India it was independence from British rule. India had once "enjoyed substantial economic growth before World War I. That growth was converted into stagnation between the two world wars by the struggle for independence from Britain, but was not reversed." They assert that "the standard of life of the poorest third of the population has probably declined [since independence]," thereby implying the superiority of the British colonial economy for India's poor.[29] This claim about how the standard of living of the poor has "probably declined" in postcolonial India denies not just the growth made in the years following independence but also the stagnancy of the Indian economy under British rule, in addition to the desperate poverty and famine of the colonial era. It also denies the "drain of wealth" from the colonies that, as Utsa and Prabhat Patnaik point out, aided Britain's "industrial transition from the eighteenth century onward, as well as the diffusion of capitalism to the regions of new European settlement."[30] Instead, by contrasting the level of economic prosperity in India and Japan, the Friedmans indirectly articulate an apology for British colonialism. In other words, just as *Free to Choose* glosses over the violence of settler colonialism in the US, it also erases the exploitative and oppressive nature of British rule in India.

In addition to effacing the progress made in the postcolonial period, *Free to Choose* presents India's postcolonial state as simply neo-feudal. This point is amplified through the audiovisual strategies of a later episode of the documentary titled "Created Equal."[31] Here, shots of bejeweled Indian women dancing for the "descendants of the Maharajas" are used to invoke Orientalizing portrayals of India as eternally exotic. Through the excess and decadence of Jaipur's former nobility, Friedman challenges the myth "that [it is] free-market capitalism [that] increases … inequalities, [and] that the rich benefit at the expense of the poor." Instead, Friedman argues, while standing against the backdrop of the ornate Jaipur City Palace, "Nowhere is the gap between the rich and poor greater, nowhere are the rich richer and the poor poorer than in those societies that do *not* permit the free market to operate, whether they be feudal societies where status determines position, or modern centrally planned economies, where access to government determines position." The City Palace and its excesses are thus made emblematic of the centrally planned postcolonial state, in which "access to government determines position." In the process, all aspects of a centrally planned economy—including interventions in defense of poor and marginalized groups—are deemed part of the state's generally regressive, neo-feudal character.

Later in this episode Friedman returns the viewer to further images of abject Indian poverty, over which he makes his concluding remarks: "Everywhere, economic progress has meant far more to the poor than to the rich. Wherever progress has been achieved, it has relieved the poor from back-breaking toil. It has also allowed them to enjoy the comforts and conveniences that have always been available to the rich." Friedman thus instrumentalizes images of India's poor to argue that the poor everywhere would have *most* to gain from a shift from planning to deregulated capitalism, thereby sealing the connection between collective progress and neoliberal economics, and implying that the former can *only* be achieved by the latter. Competitive capitalism, he suggests, would free the poor from feudalism and from "back-breaking toil," and their advancement would allow formerly colonized nations like India to finally break free from longstanding deprivation.

The Welfare "Trap"

By reframing British colonialism as relatively benign, while heightening the failures of India's postcolonial state through Orientalist imagery, *Free to Choose* stages absolute antagonism between markets and government. But to stage this antagonism, Friedman erases the centrally planned Indian state's support of big capital. This state's continued backing of textile mills and their owners, including the latter's unfair labor practices, was crucial in crushing the massive Bombay Textile Strike of 1982–1983—an event that seriously undermined the power of organized labor in India and paved the way for neoliberalization. As with the Reagan administration's breaking of the air traffic controllers' strike of 1981, and the Thatcher administration's defeat of the mine workers' strike of 1984, the Indian government's suppression of the textile mill workers' strike boosted the power of capital and enabled the formation of an expressly pro-business, neoliberal state.[32] The Indian state's protection of big business and industrial capital is completely glossed over in *Free to Choose*, which only deems state subsidies for the far less powerful handloom sector to be problematic. What is obscured is the possibility that the handloom sector might be the one vulnerable to competition from—rather than posing a threat

Beyond Alterity

to—mill-produced cloth, which, even in the late 1970s when *Free to Choose* was filmed, comprised the bulk of overall textile production in India.

Friedman's villainization of the centrally planned Indian state ultimately serves to bolster his arguments against the welfare state in the US. In an evocatively titled episode, "From Cradle to Grave," the Chicago School economist mobilizes pithy phrases and refrains to forge a connection between welfare and dependence. Welfare in the US, he argues, damages the "moral fiber" of the people who administer them as well as those who supposedly benefit from them; for, whereas the former see themselves as having "godlike power," the latter experience a damaging sense of "childlike dependence." In Britain, too, welfare causes people to be "treated like children, not like responsible adults." He characterizes those on welfare as being without "drive," given that "somebody else is taking care of their day-to-day needs, because the state has deprived them of an incentive to find jobs and become responsible people." Thus, welfare is framed as an *in*justice to poor people everywhere—something that in the guise of taking care of them in fact robs them of the capacity to become personally responsible, self-governing, and independent agents.

Unlike the episodes focused on Hong Kong and India, "From Cradle to Grave" *does* feature interviews with poor and working-class people, including racial minorities, in Britain and the United States.[33] Ultimately, though, their testimonies are stitched together to reinforce Friedman's view of welfare—even when their actual words offer little support for this view. For instance, Richard Brown, an African-American who works as an orderly in a Harlem hospital, complains that despite "liv[ing] from payday to payday," he is denied Medicaid because the US government sees him as earning too much. Brown's young daughter needs expensive treatment, which the family cannot afford since it does not qualify for government assistance. Friedman uses Mr. Brown's testimony to argue *not* for an expansion of Medicaid—so that the Brown family could become eligible—but rather for the elimination of government assistance altogether. Speaking on Mr. Brown's behalf, Friedman declares that the father of two is proud of his job at the Harlem hospital and *chooses* not to give it up in order to become eligible for Medicaid. He claims that Mr. Brown has discovered the hard way that "welfare programs destroy an individual's independence." However, when we hear from Mr. Brown directly, he does not express concerns about losing his independence; rather, he complains about the constraints placed on his family's ability to secure its health needs: "No, I don't get it, because I am not eligible for [Medicaid]. I make a few dollars too much, and [with] the salary that I make, I can't afford to really live. And to save anything is out of the question." As Mr. Brown is filmed in his living room, along with his wife and children, he notes that his family tried applying for welfare but were told they would be only eligible for $5 a month. "And, to receive this $5, we would have to cash in our son's savings bonds. And that's not even worth it," he adds. In other words, contrary to Friedman's framing, Mr. Brown's complaint is not directed at welfare *per se*, but rather at the *inadequacy* of existing welfare policy—and at the unfairness of being allowed government assistance under conditions that penalize his already poor family.

Mr. Brown's wife speaks further about this unfairness: "A lot of people are capable of working and are willing to work, but it's just the way it's set up. The mother and the children are better off if the husband isn't working, or if the husband isn't there. And this breaks up so many poor families." Mrs. Brown's comments leave ambiguous the object of her critique. When she says, "it's just the way it's set up," she seems, like her husband, to be referring to a welfare system in which benefits are doled out under highly restrictive conditions, primarily to the unemployed and to single mothers, leaving poor families like hers without the assistance they need to survive. However, the documentary frames her comments, too, as proof that the poor in America reject the very idea of welfare.

Glossing over the structural problems that Mrs. Brown's comments imply, Friedman follows up her comments with the following statement, delivered over shots of African-American children in an urban playground: "One of the saddest things is that many of the children whose parents are on welfare will in *their* turn end up in the welfare trap when they grow up." This assertion about the "welfare trap" *inscribes* meaning onto Mrs. Brown's comments about the way the system is set up. The stitching together of the Browns' testimonies within Friedman's diatribe sutures over potential tension between the interviewer's and interviewees' concerns. Indeed, the documentary's filming and editing strategies give the impression that these groups are in alignment, when in fact the Browns never speak about the "dependence" or "independence" that are so important to Friedman. Their words offer little support for Friedman's refrains about *welfare* as ultimately responsible for the constraints and vulnerability they experience.

In other words, like central planning in postcolonial India, welfare in the advanced capitalist world is scripted as the *source* of poverty and inequality. But what remains unexplained is why Mr. Brown's job in the Harlem hospital forces him to live payday-to-payday, as he puts it—and this, too, in one of the richest countries in the world. The documentary elides the reason behind competitive capitalism's failure to produce the sort of employment that allows *all* individuals to earn decent pay and to attain easy access to high-quality healthcare for themselves and their families. Friedman repeatedly sidesteps core realities of market competition—for instance, the fact that the pressure of competition and the need to stay profitable prompts capitalists to constantly cut costs and depress wages, leading to families like the Browns bearing the costs. In other words, the scripting of welfare as a regressive force enables the glossing over of a whole range of contradictions internal to the US capitalist system, including its longstanding dependence on race-based exploitation and inequality.

The Independence of "New" India

It is hard to not see Friedman's use of India in *Free to Choose* as a familiar species of Euro-American colonial discourse about the backwardness of Third-World nations. And yet, *Free to Choose* is much more than simply a work of neo-Orientalism, as is made evident in its treatment of welfare in the advanced capitalist world. Moreover, what is striking about the series is how vividly it anticipates—in both tone and substance—the discourse of Indian political and economic elites who in the wake of economic liberalization in 1991 began disseminating a Friedmanesque script about India's emergence as a new nation that had broken free of the fetters imposed by its developmental state. Structuring much of this discourse is the core opposition that animates Friedman's rhetoric as well (free market-enabled independence vs. government-fostered dependence). Invoking this opposition, Indian elites argued that the opening of the nation's economy to global competition signaled its maturation from the dependencies generated by the centrally planned state. Furthermore, these elites reactivated the memory of India's freedom struggle to argue that if 1947 marked independence from the British Raj, then 1991 marked the nation's liberation from the License Raj or era of state bureaucracy. In the 1991 annual budget speech that has since attained iconic status, then Finance Minister Manmohan Singh invoked French Romantic writer Victor Hugo: "As Victor Hugo once said, 'no power on earth can stop an idea whose time has come' … [T]he emergence of India as a major economic power in the world happens to be one such idea. Let the whole world hear it loud and clear. India is now wide awake."[34] This powerfully resonant language of coming of age and national "awakening" has played a crucial role in staging the paradigmatic neoliberal script that has circulated within India over the last decades.

A Cambridge-trained economist, Singh is widely regarded as one of the most influential proponents of economic liberalization. He exemplifies in many ways Vijay Prashad's description of Southern elites who had long wanted to turn to neoliberal policies and who allowed the IMF to "take the blame for policies that would otherwise have been politically unappetizing."[35] While at Cambridge in the 1950s, Singh studied under Keynesian economists Joan Robinson and Nicholas Kaldor. He found himself ultimately more persuaded by Kaldor's views about "how capitalism could be made to work." By the mid-1960s, as the initial growth of the postcolonial period slowed down, he came to the conclusion that, "we had … overestimated what the government could deliver. We had also underemphasized the role of private initiative in human affairs."[36] In the 1980s Singh took on the role of general secretary of the South Commission, and as part of this role he began to argue that developing economies like India had no alternative but to undergo neoliberal austerity, shrink their government expenditure, and depart from protectionist policies of the past by opening to the global market.[37] When he was tasked with the job of finance minister in the early 1990s, the Indian economy was undergoing a balance-of-payments crisis owing to its heavy international borrowing during the 1980s. Singh viewed this crisis as an opportunity to make the sorts of changes he had long believed in: "It helped us liberalise the economy," he declared openly. "There would have been difficulties in making changes without this crisis."[38] Under Singh's leadership, the Indian government accepted a loan from the IMF and implemented reforms in line with its structural adjustment principles.[39]

The economic reforms Singh helped to implement proved to be highly controversial, especially in the early days. His 1991 budget speech registers his efforts to justify them by pacifying concerns about the adverse effects of liberalization and privatization on the poor. To this end, his speech oscillates between suggesting the need for tempering structural adjustment, so as to protect the poor—what he calls implementing "adjustment with a human face"—and arguing, like Friedman, that "essential structural and policy reforms" were *inevitably* in the poor's interests, that they would lead to not just "high sustained growth with reasonable price stability" but also "greater social equity." These reforms, he argues, would "restore to the creation of wealth its proper place in the development process. For, without it, we cannot remove the stigma of abject poverty, ignorance and disease." In other words, like Friedman, Singh reframes the problem of poverty by suggesting that private wealth creation is its ultimate solution and is therefore *socially* necessary. Far from benefiting only a few (and hence being in opposition to the goal of national development), private wealth accumulation, Singh argues, is integral to the development process. Moreover, by invoking the figure of Gandhi and the anticolonial struggle, he re-casts government austerity as a form of national sacrifice:

> For the creation of wealth we must encourage accumulation of capital. This will inevitably mean a regime of austerity. We have also to remove the stumbling blocks from the path of those who are creating wealth. At the same time, we have to develop a new attitude towards wealth. In the ultimate analysis, all wealth is a social product. Those who create it and own it, have to hold it as a trust and use it in the interest of the society, and particularly of those who are under-privileged and without means. Years ago, Gandhiji expounded the philosophy of trusteeship. This philosophy should be our guarding star. The austerity that Gandhiji practised and preached is a necessary condition for accelerated economic development in the framework of a democratic polity. The trusteeship that he prescribed for the owners of wealth captured the idea of social responsibility.

Through this circuitous logic Singh suggests that those who "create ... and own" wealth need simply to follow Gandhi in seeing their wealth as a "social product." By leaving it to the wealthy to be socially responsible with their wealth, he then goes on to connect government austerity to poverty alleviation: "To my mind, austerity is a way of holding our society together in pursuit of the noble goal of banishing poverty, hunger and disease from this ancient land of ours." Thus, cuts in government spending—for instance, an increase in the price of fertilizers resulting from the elimination of fertilizer subsidies—are reframed as "freedom" from "price and movement controls" that would inevitably be good for everyone, including farmers who once relied on these subsidies.

In 2004 Singh was elected prime minister, a post he held for two terms. During this time he continued to frame private wealth creation, especially by India's richest industrialists, as being in the national interest, despite a significant rise in economic inequality. In a 2008 address to commemorate the Centenary of Tata Steel, for instance, Singh celebrated as national servants the descendants of Jamshed Tata, founder of Tata industries, one of India's oldest and largest, family-owned conglomerates: "The country owes a great deal to such dynamic leaders of business. They create wealth, they create employment, they create new capabilities and they create new possibilities ... We must salute the patriotism, the enterprise, the business acumen and the spirit of adventure of that great generation of pioneers who laid the foundation of Indian industrialization." But in order to frame India's richest industrialists and monopoly capitalists as "dynamic leaders," wealth creators, employment generators, and "pioneers" who must be saluted for not simply "enterprise" and "adventure," but also patriotism, Singh glosses over the contradictions created by economic liberalization.

Importantly, Singh delivered this address during a time when the Indian government was engaged in violent struggle with forcibly displaced populations from rural and tribal areas of Jharkhand and Orissa, where Tata Steel had been licensed to set up industrial plants. Only two years prior to Singh's address, another Tata business—Tata Motors—had been involved in pitched battle in West Bengal, once again over land acquisition that would displace rural populations. In the end Tata Motors was forced to move to Gujarat, owing to massive popular protest in Bengal. Singh's speech erases all signs of such dispossession by suggesting only that the Tatas were a vital source of employment. His comments deny the ways in which India was emerging—almost two decades into liberalization—as the "global epicenter of land grab protests."[40] Papering over popular unrest and charged public debates, Singh applauds Tata Steel for choosing to "re-invest" in the state of Jharkhand, and for its "proud record of corporate social responsibility ... [that] show[s] the way forward in deploying corporate power for public interest."[41]

Personal and National Emergence in *India Unbound*

Over the years, Singh's speeches have provided a host of memorable images and maxims in celebration of economic liberalization as a second independence for India. These images and maxims reappear as motifs in popular films and television programs, as well as in genres like the "national biography"—a medium of symbolic inculcation that gained particular currency in the late

1990s with the steady publication of titles like *India: From Midnight to the Millennium and Beyond, Imagining India: The idea of a renewed nation,* and *Rebooting India: Realizing a Billion Aspirations.*[42] Typically penned by elites and members of the professional and managerial class, these titles have proliferated an imagination of post-liberalization India as having arisen from a history of constraint and vulnerability to a future of market-enabled fulfillment. An early bestseller in the genre was *India Unbound* (2000), which yielded both Indian and foreign editions, including translations in 19 languages and a televised episode based on the book and produced by the BBC's *India Business Report*. Its author, Harvard-educated Gurcharan Das, a former CEO of Proctor & Gamble India, continues to be a prominent public figure and contributor to the nation's leading English-language daily, *Times of India*, which began in the 1990s to "legitimize the Indian state's aggressive drive towards privatization" and to promote "'New India' as [an] aspirational symbol."[43] Das's newspaper columns and bestselling books—especially *India Unbound*—illuminate some of the quintessential strategies by which elites and professionals sold neoliberal reforms to the Indian public and also recast the story of colonialism and postcolonialism.

The subtitle of Das's book, "A Personal Account of a Social and Economic Revolution From Independence to the Global Information Age," cues the reader to see it as both autobiography and biography of the nation. As reviews—most notably by Nobel Prize-winning economist, Amartya Sen—suggest, Das's personal narration is crucial to the book's broad appeal and marketability.[44] In its mobilizing of personal storytelling, *India Unbound* recalls *Free to Choose: A Personal Statement*. From the outset, Das speaks explicitly of using the first-person perspective in order "to breathe life into the clash of economic and social ideas,"[45] which are represented in the book through references to an array of philosophers (from Karl Marx to John Rawls) and economists (such as Friedrich Hayek, Deepak Lal, and Joseph Schumpeter).[46] He is also explicit in his overall aim to "sell the reforms to the people" and thereby counter "the perception ... that reforms help the rich and hurt the poor."[47] To this end, he deploys pithy chapter titles and refrains like "Bazaar Power," "The Golden Summer of 1991," and "A New Country," which succinctly and memorably link market liberalization with national rebirth.

If *Free to Choose* features a journey from the United States to India, then *India Unbound* narrates a journey in the opposite direction. Das recalls how his father's government job took the family to Washington, DC in the 1950s, leading him to eventually go to Harvard for college, where he took classes with economist John Kenneth Galbraith as well as political philosopher John Rawls. It was during this time that he developed distrust of the socialist values with which he had been raised in India. Das traces his intellectual maturation—from first believing in Development Economics and being part of a student culture that hero-worshipped Galbraith, to rejecting completely developmentalism as well as Galbraith's defense of the welfare state. It was Rawls's lectures at Harvard that convinced the young Das to privilege "equality of

Beyond Alterity

opportunity" over "equality of result" and to reassess his faith in "socialism" and developmentalism:

> [A]s a worker I would consent to the president of the company earning more than me as long it motivated the president to earn more profit for the company and I got a bigger bonus or a higher salary as a result. The greater benefits earned by a few could be justified, I realized, if the inequality improved the situation of the worst-off. Although Rawls's starting point was egalitarian, he had found a moral basis for inequality. His great insight was that free individuals would voluntarily consent to inequality in certain circumstances. This was a far more morally satisfying basis for inequality than Bentham's or Mill's ... A moral justification based on consent seemed to me superior to one based on "the greatest good for the greatest number." In an oversimplified sense, Rawls had strengthened the foundations of a market-based liberal democracy, which strives for an equality of opportunity but not an equality of result. In my eyes, Rawls had diminished the attractiveness of socialism.

As in *Free to Choose*, the power differential between worker and "president of the company" is invoked in passages like the one above, in order for it to be ultimately reframed as "improv[ing] the situation of the worst-off." Rawls's lectures lead Das to strengthen his own faith in "market-based liberal democracy" and to depart from what he describes as his hitherto "uncritical acceptance of Marx's notion of equality."[48] By thus narrating his evolution of consciousness, he prepares the reader to view the inequalities produced under capitalism as "moral" and as compatible with ideas of social justice.

Rawls's lectures lead Das to cease hero-worshipping Galbraith and to move towards greater appreciation for capitalism. He narrates a later encounter with Galbraith—in India, when the latter was appointed US ambassador under the Kennedy administration, and when Das was beginning his corporate career. In India Das finds Galbraith "gloomy and ambivalent" and confessing that "it might be better to have more private enterprise in a country at India's stage of development." According to Das, Galbraith had come to realize by the early 1960s that "His own ideas ... were more suited to an affluent society."[49] Das's perception of his former hero's ambivalence about planned economy seals his own growing belief in the superiority of free-market capitalism. When during the 1970s he is appointed manager for Richardson Hindustan—the Indian subsidiary of the American company Vicks (later an affiliate of Proctor & Gamble)—Das develops full-fledged contempt for the developmental state's controls, or what he calls its "dirigist dogma,"[50] a term he borrows from neoliberal economist and former president of the Mont Pèlerin Society, Deepak Lal.[51] His experience as a manager transforms him—from "passionately believ[ing] in [India's first prime minister] Jawaharlal Nehru's dream of a modern and just India" to strongly rejecting the Nehruvian, centrally planned state, or what he comes to see as "a rapacious and domineering state" and License Raj.[52]

The Neoliberal Script

Das's personal account of ideological transformation is strongly reminiscent of narratives of religious conversion where the "convert figure"—much like "the archetypal hero of myth"—is called to undertake a spiritual journey that "leads him to a liminal space where his old value structures and beliefs no longer apply, and his transformation often entails a break with his father or teacher." The hero must struggle against his "preconversion self" until he is finally able to abandon this "old self" and declare the new one. But because the declaration of this new self is haunted by and hence "inevitably directed against the foil of his rejected former self," "the apex of the hero's triumph is also a Sisyphean condemnation to repeat his story in perpetuity."[53] In the end, "The heroic return that follows his trials is double: it is both a return to his new community as a neophyte and a return to his old community as a prophetic revealer of error. This double return is paralleled in the double function of his text as both apology and polemic."[54] *India Unbound* functions as both apology for private capital and polemic against the redistributive state. Das is the convert whose educational experience and struggles as a corporate manager lead him to "break" from an "old self" that looked up to father figures like Nehru and Galbraith. From his new ideological position, he looks back at his college days and "pre-conversion self" with regret:

> I am shocked that we were so concerned with the distribution of wealth in those days that we ignored the whole subject of wealth creation ... Caught up in Western fashions, I did not read the great Austrians, Joseph Alois Schumpeter and Friedrich A. Hayek and Ludvig von Mises. Thus, I missed the excitement of the capitalist revolution and the romance of "creative destruction." It was overshadowed by Marx's brilliant critique of capitalism, which I read in plenty.[55]

Das ultimately emerges as both haunted by his former self (that was caught up in postwar "Western fashions"), and as "prophetic revealer" of the errors of following Marx over Hayek, Mises, and Schumpeter. Drawing on Schumpeter's notion of capitalism as "creative destruction," he glosses "wealth creation" as exciting and romantic and frames India's biggest businessmen as revolutionaries. The result is a Sisyphean repetition of stories pitting heroic businessmen and managers against a "rapacious" and "emasculating" License Raj. Such stories have played a crucial role in naturalizing the neoliberal script in India.

Bazaar Power

If the markets of New York and Hong Kong serve as potent backdrops for Friedman's performance of "The Power of the Market," then the "Bazaar Power" of postcolonial Bombay performs a similar function in *India Unbound*. Das describes finding 1960s Bombay jarring at first, with its slums and the "empty faces" of its mill workers. His relationship with the "urban stain" changes dramatically over time, however, as he goes from "feeling ambivalent about industry and 'city living'"[56] to getting "caught in the romance of the commercial world" and "adopt[ing] Bombay's heroes as my own. My eyes would grow misty when talk turned to the merchant princes like the Sassoons, Wadias, Tatas and Birlas. Instead of viewing industry with disdain, I began to see it as the nation's lifeblood and a symbol of prosperity." Whereas he is at first overwhelmed by the destructiveness of industrial capitalism—by the city's squalor and the expressionlessness of the mill workers—Das's immersion in the commercial world leads him to stop seeing the working class and to focus instead on the romantic "merchant princes" of industry, the "nation's lifeblood." Moreover, whereas he once "imagined the island city one day being swamped by a dangerous tide of humanity and crumbling into the sea," he is gradually won over by the sheer dynamism of its industry. Over time, "Even negotiating the gales on Marine Drive during the monsoon [began to seem] an adventure,"[57] he recalls—implying that he had come to see the city's natural geography itself as implicated in the "romance" of its commercial world. This description of the city's geography resonates with Schumpeter's concept of the romance of creative destruction, which is described as a "perennial gale"[58] that "incessantly revolutionizes the economic structure *from within*, incessantly destroying the old one, incessantly creating a new one."[59] Ultimately, by plotting his burgeoning recognition of the "romance of the commercial world," Das—like Friedman—builds an energetic opposition between revolutionizing markets on the one hand and stagnant government on the other. Business, condensed in the exotic image of the Bombay "bazaar," emerges as a source of vital, dynamic energy—in strong contrast with the postcolonial, developmental state.

As in *Free to Choose*, in Das's account, too, British colonialism emerges as having a far less detrimental impact on the Indian economy and culture than the postcolonial state. Early in the book Das notes that the "License Raj" "killed our industrial revolution at birth" by "persisting with the wrong model of development" and hence is responsible for the "betrayal of the last two generations by India's rulers."[60] By contrast, Britain built the railways and courts and brought the English language to India. Its problem was simply that it "did not 'exploit' India enough. Had it made the massive investments in India that it did in the Americas, India would have become prosperous and a much bigger market for British goods … a richer India would have been even a better consumer, a better supplier, and a firmer basis of Empire. Our nationalists have failed to comprehend that capital is a progressive and positive force, however exploitative it may appear."[61] Thus, Das uses colonial India's poverty to defend capitalism in general as a progressive force, its exploitation leading to gains for everyone—exploited as well as exploiter.

In later pages, the market becomes—as in Friedman's account—a harbinger of not simply economic gains but democracy as well. Das's account of how he helped to promote and make affordable Vicks's cold remedies

The Neoliberal Script

even in the poorest Indian households conveys the progressive qualities of "bazaar power." Das's experience of working for Vicks leads him to learn the importance of physically occupying and spending time talking to consumers and ordinary people. He thereby suggests that those in the corporate world are far more connected to ordinary people than government elites. In stark contrast to business's revolutionizing energy and populism, the Nehruvian state emerges as a static, elitist, "'top down' rather than 'bottom up'"[62] entity that is unreceptive to industrialists and uninterested in their experiential, physically engaged, "bottom-up" knowledge.

By conjuring the imagination of a revolutionary and democratizing "bazaar," Das argues that business is better for the poor than the welfare state. He describes the "victims" of the Nehruvian state as "unorganized private citizens—farmers, businessmen, the unemployed, consumers,"[63] thereby implying parity between the concerns of farmers and businessmen, given that these are both "unorganized private citizens." However, just as Friedman refrains from interviewing the working poor of India and Hong Kong, *India Unbound* features no conversations with Indian farmers—an omission that erases the crushing poverty many of them experience. On the other hand, the book is filled with accounts of Das's meetings with India's richest businessmen, such as chairman of Tata industries, J.R.D. Tata, who complains to Das during the 1970s that the government had called him "a monopolist with 'great concentration of power.'" But "I am powerless," the industrialist tells Das.[64] A common friend then confirms J.R.D.'s self-constructed portrait by testifying that "His entire income goes in taxes, and he has to sell some assets each year to live on."[65]

But the industrialist who is most clearly cast as revolutionary hero in battle with a repressive state is Dhirubhai Ambani, founder of Reliance, "India's largest company and among the world's top five producers of petrochemicals."[66] Das describes Dhirubhai as "a master gamesman who managed the post-colonial License Raj to his advantage and came out on top." His rags-to-riches story of entrepreneurial emergence—in which Das describes Dhirubhai's rise from poor boy of the "Bania" or merchant caste to one of the richest men in the world—is filled with proclamations about the latter's "audaciousness," which, we are reminded, had benefits for the wider public.[67] When the banks would not lend to Dhirubhai, "he turned to the public." "Thanks to him," Das declares, "Indian shareholders increased from one to four million between 1980 and 1985."[68] When, "In 1991, the government's economic reforms unshackled Dhirubhai," the head of Reliance "decided to build the world's largest refinery." "The start of his refinery in July 1999 sent a powerful message to all Indians with global ambition that dreams could become real."[69]

The stories of businessmen like Dhirubhai Ambani are then paralleled with stories of the aspiring poor—those whom Das refers to as "the million reformers" and as "a different type of businessman."[70] These include 14-year-old Raju, who hustles between tables at a roadside café in South India and dreams

61

Beyond Alterity

of starting a computer company like Bill Gates, whom he knows from TV to be the richest man in the world; or a young girl selling flowers at a traffic light in Delhi who stores her flowers in a refrigerator to keep them fresh and to give her "competitive advantage" over her fellow flower vendors.[71] By paralleling these various stories of entrepreneurialism, the difference between small businesses and big business monopolies—just like the difference between major industrialists and flower vendors, hustlers, and farmers—disappears. In fact, Das uses these stories of the aspiring poor to challenge critics of liberalization that "remind us ad nauseam that liberalization will only make the rich richer." He counters these critics by arguing that "The new millionaires did not inherit wealth. They have risen on the back of their talent, hard work, and professional skills."[72]

Mutations in the Neoliberal Script

Through the story of Dhirubhai Ambani, Das also reframes caste as an *asset* rather than an impediment to India's emergence. Dhirubhai, Das reminds us, belonged to the Bania or merchant caste, and it is this *caste* background that is deemed essential to the industrialist's success. More generally, Das views the caste system as a "source of advantage in the global economy": "Bania traders know how to accumulate and manage capital. They have the financial resources and, more important, financial acumen," he writes.[73] In celebrating the entrepreneurial potential of the Bania caste, Das implies that the caste system's rigid hierarchical delineation of social groups is not a moral problem but rather an enabler of India's economic growth. In another instance, he connects caste to Indians' success in the information technology industry. Caste "may have positive consequences in the knowledge age," he proclaims,[74] thereby implying that caste is more crucial to this industry's success than the developmental state's active funding and institutional support.

By presenting caste as a source of "interdependence" and "equilibrium" rather than exploitation,[75] *India Unbound* makes visible the alliance between neoliberal storytelling and cultural essentialism, which is further solidified in Das's more recent work, including *India Grows at Night: A Liberal Case for a Strong State* (2013). When celebrating caste-based interdependence, Das sounds most *un*like Friedman, whose emphasis lies on individual autonomy rather than on interdependence. However, differences in these versions of the neoliberal script attest less to an *essential* difference between the Indian and US contexts than to neoliberalism's flexibility as an ideology. This flexibility has come into relief in the aftermath of falling growth rates and rising inequality since the Great Recession of 2008–2009. In this context, neoliberal proselytizers like Das have increasingly tempered their rejection of state intervention, and articulated free-market ideas with culturalist discourses such as those of the nativist right. These developments in Das's writing attest to broader adaptations and mutations by which neoliberalism has retained its position as an ideological dominant, even in the face of its declining legitimacy as a mode of political economy.

Das began modifying his anti-state polemic in *India Grows at Night*, which appeared at the end of India's "boom" years—the high-growth first decade of the twenty-first century. In this book Das builds a far less utopian argument, even if ultimately the book continues to provide an apology for the creative destruction unleashed by economic liberalization. He admits that the heroism of "unorganized private citizens" progressing despite the state's controls and without its help "cannot be a long-term virtue"—that "Prosperity does not magically appear 'when the government sleeps.'"[76] He claims to have come to the realization that "While economic growth is a necessary condition for lifting the poor, it is not a sufficient condition. People also need honest policemen and diligent officials, functioning schools and primary health centres."[77] Das makes clear, though, that his renewed belief in the need for state intervention is distinct from the view of leftists who attempt to achieve "equality of result"[78] and also from that of left liberals who "advocate state intervention in providing social and economic services."[79] A "strong" state, he maintains—by drawing on Hayek as well as Francis Fukuyama—is one that does not try to manufacture "equality of result" but is concerned merely with protecting "equality of opportunity" and "has a strong authority to allow quick and decisive action." "The state's ability to act," he argues, "has been undercut by enfeebled enforcement of the law; but also, ironically enough, by civil society's success in holding the state accountable. What was always a timid and soft state is now almost paralysed in its ability to make bold decisions."[80] As an example of the weak state, he turns to the city of Gurgaon, located on formerly rural land on the outskirts of Delhi and home to major industries catering to both domestic and foreign markets. Das notes its contradictions: on the one hand, this "symbol of a rising India" is filled with "shiny skyscrapers, twenty-six shopping malls, seven golf courses, countless luxury shops belonging to Chanel, Louis Vuitton and others, and automobile showrooms of Mercedes-Benz, BMW and Audi";[81] on the other, it has no "functioning sewage or draining system; no reliable electricity or water supply; no public sidewalks; no decent roads; and no organized public transport."[82] "To rise without the state, as Gurgaon has done, is a brave thing, but it is not sustainable," Das declares. What Gurgaon needs, in his view, is a state that "allow[s] the private sector to build [infrastructure] in adequate quantity."[83] Thus, although he defends the need for state intervention, Das's view of the strong state is continuous with his critique of the developmental state in *India Unbound*. A desirable or "strong" state, for him, is simply one that enforces contracts quickly so that private capital can do the job of building infrastructure. While obscuring private capital's increasing corruption, as well as capitalist dispossession of the poor in both urban and rural areas, Das argues that a privatizing state is necessary to fight corruption; for corruption, like "crony capitalism," results only when states have failed to privatize sufficiently.[84]

Beyond Alterity

In *India Grows at Night* Das also turns in more deliberate fashion to ancient Hindu texts like *The Mahabharata*, in order to indigenize his defense of strong state-enabled privatization. His coining of the phrase the "dharma of capitalism," for instance, gives a Hindu cast to his apology for capitalism's creative destruction, during a time of increasing popular distrust of markets, coupled with the growing legitimacy of the Hindu right. Disavowing the Hindu provenance of the concept of *dharma*, Das defines it simply as that which "provides the underlying moral norms that promote trust and give people a sense of security when they cooperate in the marketplace."[85] "[D]harma is especially useful for public policy" Das argues, "because it is a pragmatic concept and does not seek moral perfection; it views men to be social but imperfect, with strong passions that need to be restrained."[86] In other words, *dharma*'s capaciousness as a concept, and its professed accommodation of imperfection, allow Das to gloss over the failures of liberalization and to construct a more updated, seemingly indigenous, defense of neoliberal capitalism.

Das's centralizing of the notion of *dharma*, advocacy for a strong state, and continued defense of the caste system, are symptomatic of the mainstreaming of arguments that problematically identify Indian culture with an ancient Hinduism deemed constitutive of the nation's essence.[87] Meera Nanda describes this mainstreaming as the "growing banalization, [and] the everydayness, of Hindu nationalism in polite society."[88] "[T]he current neo-liberal economic regime," Nanda notes, "is bringing the state, the religious establishment, and the business/corporate elite in a much closer relationship than ever before."[89] Although Das is opposed to an explicitly nativist Hindutva politics, especially its protectionist or "Swadeshi" economic policies,[90] his defense of caste and his use of Hindu texts to apologize for capitalism's injustices resonates in important ways with banalized Hinduism. As Nanda notes, "As long as Indian liberals [like Das] do not actively challenge the illiberal world view of Hindu traditionalism, they run the risk of co-opting and getting co-opted by the Hindutva neo-liberals."[91]

Nanda's fear about the cooptation of secularists like Das by Hindutva neoliberals is not unfounded. In the wake of Prime Minister Narendra Modi's highly successful 2014 electoral campaign, in which he ran as the son of an ordinary tea seller, Das celebrated what he saw as democratizing possibilities inherent in Modi's far-right regime. In the introduction to the fifteenth anniversary Indian edition of *India Unbound*, Das frames Modi's rise as a rags-to-riches story, and as a real-life parallel to the blockbuster hit *Slumdog Millionaire*. In this 2015 edition to his bestselling national biography Das notes, "By electing a chaiwalla's son who affirmed the aspirations of the millions who had pulled themselves up in the post-reform decades through their own efforts into the middle class," Indians had been forced to challenge their internalized class bias.[92] Das welcomes Modi as not only an icon of progressive social change in India but also a welcome departure from Manmohan Singh who, in his view, failed to sell neoliberal reforms even to his own Congress

Party members. By contrast, Modi is "an outstanding salesman of ideas who could transform the master narrative of [India's] political economy," Das predicts. He therefore encourages Modi to frame his discourse on *vikas*, or development in terms of market liberalism: "When he talks about making vikas [*sic*], 'development', a *jan andolan*, 'mass movement', [Modi] should go a step further and explain how vikas happens via an 'invisible hand' in a free market democracy." Then, anticipating resistance to this Smithian language by those in Modi's BJP party who are wary of all things Western, Das qualifies his assertion: "It might help [Modi] if he used the language of the nationalist right and alluded to India's great trading past: not speak about Adam Smith's market but the famed market of Hampi."[93] In this manner, Das gives advice to the far-right leader and entrusts him with appropriately indigenizing market ideology by attaching it to the project of recovering India's "trading past."[94] If the Modi regime's success in winning a second term in 2019 is in part the product of its material backing by corporate elites, then Das's comments point also to the ideological backing it has received from non-Hindutva neoliberals who have enabled the regime by masking its bigotry and parochialism while celebrating it as an agent of democratizing, competitive capitalism.

The increasing dominance of the Hindu right evidences the fact that, contrary to Friedman's predictions in *Free to Choose*, the liberation of market competition has not set India on the path to freedom from feudalism and poverty. On the contrary, three decades of economic liberalization have deepened problems of poverty and inequality in the nation. As Prabhat Patnaik puts it, "neoliberal policies are [now] even more highly associated with the growth of income inequality than with the growth of GDP."[95] The literary and filmic texts examined in the following chapters index the effects of growing inequality—even as they also at times perform the neoliberal script through fictionalized plots of personal and national transformation.

CHAPTER 3

The Maturing Entrepreneur of Popular Indian Fiction

[I]t is the market order which makes peaceful reconciliation of the divergent purposes possible—and possible by a process which redounds to the benefit of all.

—Friedrich Hayek[1]

Talent is the only way the poor can become rich. Otherwise, in this world the rich would remain rich and the poor would remain poor.
—Chetan Bhagat, *The 3 Mistakes of My Life*[2]

It felt like he was racing towards the epicentre of ideas and entrepreneurs, of profits and progress and prosperity. The blood in his veins jumped with anxiety and hope.
—Parinda Joshi, *Made in China*[3]

Alongside the national biography and its narration of India's neoliberal turn, genres of personal transformation have attained considerable currency since the 1990s, owing in part to a sizable expansion in India's book publishing industry. In the late 1990s, self-help books like Shiv Khera's *You Can Win: A Step-by-Step Tool for Top Achievers* and inspirational memoirs like *Wings of Fire* by former Indian President A.P.J. Abdul Kalam became bestsellers.[4] Published in English by multinational as well as Indian presses, such nonfiction books circulated widely, including through translation into regional languages, and became familiar sights in bookstores and at the ubiquitous pavement booksellers of urban and semi-urban India. This chapter turns to a category of domestically oriented English-language fiction that rose to prominence within this publishing ecosystem. Unlike the internationally recognized novels of Amitav Ghosh, Vikram Seth, or Arundhati Roy, which are deemed "literary" and are sold to metropolitan readers in India and abroad, this new species of English fiction is addressed to a wider cross-section of Indian society, sold at affordable prices, and frequently translated into other South Asian languages as well as film and television series. The bestselling novels of Chetan Bhagat, also known as India's "paperback king," are some of the most emblematic of this new Indian English fiction,[5] and they have circulated partly through translation into languages like Hindi, Tamil, Gujarati, Marathi, and Malayalam.[6] Here I focus on one of his early novels, *The 3 Mistakes of My Life* (2008), which "sold a million copies in ten months"[7] and encapsulates why Bhagat's brand of commercially successful storytelling has earned him a reputation as the "voice of India's rising entrepreneurial class."[8] The influence of Bhagat's brand is palpable in a number of recent works, including *Made in China* (2019), a lesser-known novel by author Parinda Joshi, which I will discuss in conjunction with *3 Mistakes*. Both novels track the struggles of small-town businessmen from Gujarat by following a "model of progressive maturation, insight, and social adjustment,"[9] and they have each been adapted into popular Bollywood films. Together, these novels and films reveal the potency of narratives of entrepreneurial development in post-liberalization India, and they point particularly to the role of fiction in animating the neoliberal script by fleshing out its skeletal cause-and-effect sequence with expressive and imaginative storytelling.

The social function performed by these fictional narratives is quite consistent with that of the classic *Bildungsroman*, which, as Joseph Slaughter notes, is "a literary artifact from that historical period of social evolution that sociologists of modern Europe describe, 'in many idioms,' as the 'Great Transformation': 'the transition from feudalism to capitalism, the emergence of market society, the emancipation of civil society from the state, the increasing division of labor, and the rationalization of the modern world.'"[10] Amidst the "Great Transformation" the *Bildungsroman* emerged as a form that could "patriate the once politically marginal bourgeois subject as national citizen," by projecting "individualized narratives of self-determination as cultural alternatives to the eruptive political act of mass revolt."[11] The Indian *Bildungsromane* described in this chapter similarly "patriate" readers. In both *3 Mistakes* and *Made in China*, a small-town Gujarati businessman contemplates suicide but survives in the end: his trials and tribulations, as well as his collaborations with male friends, teach him to suffer the challenges of the business world. In relaying the small businessman's struggles, the novels provide a counterpoint to the romantic tales about India's biggest industrialists narrated by elites like Gurcharan Das and Manmohan Singh. Bhagat's small businessman must learn to tame his expectations, not simply aspire to be Dhirubhai Ambani (whom he admires), and realize that that sort of ambition might in fact erode his capacity to become resilient in the face of challenges arising from factors beyond his control. Similarly, the protagonist of Joshi's novel must learn to recognize the hollowness of mere material success and to get in touch with the moral imperatives driving his business. Each of these narratives of maturation helps to imaginatively reconcile an out-of-reach, idealized picture of entrepreneurship with the material realities and constraints of succeeding in business. By working through the challenges of post-liberalization India's enterprise culture, the *Bildung* plots of novels like Bhagat's and Joshi's ultimately imagine subjectivities that are flexible and resilient enough to withstand the pressures imposed by neoliberal capitalism.

Much like the classic *Bildungsroman*, then, this fiction performs the key function of "reconcil[ing] the subjective condition of the human being with the objective social world."[12] Moreover, its currency within the cultural landscape of contemporary India testifies to the ways in which, as Francis Mulhern argues, "the tropology of the Bildungsroman, its store of situations and sequences, is everywhere in modern narrative culture, far exceeding the recognizable boundaries of the genre proper."[13] Whereas it is sometimes assumed that "post-colonial and post-settler coordinates [of the Bildungsroman] challenge the familiar delineations of the Bildung as such,"[14] this popular Indian fiction has in fact furthered the familiarity of "delineations of the Bildung" within India. Also, by emotionally engaging readers in the maturation process of budding entrepreneurs, this fiction has helped catalyze the formation of a new, pan-Indian middle-class identity.[15] Its aspirational characters and plots of personal development have fueled the middle class's self-perception, as well as public promotion, "as the central agent that can effectively realize the potential of a newly liberalizing Indian nation."[16]

A graduate of the Indian Institute of Technology (IIT) and a former investment banker at Goldman Sachs and Deutsche Bank, Bhagat emerged as a major public figure in the early 2000s following the enormous success of his first novel, *Five Point Someone: What Not to Do at IIT* (2004), which was adapted as the Bollywood hit *3 Idiots* (dir. Rajkumar Hirani, 2009). The author draws actively on this reputation in his novels, by appearing at times as a character and by intervening directly in the fates of his various aspirational protagonists—from students and call-center workers, to businessmen and women in the corporate sector. Outside his fiction, Bhagat has consciously constructed the persona of an author who is in service to "reader-customers."[17] Thus, he has earned the status of self-help expert,[18] which in turn has afforded him the opportunity to give inspirational talks and to write popular essays and columns, some of which are compiled in nonfiction books like *What Young India Wants* (2012), *Making India Awesome* (2015), and *India Positive* (2019).[19] Bhagat's success in producing "self-help spun into fiction or pep talk"[20] has, as Manisha Basu notes, "radically transformed the [publishing] industry itself—so much so that Indian publishing in English could henceforth be divided into pre- and post-Chetan Bhagat periods."[21] One Indian publisher describes Bhagat, together with fellow bestselling novelist Amish Tripathi, as "a new kind of Indian writer—one who believes the author is the CEO of his book—unlike Amitav Ghosh or Vikram Seth, who leave promotion to the publisher."[22]

The commercial success and public prominence enjoyed by popular writers like Bhagat and Tripathi has fueled a boom in India's publishing industry. This domestic boom might appear in sharp contrast to the faltering publishing industries and declining book cultures of the global North.[23] In the advanced capitalist world, as Sarah Brouillette observes,

> The things that are necessary to the development of the specifically literary disposition, which were always relatively distinguishing and elite, are now decreasingly available in [the] context [of growing precarity]. These include the leisure and focus to read for relatively long periods of time, exposure to the kind of education that inculcates the value of the literary and other aesthetic experiences, [and] available and relatively welcoming public institutions of expressive art and culture.[24]

India's booming publishing scene suggests a markedly different state of affairs, and rising literacy rates during the last decades promise further expansion and diversification of the book market. But even as the number of books sold in India is high relative to other parts of the world, this results in large part from sales of educational books, rather than of literature.[25] Indeed, similar aspects of the "real economy" that Brouillette highlights have restricted, and continue to place limits on, the reach and consumption of imaginative literature in India. As one Indian publisher puts it, "The way middle-class Indians see books isn't strong enough [to drive sales]." For, "Indians don't read for fun. They read for a job, they read purposefully. So educational books have grown massively." Novels like Bhagat's that sell in the millions—by attracting traditional readers as well as non-readers—are the exception, rather than norm within this publishing landscape.[26] In other words, the "scale of leisure readership"[27] in India remains limited, which is not surprising given that leisure time—or for that matter an education that privileges reading—remains a luxury affordable to only a small minority. Within this narrow "leisure readership," readers of the "literary" novel comprise a still smaller subset. Not surprisingly, then, Indian publishers have welcomed the turn to popular fiction and to the construction of novelists like Bhagat as cult figures whose works can attract new readers, elicit translation into vernacular languages, and be adapted into film and web-based television series.

Novelists of this new Indian English fiction often work as screenwriters for the cinematic and serialized adaptations of their works. *3 Mistakes* was made into the blockbuster hit *Kai Po Che!* (dir. Abhishek Kapoor, 2013), to which Bhagat contributed as screenwriter. And the commercial success of this film, in conjunction with other Bhagat adaptations,[28] set the stage for the Bollywood version of *Made in China* (dir. Mikhil Musale, 2019), which was co-written by novelist Parinda Joshi. In the latter case, the film in fact *preceded* the novel's release, pointing to how sales of popular Indian English fiction are not merely being facilitated by, but might even be *led* by their Hindi film adaptations. While historically, as Sangita Gopal notes, "there was little intersection between the social and imaginary milieux of the English novel and its (ideal) readership on one hand and the so-called masses to whom the Hindi film was supposedly addressed on the other," since the early 2000s there has been increasing overlap between these modes of communication and their "social and imaginary milieux." Gopal observes that "this unprecedented exchange between the worlds of English fiction and Hindi cinema ... [constitutes] a transmedia—or multiplatform—phenomenon, in which a narrative is constructed and dispersed differentially across multiple platforms, in this case print and celluloid."[29] If the gap between the English novel and Hindi film has narrowed in the post-liberalization period, then this is in part due to the eminently adaptable scenarios of entrepreneurial development in popular fiction like Bhagat's and Joshi's. In turn, the ubiquity of these scenarios within contemporary Hindi cinema has further reinforced their centrality in English novels.

Since both Bhagat's and Joshi's novels foreground friendships and business partnerships, they may at first glance appear quite unlike the prototypical individual-centered narratives of Anglo-American neoliberalism. Yet, like Wendy Brown's "human capital," the middle-class subject portrayed in Bhagat's and Joshi's fiction is perpetually engaged in pursuit of investment opportunities. This subject is, moreover, responsibilized, in that he assumes a sense of personal responsibility for social problems and expresses cynicism about the government and public sector's contributions. In *3 Mistakes* the business partners, who are middle-class Hindus, commit to personally training a poor Muslim cricket prodigy; and in *Made in China* similar protagonists collaborate to help counter narrow-minded views about male sexuality. Although the individualism portrayed in this new commercial Indian fiction is not as stark, and although the pleasure in its consumption arises partly from the collaborations that are central to the plot, this fiction nevertheless suggests that the norm of the responsibilized entrepreneurial subject has exerted significant pressure on middle-class consciousness in India. In fact, this fiction's emphasis on partnership and social engagement might be seen as offering relief from the alienation and *ressentiment* that characterize the subjective experience of so many people living under contemporary global capitalism.

As the protagonists grow into entrepreneurs engaged in challenging class and communal tension, or conservative gender and sexual norms, they come to embody the promise of a maturing Indian capitalism that is rooted in the nation's hinterlands, grounded in values of talent and enterprise, and committed to ethical and socially engaged business practices, which are represented as moving India beyond the parochialism and crony capitalism of the past. In other words, it is precisely by modeling a collaborative and socially responsible business model that Bhagat's and Joshi's novels uphold private enterprise as the key to national transformation. These novels suggest that if the new commercial English fiction has provided "an arena for considering the unsavoury features of domestic hierarchies, sexual repression, class and gender inequalities, [and] caste oppression," as Suman Gupta points out,[30] then it has often done so by reanimating India's neoliberal script—including its particular Hindu nationalist iterations. Indeed, Bhagat's and Joshi's novels as well as their filmic adaptations point to how this

Beyond Alterity

fiction, while performing social commentary and critique, has emerged as an entangled participant in the marriage between neoliberalism and cultural nationalism in contemporary India.

From "Nationsroman" to Nationalist *Bildungsroman*

From its beginnings in the nineteenth century, the Indian novel in English has been a source of contention in India, primarily because of the status of English—the language of the former colonizer and, still, the language of the elite and an essential means to privilege.[31] As Rashmi Sadana notes, "English is spoken fluently by close to 5 percent of Indians and is 'known' by as much as 10 percent of the population (i.e., about 50 million to 100 million people of a population of just over one billion)."[32] Given the status of English in India the Indian English novel legitimated its existence through what Priyamvada Gopal calls "the narration of nation." As Gopal puts it, "the narration of nation gave the Anglophone novel in India its earliest and most persistent thematic preoccupation, indeed, its raison d'etre, as it attempted to carve out a legitimate space for itself."[33] The 1930s witnessed the first flowering of Indian novels in English, with most of these texts explicitly thematizing British colonialism and anticolonial resistance.[34] The 1980s then marked what Jon Mee calls "a second coming," its "messiah" being Salman Rushdie, and its inaugural text the Booker Prize-winning *Midnight's Children*, which narrated the formation of postcolonial India.[35] Priya Joshi sums up the difference between these two generations of the Indian English novel by arguing that whereas the 1930s generation wrote "national*ist*" novels, the post-1980s new wave was characterized by a more pessimistic kind of "nationsroman":

> *Midnight's Children* inaugurated what seemed like an endless stream of 'nationsroman' in the 1980s—novels of the nation … Paradoxically, however, the most striking feature of this wave of 'nationsroman' is exactly how *un*nationalistic they are. Unlike Bankim [Chandra Chattopadhyay]'s unmistakable albeit contradictory nationalism or [Rabindranath] Tagore's more probing version of almost a century earlier, the English novelists of the 1980s seem more elegiac over than celebratory of the nation. These are national novels, yes; but hardly national*ist* ones.[36]

Joshi elaborates that this "*un*nationalistic" 1980s novel was characterized by "a curious obsession: to mythologize the nation not at its moment of birth when it was the glorious victor of a liberation struggle, but in its unglamorous middle age, riddled by the maladies of modernity and despair that the novels proceed to catalogue in painstaking detail."[37]

Beginning in the '80s, the nationsroman traveled as part of an expanding "alterity industry"[38] in which India was marketed in the West as a site of exotic difference. The international recognition earned by novels like *Midnight's*

Children, *The Shadow Lines,* and *The God of Small Things* conferred on this fiction the expectation that it would inevitably bring formerly colonized spaces "to the modern British [or American] reader as exotic sites for consumption within a revisionist view of the past."[39] Moreover, like international prize-winning fiction from other nations of the global South, such as South Africa, the globally mobile Indian English novel came to be identified with what Ronit Frenkel calls a "politics of loss" or "postcolonial pathos," and with character-types that tended to be "overwhelmed by their histories and marked by the triumph of loss or instability over love."[40]

During the 1990s Indian English writers started receiving lucrative contracts from Anglo-American publishing houses that were looking to the attractions of "exotic" postcolonial fiction as a means of staying afloat amidst declining reading publics in the advanced capitalist world. Vikram Seth's 1993 novel *A Suitable Boy*, Rashmi Sadana notes, was "an economic watershed in terms of the kinds of book advances ($375,000) that Indian fiction writers could hope to attain."[41] The success of *Midnight's Children* and the lucrative contracts received by writers like Seth contributed to a "boom" in the international marketing of Indian writing which, Roanne Kantor points out, "achieved its recognizable shape with the 1998 bidding war over Arundhati Roy's subsequent Booker winner *The God of Small Things*, and probably reached its peak in 2008, when Aravind Adiga's *The White Tiger* won yet another Booker Prize and Danny Boyle's *Slumdog Millionaire* received the Academy Award for best picture."[42]

As this international boom subsided in the early 2000s, the market for Indian English fiction *within* India—which had started to grow with the arrival of new Indian and multinational publishers in the late 1980s—underwent significant expansion and diversification.[43] The emerging body of fiction—intended not for the "alterity industry" but rather for India's middle classes, including those from smaller cities and towns—deployed a notably different English than that used previously in Indian writing. As Amardeep Singh describes it, this is "a version of English that is much closer to the version of Indian English spoken in contemporary India—with a frequently intense sprinkling of terms and ideas from Indian languages that are presented matter-of-factly and without annotation."[44] Manisha Basu describes this as not just Indian English but also, specifically, "a nationally viable, cyber-savvy, managerially endorsed English"[45] that is spoken on urban college campuses across India and routinely in combination with other Indian languages. This address to middle-class readers and use of spoken English has made this fiction more readily translatable into vernacular Indian languages and also more amenable to cross-media circulation—chiefly through film and television, though in the case of Amish Tripathi's mythological fiction, through musical soundtrack as well.[46] Moreover, the *Bildungsroman* has acquired an undeniable centrality as narrative mode structuring a variety of genres, including science fiction, detective fiction, chick-lit, fantasy, romance, graphic novels, campus novels, mythological thrillers, and, as Priya

Beyond Alterity

Joshi puts it, "the very Indian form of crick(et) lit"[47] to which Chetan Bhagat's *The 3 Mistakes of My Life* belongs.

Bhagat has spoken explicitly of his antagonism to the canonized, "literary" Indian English novel and of his attempts at meeting the needs of readers who, he argues, "have had enough of old-style depictions of rural poverty and immigrant angst."[48] His statement attests to how, if the Rushdiesque "nationsroman" was elegiac in its tone and critical of the nation-state, then the new English-language fiction tends to be largely optimistic, even overtly nationalistic in tone. Furthermore, unlike the metropolitan and cosmopolitan protagonists of much "literary" fiction, who often experience a sense of alienation either in India or abroad, the protagonists of fiction like Bhagat's are firmly rooted in the national context, their anxieties emanating not so much from the weight of colonial history as from the aspiration to succeed in contemporary India. These protagonists of new Indian fiction are constructed not simply as vehicles for allegorizing the nation but also as projects to be improved and matured, in order to enable India's rise in a competitive global order.

In *3 Mistakes*—as in Bhagat's later novel, *Revolution 2020* (2011)—the author appears as himself in the role of patriot, life expert, and guide. The author's appearance begins on the Acknowledgments page, with Bhagat invoking his public persona as a commercially successful author-businessman to directly address the reader and to frame his writing as a form of national service. "My life belongs to you now, and serving you is the most meaningful thing I can do with my life," Bhagat declares to the reader, following which he thanks his "friends in the film industry, who have given me a new platform to tell my stories" and "friends in the media, especially those who have understood my intentions for my country."[49] He then reappears in the novel's Prologue—this time as a character within the diegesis who encounters the protagonist, Govind, a suicidal Gujarati small businessman and fan of Bhagat's fiction. The Acknowledgments page and Prologue thus blend into one another, leaving unclear the boundaries separating nonfiction from fiction, or the extra-diegetic from the diegetic, and suggesting that the novel's *Bildung* plot is be read as a fluid continuation of the author's direct address to the reader. This unabashedly direct and didactic author figure is a striking departure from the author-stylist of canonized "literary" Indian English fiction, whose voice tends to cultivate distance from the reader. In Bhagat's novels we see how, rather than clearly demarcating the bounds of the fictional universe through the adoption of a distinct literary voice, the author maintains a consistent persona within and outside the narrative frame.

Subtitled "A Story of Business, Cricket and Religion," *3 Mistakes* opens with the dedication, "To my country, which called me back." This dedication, like the subtitle, speaks to the book's ambitions to narrate a story about the promise of contemporary India—a place populated with globally mobile citizens like Bhagat who feel pulled to return home to serve their countries. The story begins with Bhagat's proxy—who lives in Singapore—flying to

Ahmedabad to find Govind, after receiving the latter's suicide note. When the two men meet, Govind narrates to Bhagat the story of his friendship with Ishan and Omi—who stand in, respectively, for "cricket" and "religion"—and with whom Govind had started a sporting goods business and cricketing academy for young talent. From the outset, Govind's earnest narration resonates with Bhagat's own patriotic pronouncements. For instance, the Gujarati businessman describes Ahmedabad as "the real India"—unlike the "fake" India of big cities (8)—thereby echoing Bhagat's claims of attachment to "[his] country." Through Govind, and especially through the relationship forged between the Singapore-residing bestselling author and the Ahmedabad-based small businessman, the novel presents itself as giving voice to the "real India," in which business functions as a catalyst for overcoming social divisions and actualizing large-scale transformation.

Govind describes himself as someone whose "love for business" (11) leads him to push back against his mother's entreaties to become an engineer. When starting off as an independent tutor, he describes the "thrill" of business: "I was making money, not earning it under some boss or getting a handout. I could decide my fate, how many students to teach, how many hours per class—it was my decision" (11). In other words, he presents himself as Milton Friedman's market agent—he is "free to choose," free to decide how and how much he wants to work, and not compelled by his circumstances to accept "handouts" or to work for a boss. In addition to being a free agent, Govind is a dreamer, whose "biggest dream" was "to be a big businessman one day." "The only hitch," he adds, "was my lack of capital. But I would build it slowly and make my dream come true" (12). Thus, the novel lays the groundwork for a familiar story of the entrepreneur's rise. As the plot unfolds, this familiar story is somewhat complicated through the introduction of challenges and obstacles. Govind's dream of becoming a big businessman leads him to take premature and costly risks, such as putting all his money into a new shop in a high-end mall, which ends up being destroyed in an earthquake that strikes Gujarat in 2001. His friend and business partner Ishan, or Ish, anticipates Govind's weakness early in the novel when he says, "We have only started and he already aspires to be [Dhirubhai] Ambani" (25). The novel thus exposes the dangers of an aspirational culture that makes men like Ambani into heroes and prompts strivers like Govind to dream in ways that might ultimately cost them materially as well as emotionally.

Jonathan Shapiro Anjaria and Ulka Anjaria therefore see Bhagat's fiction as "outlin[ing] the limitations of enterprise culture ... [and offering] a deep, even at times poignant condemnation of the price of narrow entrepreneurialism that must be paid by India's young people." This attentiveness to the experience of young Indians leads, in their view, to a "surprising ironization of entrepreneurship."[50] But the example of *3 Mistakes* suggests that even as the "limits of enterprise culture" are raised in Bhagat's fiction, this does not necessarily result in a questioning of the culture as such. Rather, the narrativizing of limits functions as a device through which the novel exposes—in order to work through and manage—the actual contradictions that come with enterprise. Put differently, the *Bildung* plot with its dynamic energy and characteristic arc allows for imaginatively entertaining and emotionally processing the challenges that accompany the running of a profitable small business. In the end the novel suggests that, precisely *because* of the challenges he has had to endure and overcome, the mature small businessman is the best hope for the nation's economic and cultural transformation. The reader, by being taken along in the entrepreneur's journey of maturation, is similarly allowed to process and work through the risks and challenges attending enterprise culture. This is not so much an ironizing of entrepreneurship as an affirmation of the concept delivered through a realistic—as opposed to utopian—narrative about the small businessman.

To fully mature, the small businessman of *3 Mistakes* needs first to depart from the culture of a prior era of state-led developmentalism which, the novel suggests, continues to pollute the business world and mar free exchange between "talent" and capital. Ish, the free-spirited cricket lover and coach, gives voice to the novel's deep cynicism about the public sector, which is represented as a site of corruption and a foil against which a new private sector, based on talent and enterprise, needs to be constructed. Echoing Gurcharan Das's commentary on the ethos of postcolonial developmentalism, Ish declares:

> The young generation from the Sixties to the Eighties is the worst India ever had. These thirty years are an embarrassment for India ... We remained poor, kept fighting wars, electing the same control freaks who did nothing for this country. People's dream job was a government job, yuck. Nobody took risks or stuck their neck out. Just one corrupt banana republic marketed by the leaders as this new socialist, intellectual nation. (75)

Like Das, Ish expresses impatience with the political corruption, economic stagnation, and "socialism" of the developmentalist era. He critiques this corruption and stagnation by opposing an older generation's preference for the safety of a "government job" with a younger generation's openness to risk-taking. Ish's decision to train Ali, a poor Muslim cricket prodigy, comes to emblematize the new generation's social commitment, which is expressed through private acts and by rejecting the state. Relative to Ish's social commitment, Govind's orientation is more pragmatic; yet he, too, expresses passion for some form of large-scale social transformation. Early in the novel he declares, "There are things about my small town neighborhood that I want to change ... the whole old city could be a lot cleaner ... I want to stop the gossip theories people come up with about other people" (8). Through the course of the narrative, Govind learns to incorporate some of Ish's raw passion, including the latter's investment in transforming the nation through acts of private charity and the training of young talent.

It is Govind's pragmatism that leads him to conceive of the novel idea of starting a cricket shop with his friends in the middle of a temple complex.

But, acting as "the parent of [his] friends," he is reluctant when Ish expresses his desire to coach the poor Muslim cricket prodigy, Ali. For Govind, the impoverished Ali's "gift" is a naturally occurring "unfair talent [which] actually creates a balance, helps to make the world [that otherwise favors the rich] fair" (97). But Ish sees Ali as a "national treasure" (230) that needs to be actively "groomed" (140) and molded (162). Ultimately, Govind agrees to coach young talent, and the friends' faith in Ali is later rewarded when the boy is offered a scholarship from an Australian cricket association. Thus, "talent" is shown to have the power to trump racial difference abroad (between white Australians and Indians) as well as class and religious difference at home (between Ali on one hand and Govind, Ish, and Omi on the other). Through the alliance between Ali (the talent), Ish (the passionate cricket coach), and Govind (the pragmatic businessman), the novel suggests that a new Indian capitalism that combines passionate patriotism with pragmatism can create a level playing field for the (talented) poor to rise.

Moreover, the success of the cricket store in attracting not just Hindu but also Muslim and Christian children suggests that this new Indian capitalism can provide also a powerful *equalizing* force, capable of replacing religion-based parochialism. Omi's uncle, Mama—whose business is explicitly in service of politicized religion, and who laments the younger generation's unwillingness to understand Hindutva "properly" (33)—represents an older, corrupt way of doing business. At the novel's end, Govind tries to save Ali and his family from the anti-Muslim violence that erupts in Gujarat in the post-9/11 moment. But because Govind fails to act on time, Ali is compelled to have a wrist operation to ensure that he can continue to play cricket; and Omi dies in the violent attacks—a victim of the extremism of Mama and the rest of his fundamentalist Hindu family. It is his trauma and sense of failure resulting from these events that leads Govind to become suicidal and to solicit the intervention of Chetan Bhagat.

Although the novel critiques the backwardness of Omi's Hindu fundamentalist family, it is important to note that it nonetheless ascribes primacy to *Hindu* entrepreneurs, with the Muslim characters functioning mainly as enablers of Govind's maturation into the sort of businessman who is driven by both pragmatism and a desire to contribute to social uplift. Relatedly, whereas it celebrates the rebelliousness of Hindu characters like Ish, it remains anxiously invested in portraying the Muslim characters—Ali and his father— as compliant and averse to rebellion. Ali's and his father's roles as catalysts for Govind's maturation process reinforce the power differential between India's Hindu majority and Muslim minority. Furthermore, whereas the Hindu characters are not always overt in their expressions of nationalism, the Muslim characters are explicit in their performances of commitment to the nation. Ali barely speaks throughout the novel; but in one of the few moments when we do hear his perspective, he refuses a cricket scholarship and citizenship in Australia with dramatic declarations of his fidelity to his (Hindu) coach and nation: "It's ok if I don't become a player, but it's not ok if I am not an Indian," he announces (178). The lack of complexity in Ali's character is justified with numerous references to his exceptional talent: he has a "freakish gift" (97); his "brain is wired differently" (61); and it is because he "sees the ball in slow motion" (60) that he is able to magically hit consecutive sixers. Ali is thus at once an embodiment of "The Victorian idea of the 'deserving poor'"—which, Paroma Chakravarti notes, has enjoyed currency in post-liberalization India[51]—and of the "good" Muslim—which, as Mahmood Mamdani has argued, appears repeatedly in post-9/11 discourse as the patriotic "other" to the "bad" Muslim or terrorist.[52]

Along with Ali, his father illustrates the workings of what Evelyn Alsultany calls "simplified complex representations," which expressly perform the balancing of negative representations ("bad" Muslims) and positive ones ("good" Muslims)—and in doing so reframe religious fundamentalism as a moral rather than political problem.[53] A respectable former college professor, Ali's father was once in a "hardline party." Speaking to Ish, Govind, and Omi, he admits to having made mistakes before he finally embraced "secular politics" (68). In this moment, Ali's father performs his transformation from "bad" to "good" Muslim. His subsequent trust in Ali's Hindu benefactors confirms for the reader the success of his evolution into a broadminded Muslim. Moreover, like Ali, the father performs his patriotism and investment in the nation when he tells Omi: "Son, India is a free country. You have a right to your views. My only advice is Hinduism is a great religion, but don't get extreme" (69). These lines consolidate his identity as a good Muslim—one who can respect Hinduism, and who, unlike "hardline" Muslims, who might question India's democratic credentials, affirms India to be a "free country" where all are entitled to their views and differences of opinion (70). This performance of patriotism by Ali's father does not merely decontextualize communalism in India, it also shores up the professed liberalism of the key middle-class Hindu characters (Ish and Govind) and, indeed, of the novel itself. In the end, the construction of "good Muslims" and exceptional "talent" enables the glossing over of actually existing, structural impediments to the rise of poor Muslims in India.

The novel ends with a rejuvenated and more mature Govind working with Ish to raise money for Ali's successful wrist operation in London. In the novel's final moments, Ali returns to the pitch to hit his characteristic sixer—the ultimate sign of his talent or "gift." The ending thus suggests that Govind's maturation has enabled a transformed and more resilient business culture to take hold in India—a culture that resists the public sector's corruption, as well as the influence of politicized religion, and that is infused instead with realism and passionate commitment to nurturing the equalizing force of talent. In other words, even as *3 Mistakes* cautions against the dangers and trappings of aspirational culture and exposes the impediments to the small businessman's success in "new" India, the novel ultimately regurgitates the official neoliberal script—by suggesting that a resilient and socially responsible form of entrepreneurship is what is most needed for engendering progressive transformation in the nation.

Enterprise as Healer

The Hindu small businessman protagonist is a crucial and recurring figure in much early twenty-first-century Indian fiction, beyond Bhagat's *3 Mistakes*. In fact, increasingly, this figure functions as a vehicle through which the anxieties and maladies attending neoliberalization are addressed and managed, sometimes in comic mode—as is the case with the novel *Made in China*, also set in Gujarat, and adapted into a popular Hindi film of the same name. Author Parinda Joshi, who also co-scripted the film version of *Made in China*, was born and raised in Ahmedabad before migrating to the United States. Business is an important character in much of her work, which is primarily genre-based and addressed to middle-class audiences within India as well as the Indian diaspora. In an earlier novel, *Powerplay* (2013), the business of cricket functions as a setting for romance between a male corporate executive acquiring an underperforming cricket team and a female employee in the team's marketing department. If *Powerplay* fits the mold of Chick Lit—as well as "Crick Lit"—then *Made in China* is structured as a traditional narrative of entrepreneurial development whose plot unfolds in Surat, Gujarat's second-largest city after Ahmedabad. Once again, a Gujarati city becomes the face of non-metropolitan Indian capitalism, and two Gujarati Hindu men and business collaborators act as representatives of "a changing, evolving India."[54] Through an involved plot that ultimately traces the internal maturation of one of these men, Raghu Mehta, Joshi's fiction channels some of the problems with India's capitalist culture, in order to eventually reframe these problems as sources of the nation's superiority over its economic rival, China. In the process, Indian entrepreneurialism is aligned with the ancient wisdom of Ayurveda—a conflation that allows the novel to resonate with elements of Hindu nationalist discourse.

As in *3 Mistakes*, the paratext of *Made in China* contains the author's direct address to the reader and sets up the novel as both a work of fiction and a self-help guide. Joshi compares the novel to its central character: "It takes pride in its resilience," she declares in the Author's Note. In asserting that "This story is about every man and woman; about our innate desires, about those times when we put everything on the line for something, lose our way, how that transforms us," the Author's Note prepares the reader to expect the central character to go through a transformative personal journey. In the process, Joshi, like Bhagat, also establishes herself as an entrepreneur who has been on a similar journey of engaging the support of publishers, marketers, and movie producers, whom she thanks for "investing" in her work. The middle-class small businessman-protagonist of *Made in China* appears, then, as a reflection of the author, whose own entrepreneurial persona supplies a frame for the story-world as well as a vital cue to readers for how to read and interpret this world. As with *3 Mistakes*, the authorial voice and voice of the third-person narrator appear as overlapping rather than distinct.

The Author's Note also appeals to the reader's nationalist sentiments: "Despite what its title might lead you to believe, it is one hundred percent Made in India,"[55] Joshi declares at the outset, thereby establishing her legitimacy among Indian readers who may see her as an outsider, given her migration to the United States. Through the rest of the book China emerges as both a source of competition and a foil against which India's unique entrepreneurial spirit is at first tested and ultimately confirmed. Raghu, the somewhat comical struggling small businessman travels to China for new business opportunities after several failed ventures and bad decisions in Gujarat. He is prompted to take the trip by Dev, a wealthy friend who gives voice to Indian anxiety about China's greater competitiveness: "These Chinese businessmen are bloodsuckers of the first order; they beat Gujju businessmen at their own game ... They see a new importer, they swallow him alive."[56] In another moment, Raghu himself gives expression to this anxiety when he tells a Chinese policeman, "You know in India everything has a Made in China label? Electronics, shoes, clothes. My jersey is *Made in China* too, see?"[57] While Dev is cartoonishly coarse, and Raghu is somewhat of a comical trickster, their characters nonetheless expose one of the novel's overarching questions: will the middle-class Indian—and more specifically, the Gujarati or "Gujju"—businessman be defeated at his own game, or will he triumph over the predatory Chinese?

During his business trip Raghu encounters an intriguing Chinese remedy that claims to use tiger body parts to treat erectile dysfunction. On returning to India, he partners with an Ayurvedic doctor, Dr. Vardhi, with the aim of making and selling this product in the Indian market as an elixir. While the product the partners eventually create is based on an Ayurvedic formula, it is marketed, falsely, as derived from tiger parts originating from China, to endow it with a sense of the exotic. This marketing gimmick proves to be popular, but it also embroils the business partners in much controversy—first for confronting social taboos regarding the overt discussion of sexuality and second for making a product that is deceptive and that appears to be the result of tiger poaching. In the process of defending himself against the criminal charges levied against him, Raghu finds himself estranged from his wife and learns to recognize the shallowness of his dogged pursuit of material gain. By the novel's end, he learns that he does not need deception in order to succeed. The product he creates with Dr. Vardhi is "Made in India" and even has a Sanskrit-derived brand name, *Ashvardhi*, that speaks to its origins in Dr. Vardhi's Ayurvedic clinic. This indigenous product attracts sponsorship from a powerful Indian pharmaceutical company. Raghu continues to work with his Chinese collaborator, though, and declares his intention to "expand within [India] at first, and then to China, which is a huge market." "We've got the learnings and you've got the infrastructure. We join hands and take this to the next level," he declares in his new, confident voice that is able to set the terms of his dealings with big pharma.[58] Thus, the anxieties surrounding China's greater competitiveness are addressed and managed through the Gujarati small businessman's spearheading of a business deal with China—a deal to sell in *Chinese* markets a product created from *India's* ancient "learnings." This authentic, indigenous product confirms India's superiority by promising to restore the virility of modern Chinese men as well.

Although the narrator's tone remains mildly mocking of the maturing protagonist's foibles and deceptions, by following the twists and turns in his journey to success, it also elicits empathetic identification with his maturation process and thus with the idea of a maturing middle class in "new" India. If in Bhagat's *3 Mistakes* the author serves as a therapist of sorts who supports the small businessman through his crisis of confidence, then in Joshi's *Made in China*, the process of starting and consolidating a business functions by itself as a form of therapy and healing—for both Raghu and the potential consumers of his product. Business leads the protagonist to the depths of despair and thoughts of suicide, but ultimately awakens him to repressed memories that disclose the source of his inspiration. Here his collaboration with the nonconforming but well-meaning Dr. Vardhi is vital. On Dr. Vardhi's prompting, Raghu is forced to look deep into his past for the real reason behind his investment in making and selling tonics for erectile dysfunction. This looking within results in an epiphany—that he has been inspired all along by his mother's role as healer in her community. At this moment, "Words poured out of him, as if a dam had burst open," and Raghu realizes that he had in fact always been motivated not by greed but rather by a deep desire, much like his mother, to heal people.[59] He also recalls that an accident had negatively affected his father's reproductive capacity and left him insecure about his virility—all of which, Raghu believes, denied him the possibility of having a sibling. The young Gujarati resolves to channel his personal trauma into business—specifically the business of selling a remedy for erectile dysfunction. Inspired by Dr. Vardhi, he then works to contest the silence that surrounds issues of male sexuality in India. Raghu's epiphanies and uncovered memories make him realize that "The reason had been within him all along, and finding it ... liberate[s] him." In other words, this portrait of the young entrepreneur's maturation is framed much like the portrait of an *artist*'s development: the process of starting and maintaining a business prompts Raghu to look within and to uncover repressed and traumatic memories, which are then funneled into an act of creation.

As Raghu gets in touch with his deepest aspiration, "The goal," he comes to see, "was simple; to negate misinformation. To create awareness about health and hygiene. To dispel age-old myths about what should and shouldn't be considered discussion-worthy in polite society."[60] Thus, much in the way that Govind and his partners' cricket shop in the temple complex compels Ahmedabad's residents to get past longstanding parochial attitudes through acts of consumption, Raghu's marketing of his product leads residents of Surat to talk about and to address the taboo topic of erectile dysfunction. Even though the product that Raghu and Vardhi jointly create relies on fraudulent marketing strategies, it is finally redeemed, owing to its capacity to mobilize the maturation of the small businessman in India—to take him from corruption to honesty and to make him into a catalyst for the transformation of traditional societal attitudes towards sex and sexuality. In other words, *Made in China* reveals the struggles and anxieties of the small businessman in order to eventually celebrate the potentiality of business, which is presented as an energizing, revitalizing force for the middle class in particular and the nation in general.

The novel's arc leads the reader to the conclusion that solutions to India's social problems lie in the marrying of "profits and philanthropy." Early on Raghu wonders in one of his daydreams, "Profits and philanthropy; the two could go hand in hand, couldn't they?"[61] The plot's resolution helps to answer this question by clearing the business partners of all charges and thereby affirming the sincere aspirations of the small businessman and doctor of traditional Indian medicine. Their collaboration, with all its problems, models for the reader/viewer what is needed for the emergence of a socially conscious and accountable business culture in India. If Ali's sixer at the end of *3 Mistakes* signals the fruits of successful collaboration between "business" and "talent," then *Made in China* ends by vindicating on social grounds the collaboration between business and medicine.

In the process of tracing the Gujarati businessman's maturation into a harbinger of sexual healing and social change, *Made in China* presents a Gujarat that is devoid of significant inequality and demographic diversity, and effectively cleansed of the memory of the 2002 anti-Muslim pogrom featured in *3 Mistakes*. Instead, there appears to be an automatic and effortless coincidence between the Hindu, middle-class small businessman's maturation—into a confident man who sets the terms of his dealings with big business—and his community and nation's advancement and (sexual) awakening. Indeed, Raghu's internal healing, his successful collaboration with Dr. Vardhi, and their creation of a socially useful product, all function as proof of the power of the market to, as Hayek put it, "make peaceful reconciliation of ... divergent purposes possible—and possible by a process which redounds to the benefit of all." Furthermore, the construction of Dr. Vardhi as a noble and progressive Gujarati doctor of traditional medicine contributes to the novel's connection of Gujarat with an authentic, indigenous wisdom which, through Ayurveda, is imagined as Hindu. This construction resonates with the cultural essentialism of Hindu nationalists, as does the novel's presentation of Gujarat as a model for successful capitalist development in India. The film version of *Made in China* then reinforces this portrayal of Gujarat, right from its opening scene that reveals clean and modern roadways in what a newscaster's voice describes as "glorious" Gujarat.

Filming the Entrepreneur's Journey

The Bollywood adaptations of Bhagat's and Joshi's novels—*Kai Po Che!* (2013) and *Made in China* (2019), respectively—illustrate the increasingly "fluid interchange between English and other Indian languages (preeminently Hindi)"[62] within contemporary Indian cultural production. Hindi film adaptations afford English-language novelists the possibility of reaching and engaging an even larger national audience—one that includes non-English speakers as well as non-readers. Linking the adaptations of Bhagat's and Joshi's novels is the prominent Bollywood actor Rajkumar Rao, who brings an everyman persona to his portrayal of the Gujarati Hindu businessman in both films. Rao's casting as the struggling and sympathetic middle-class entrepreneur contributes to the films' framing of "business" as an essentially empowering as well as progressive force.

In his role as Govind in *Kai Po Che!* Rao plays the meditator between Ish's liberalism and Omi's conservatism. Rao/Govind is conspicuous in this mediating role, appearing often between Ish and Omi in the frame, especially in early scenes that establish the friendship between the three young men. In a key song sequence, Ish and Omi, who appear bare-chested and in precarious positions, clearly represent two extremes; Govind, by contrast, appears fully dressed throughout and invariably on solid ground. Always the businessman, Govind is shown as wanting in his friends' passion. But as the narrative unfolds, he is repeatedly validated for his apolitical pragmatism and his ability to occupy the middle ground. By contrast, the nonconforming Ish turns out to be often irresponsible and the conformist Omi overly deferential.

The tension between Ish and Omi structures much of the film and is made especially visible during a monumental India–Australia cricket match when Ish emerges draped in the flag of postcolonial India, while Omi appears in a saffron *kurta* that speaks to his growing absorption into his uncle's far-right Hindu nationalist party. A subsequent sequence of scenes alternates between the Hindu nationalists' political campaigning and a cricket match in which

Ish's Muslim protégé, Ali, scores a century. Thus, the film clearly opposes the passion, vitality, and liberalism of cricket to Omi and his uncle's adherence to politicized religion, which it represents as outdated and dangerous. This sequence prepares the viewer to expect a final confrontation between secular and religious nationalism that occurs in a scene depicting the communal violence that erupted in 2002. In the film, though, it is Ish rather than Omi who is killed at this time—a tragic victim and cautionary reminder of the dangers of religious nationalism. In fact, it is Omi who kills Ish, and ends up in prison. The film's final scenes show the resilient businessman, Govind, as the only one capable of surviving and transcending the ideological division that destroys his friends.

If in the novel Govind's character is suicidal and acts as a reminder of the pressures imposed by market competition on young Indians, then his counterpart in the film appears to be far less embattled. Indeed, the film—to an even greater extent than the novel—celebrates enterprise culture as the ideal path towards national progress and unity. In the end, Govind manages to open the fancy sporting goods store he always dreamed of—and which was at first destroyed in the 2001 earthquake—while a grown-up Ali makes his debut with the national cricket team. Thus, "business" enables "talent" to rise, and through the joining of the Hindu businessman with the Muslim talent the film suggests that the unleashing of politically neutral market forces is the best way of generating economic growth and upward mobility while simultaneously moving India away from longstanding bigotry and political corruption.

Although a progressive message that seems to reject Omi's Hindu nationalism, it is nonetheless, as in the novel, delivered by framing the Muslim characters as dependent on training and protection by liberal Hindus. In fact, the film's portrayal of the relationship between Ish and Ali is far more blatantly paternalistic than the novel's. In the final moments, when a grown-up Ali hits a winning shot, it is not one of his characteristically reckless sixers—the quintessential sign of his innate talent or "freakish gift" with which the novel ends—but rather a restrained cover drive boundary, which does not come naturally to Ali and serves as an overt reminder of his training by Ish. Following the boundary, the film confirms Ish's role in Ali's success by flashing back to a slow-motion close-up of the martyred Hindu coach looking on approvingly at his Muslim protégé's transformation from raw to mature talent. Ish's approval of Ali conveys the film's social vision: Ali is the "good Muslim" whose skillful play and material success index the excellence and agency of his liberal Hindu mentors.

In contrast to the earnestness and didacticism of *Kai Po Che!*, the film adaptation of *Made in China* is comedic and self-consciously ironic. It frames Raghu as an entrepreneur whose determination to succeed means that he comes up with various outlandish business ideas, from selling emu eggs to marketing square watermelons. Early in the film, a man stumbles when pronouncing the word "entrepreneur," which he uses to characterize Raghu

The Maturing Entrepreneur of Popular Indian Fiction

and to describe him as someone who "makes ideas" rather than simply selling them. As the man speaks, a montage of exaggerated comic snippets of Raghu's failed ventures reactivates the audience's prior knowledge of the actor Rajkumar Rao's filmic persona as an ordinary middle-class Indian with an innate desire to succeed. We later watch an earnest Raghu/Rao in the privacy of his office, where he stays after hours watching inspirational videos by self-help expert Mr. Chopra (reminiscent of New Age guru, Deepak Chopra), who lectures animatedly on the importance of nonconformity and risk-taking. "You can be Dhirubhai Ambani," he proclaims loudly, as Raghu listens in apparent agreement. In moments such as this, the film *Made in China* appears to not simply represent but also parody India's enterprise culture. Ultimately, though, as in *Kai Po Che!*, its narrative arc affirms through Raghu's journey the value of the qualities that Mr. Chopra promotes and that the film, like the novel, suggests are essential for both private success and social change. In other words, despite its lighter approach to the entrepreneur's journey and to India's enterprise culture, the film nonetheless performs a version of the neoliberal script.

A scene that makes clear *Made in China*'s performance of this script occurs when Dr. Vardhi breaks social taboo by speaking in public about sexual intercourse and erectile dysfunction. Although he uses metaphor and euphemism, Vardhi's lecture is framed as transgressive and transformative, even for Raghu, who watches in amazement as he records his partner's lecture on camera. As the film cuts between the brave doctor, his entrepreneurial colleague, and the transfixed audience that snickers, protests, but ultimately is won over, the (Indian) viewer is in turn prompted to confront sexual repression and taboo. In other words, the large audience gathered in the cinema-like auditorium in which Dr. Vardhi speaks becomes a stand-in for the imagined cinematic audience of *Made in China*, revealing the film's self-perception as a platform for educating and liberating Indians to be bold in relation to matters of sexuality and self-expression. This focus on the liberation of private sexuality makes the film's politics appear at first to be quite distinct from *Kai Po Che!* But what links these film adaptations is their shared representation of maturing, middle-class Gujarati entrepreneurs as

Beyond Alterity

the ideal conduits for upending narrow-mindedness—whether emanating from parochialism or sexual conservatism—and for forging thereby a new middle-class identity in India. Moments like the auditorium scene in *Made in China* model for the viewer an imagination in which private enterprise—figured as apolitical, pragmatic, yet transgressive—becomes the trigger for actualizing progressive change in the nation.

***

In her remarks about *Made in China* in an essay titled "The Entrepreneurial Gene," Joshi describes Raghu as part of a "long line of people who have kept the entrepreneurial spirit alive," and as "the epitome of Gujarati spirit … a spirit that is characterized by adventure, risk-taking, ability, grit, gumption and enterprise." Gujarat, she argues, has been "at the forefront of Indian trade and commerce since ages [sic]," and therefore Gujaratis like Raghu are naturally—even genetically—predisposed, as the essay's title suggests, to being entrepreneurial. Moreover, entrepreneurship is "no less than a religion in Gujarat." This is a religion that is committed not to the pursuit of political power, but rather to "peace and prosperity [for] all," she adds. Therefore, "Gujaratis, more than any other Indian people … are … perhaps what defines the term progress in India." In this manner, Joshi produces an essentialist argument about Gujarati "people" and about Gujarat, which is portrayed not so much as a modern, political entity with a religious majority and minorities, but rather as a longstanding home to those for whom entrepreneurialism itself is a religion.[63] The essay as a whole articulates explicitly the cultural essentialism that is only implicit in Joshi's novel and its film adaptation. Appearing in the context of Narendra Modi's rise to power, this sort of cultural nationalism indirectly gives fuel to the ruling party's disavowal of the 2002 pogrom, by reframing Gujarat as primarily an emblem of India's economic revival.

Because Bhagat's *3 Mistakes* and *Kai Po Che!* invoke the memory of the Gujarat violence and cast Hindu fundamentalists as key antagonists, these texts can reasonably be read as critiques of Hindutva. Yet, with plots tracing the ordinary Gujarati-Hindu entrepreneur's maturation into a successful capitalist who represents the best hope for the nation, these texts similarly manage and provide imaginative resolutions to the political and economic contradictions arising out of neoliberalism's marriage with cultural nationalism in contemporary India. In fact, given Bhagat's belief in the power of capital to transcend religious fundamentalism, it is not surprising that in 2014 he supported the candidacy of Narendra Modi, who downplayed his party's Hindutva politics and ran as the business-friendly former Chief Minister of Gujarat who had professedly transformed the state into a model of successful development. As Basu argues, this sort of support provided by Bhagat and other liberal writers and public figures has contributed to giving "millennial Hindutva an important image makeover."[64]

To speak of recent Indian fiction's entanglements with neoliberalism and Hindu nationalism is by no means to discount its challenging of social rigidities, and, in Bhagat's case, its contribution also to a much-needed bridging of the gap between English- and non-English-language cultural production.[65] Rather, it is to complicate this fiction's too-easy celebration as the voice of India's middle class. For, while novels and films like *3 Mistakes*, *Kai Po Che!*, and *Made in China* reflect and respond to the anxieties experienced by middle-class Indians, these texts nevertheless channel a script which has been championed by political and economic elites. Old ways need to be rejected to make way for a new India, they suggest, where all that is needed is raw talent, entrepreneurial ingenuity, and a mature and liberated middle class.

CHAPTER 4

Undercity Fiction and the Crisis of Urbanization

They came to Mumbai, the city of gold, with dreams in their hearts of striking it rich and living upper-middle-class lives. But that gold turned to lead a long time ago, leaving behind rusted hearts and gangrenous minds.

—Vikas Swarup, *Q&A: A Novel*[1]

He was lord of his own disillusion … He was vermin born under the sign of Gemini.

—Paulo Lins, *City of God: A Novel*[2]

Perhaps the most iconic as well as controversial representation of neoliberal India is the film *Slumdog Millionaire* (2008). Although co-directed by Danny Boyle and Loveleen Tandan, it is typically to the British director, Boyle, that the film is credited, leading many to argue that its view of Indian poverty comes from the West and involves a familiar regurgitation of Orientalist tropes and ways of looking at India.[3] The film's adaptation from an Indian novel—Vikas Swarup's *Q&A* (2005)—complicates this argument, as Ana Christina Mendes and Lisa Lau point out in their reading of the book.[4] They see Swarup's English-language novel as simultaneously deconstructing and *strategically* reinforcing Orientalism. They refer to *Q&A* as "re-Orientalist" and place it within a body of Indian English writing that includes Indra Sinha's *Animal's People* (2007) and Aravind Adiga's *The White Tiger* (2008) and that at once caters to and subversively challenges the expectations of a "western literary marketplace."[5] In their view, authors like Swarup, Sinha, and Adiga feed an appetite in the West for narratives of Indian poverty; but they do more than this—specifically by producing a rich commentary on "Dark India" that effectively challenges the Indian government's propagandistic rhetoric of "India Shining."

Beyond Alterity

Mendes and Lau are right to complicate the familiar East–West binary by pointing to the engagement of *Indian* authors—and not simply Europeans—with Orientalist discourse. However, their use of "re-Orientalism" as a critical lens also has the unintended consequence of locking Indian fiction further into this binary and, moreover, reinforcing the practice in postcolonial studies of reading this fiction primarily for its "construction of … [national] identities" which are assumed to be in opposition to the West.[6] This critical focus on national identity and specifically on Indian novels' subversive responses to the West obscures insight into contemporary Indian fiction's domestic context and politics, as well as its affinities with fiction from other areas of the global South that are not part of an imagined, Orientalized East. This chapter turns to Swarup's novel and its infamous adaptation, not for their constructions of a unique non-Western Indian identity but rather for their illumination of core features of a popular, international genre of cultural production about poverty—that I refer to as "undercity" fiction. The most celebrated examples of undercity fiction in recent years have been adaptations of literary works from the global South. These include the acclaimed films *City of God* (2002) and *Tsotsi* (2005), as well as the recent web series *Sacred Games* (2018–2019), that are adapted respectively from Brazilian, South African, and Indian novels—Paulo Lins's *City of God* (1997), Athol Fugard's *Tsotsi* (1980), and Vikram Chandra's *Sacred Games* (2006). Uniting these texts is a shared focus on socially marginalized urban characters—including gangsters and others involved in criminal underworlds—that expose unseemly truths about the political and economic realities of major cities of the South. The staging of violent criminality against backdrops of urban squalor in these works serves to expose global capitalism's underbelly. But it often also risks reinforcing perceptions of impoverished urban areas as simply crucibles of crime. I argue that these internationally circulating works of undercity fiction are relevant not just for the fact that they prompt audiences to notice global poverty, but also for how they prepare audiences to understand the causes and consequences of this poverty—specifically in neoliberal terms. These narratives' framing of poverty in the South as a toxic or diseased state that can only be overcome through acts of entrepreneurial dynamism has contributed to familiarizing the notion that private enterprise is the best means for improving the plight of—as the epigraphs above frame them—"vermin"-like, disillusioned poor, with their "rusted hearts and gangrenous minds."

My use of the term "undercity" derives from American journalist Katherine Boo's *Behind the Beautiful Forevers: Life, Death & Hope in a Mumbai Undercity*—an account of life in the Mumbai slum of Annawadi that won the 2012 National Book Award for Nonfiction in the United States.[7] In her work Boo uses "undercity" as a provocation to draw attention to the segregation of Mumbai's slums from centers of wealth and power, or what she terms the "overcity." In what follows I extend her provocative language to the realm of fiction—to describe some of the contradictions informing popular fictionalized representations of urban poverty, where the legally sanctioned depredations of corporate and finance capital in the overcity remain outside the diegesis, or else appear insignificant relative to the spectacular, sordid violence taking place in the undercity. The core problem, then—as it is presented in much of this fiction—lies not in the overall capitalist system and its production of uneven development, but only in a blatantly predatory form of capitalism—gangsterism—that is headquartered in the slums. As a result, the poverty experienced by slum dwellers is attributed largely to the villainy of mafia dons, and audiences are set up to respond to this poverty by consuming the thrill of spectacular criminality or the titillation of escape from gangsters, pimps, and drug dealers.

While *Q&A* and *Slumdog* will serve as my primary examples in this chapter, I begin by examining the parallel case of Brazilian author Paulo Lins's commercially successful novel *City of God*, together with its internationally celebrated film adaptation directed by Fernando Meirelles and Katia Lund. Tracing the parallels between these popular Indian and Brazilian texts helps to bring to the surface the contradictions informing much contemporary undercity fiction and its response to actually existing problems of overcrowding and growing inequality in urban centers like Mumbai and Rio de Janeiro. As Mike Davis has noted, "The scale and velocity of Third World urbanization" under contemporary, neoliberal capitalism "utterly dwarfs that of Victorian Europe."[8] In India, where capital has historically been concentrated and centralized in the big metropolitan cities, rural areas have tended to remain relatively impoverished and underdeveloped (first in the era of developmentalism and now more dramatically under structural adjustment), leading rural populations to flock to major urban centers for employment and to join vast, highly exploited, informal labor forces.[9] This influx of rural migrants to cities like Mumbai has continued even in times of deindustrialization and slowdown in urban growth, making newcomers to the city especially vulnerable to joblessness and precarity.[10] Similar dynamics of urbanization have been at work in Brazil, too, which, like India, began an accelerated project of neoliberalization in the 1990s. In recent years the growth of *favelas* in Brazil has resulted from not just the influx of rural migrants to cities but also the rise of unemployment nationally, as well as cuts to social spending. As in India, slums have expanded amidst growing concentration of wealth in the major cities.[11]

It is within this context of exacerbated inequality that popular undercity narratives like *Q&A*, *Slumdog*, and *City of God* raise consciousness about poverty through stark depictions of abjection in cities like Mumbai and Rio. In doing so, these texts puncture the grandiose promises and proclamations of India's and Brazil's elites. At the same time, with their depictions of anarchic slums, where police and government agents are completely enmeshed in the reigning culture of gangsterism, these narratives make it hard to imagine possibilities for successful government intervention. The protagonists in these narratives are from the outset separated out—owing to their talent, enterprise, or moral steadfastness—from what is presented as an internal culture of toxic stagnation and corruption in the slums. This implies that the only way out

Beyond Alterity

of the slums is to be exceptional. Moreover, because the slum is depicted as a site of "messy and hidden" urbanization,[12] as well as of unending brutality and corruption, spaces of capitalism *outside* the slums—and within the "overcity"—appear as relatively tame arenas of modernization that signify uplift for the exceptional protagonists.

Crucially, then, these texts' portrayals of slums and *favelas* as containers of violence and anarchy reproduce on an imaginative level the physical separation of areas of concentrated poverty from the rest of the city—thereby fueling the sense that urban poverty inheres within the culture of seemingly self-contained "undercities" rather than in the broader economic system. Furthermore, the horrifying yet exhilarating portrayals of urban poverty, particularly in the spectacular film versions, have produced slums as fetishistic attractions. Elmo Gonzaga notes how in recent years "emotive images and narratives of everyday life in the global South have been appropriated by an emergent tourism industry that offers visits to informal settlements in megacities like Mumbai, Johannesburg, Jakarta, Nairobi, and Rio de Janeiro."[13] The enormously successful *Slumdog Millionaire* has played a crucial role in spurring this tourism and, moreover, promoting the notion that there is no alternative to capitalism—especially if we are to transform slum-ridden urban centers of the South into "world class cities."[14]

Undercity as Hell in *City of God*

Published in Portuguese as *Cidade de Deus* (1997), Paulo Lins's semi-autobiographical novel appeared amidst a surge in the population of favela residents in Rio de Janeiro. This population surge was driven partly by the influx of poor migrants from the Brazilian countryside, but also from "growing downward social mobility ... accompanied by residential movement, either voluntary or involuntary, from formal to irregular favela housing."[15] Within this context, Marta Peixoto notes, "many of the well-off conduct[ed] their lives in gated and protected spaces, [and] the film and publishing industries ... found a thriving market among them for cultural products that represent impoverished spaces."[16] Lins's novel emerged as part of "a boom in neo-naturalist fictional narratives and images that 'focus on marginal characters, urban violence, poverty and extreme experiences (and) avoid avant-garde experimentation.'"[17] In the vein of naturalist fiction, Lins's narrative keeps the reader confined within the bounds of the favela, which is portrayed as besieged by both villainous gangsters and a racist police. But the third-person narrator—who speaks in a detached and educated voice while relaying the street slang used by gangster-villains—models for middle-class readers how to look at *favela* life from both the inside and the outside.

Having grown up in the actual Rio *favela*, Lins drew on his own experience in addition to interviews with his neighbors to construct his sprawling novel, which narrates life in the City of God from its origins in the 1960s to its descent by the 1980s into a dangerous zone of relentless gang warfare. This is the period of Brazil's dictatorship (1964–1985), which is not directly addressed by the novel, except that, as Michael Niblett points out, the "violence of the dictatorship finds expression in the violence and corruption of the police force."[18] The City of God *favela*, we learn, was formed as a result of the state's apartheid-style relocation of poor residents to the margins of the city. This relocation sets the stage for the creation of an increasingly dangerous life-world in which even righteous civilians become engulfed in a culture of predatory violence.

By the end of the novel we see the formation of a new breed of gangsters with a "dog-eat-dog attitude" that, Niblett claims, "speaks to the direction in which Brazilian society was headed under the pressures of neoliberalization."[19] He argues that the novel "consistently enforces a critical distance between text and reader," and that the "relative lack of interiority to the protagonists ... deliberately forestall[s] any absorption in the novel's characters ... [and] problematizes this as a site of identification." In other words, "The novel pursues a form of critical pedagogy: its characters and the world they inhabit, as well as hitherto dominant ways of apprehending this world ... are presented to the reader as a matter for careful study and critique. In this way, the novel seeks to encourage new attitudes towards the contemporary situation."[20] I would argue, however, that the novel's ability to "encourage new attitudes" towards the poverty and violence of the slums is severely compromised by its repeated focalization of the perspectives of rageful and megalomaniacal gangsters who, with their sexist and homophobic attitudes, reinforce the bourgeoisie's assumption that the *favela*'s descent into crime and violence is largely a product of its residents' own, *internal* culture of "hot-blooded" men embarking on adventures of stealing, killing, rape, and revenge.

Further contributing to this view of the *favela* and its residents is the narrative strategy of relentless movement between episodes of shocking brutality: for instance, the gangsters' violent robbery of a motel early in the novel is shown to occur simultaneously with a betrayed husband's decapitation of his wife's lover and the dismembering of his newborn baby's body in the kitchen sink. Such provocative use of juxtaposition frames the *favela*'s violence as an unstoppable, autonomous, pathological force that, as the narrator declares, "imposed its absolute sovereignty and came to claim anyone who didn't keep their wits about them" (4). This framing of violence undermines any attempt the novel might make at presenting the *favela*'s residents and the world they occupy "as a matter for careful study and critique." Or, if the reader is prompted to form a critique, then it is most likely a critique of a culture that is assumed to be particular to the *favela*, and not a reflection of the broader social and economic system.

The one exceptional figure in the arena of violence that is City of God is Rocket—a budding photographer who, although a relatively marginal character in the novel, is introduced early on as a model, aspirational subject "disillusioned about his chances of getting a job so he could continue his studies, buy his own clothes, and have a little money to take his girlfriend out and pay for a photography course" (2). His modest aspirations mean that while gangsters and drug dealers—with names like Got it Made and Good Life—engage in armed warfare, Rocket sells ice pops on the *favela* streets and eventually manages to finish school, "establish himself as a photographer," and move out of the *favela* (428). Moreover, in contrast to the delusional, psychopathic, and "vermin"-like gangsters (429) such as Pipsqueak—who renames himself Tiny and represents the new breed of hardened mercenary gangsters that is incapable of forging human relationships—Rocket gets married and also becomes an activist who fights for rights with the Residents' Association. Apart from his exceptional story, which unfolds within an era of heightened brutality in the *favela*, the book's narrative is bleak, its final pages leaving the reader to contend with seemingly endless gang war that conscripts the *favela's* young men, unless they are smart, talented, and healthy enough to dodge it.

The commercial success of Lins's novel in Brazil laid the foundation for Fernando Meirelles and Katia Lund's widely acclaimed and globally distributed 2002 film adaptation. The film's subsequent success in turn sowed the seeds for the novel's translation into English and launched its marketing in the anglophone world and beyond. The cover of a 2006 Bloomsbury paperback edition is particularly revealing of the ways in which the film served to market Lins's novel internationally. An image from the film adorns this edition's front cover and is accompanied by the refrain, "Drugs, Guns, Fashion, Music, Love, Friendship, Corruption, Blood and Guts." Thus, the sensorium of a violent, exotic *favela* is invoked to lure touristic readers. The book's back cover confirms its address to this sort of reader, who is "welcome[d] to one of Rio's most notorious slums. A place where the streets are awash with drugs, where violence can erupt at any moment—over drugs, money … or love … But also where the samba beat rocks till dawn, where the women are the most beautiful on earth, and where one young man wants to escape his background and become a photographer."[21] The reader is thus lured by the promise of a distant world of sensuality, violence, and sex. The novel's commodification for foreign audiences reinforces Lins's textual framing of the *favela* as a sealed-off world, with its particularly pathological culture of violence—leading one reviewer of the English translation to describe it as a "Postcard from Hell."[22]

In order to give an easily recognizable shape to Lins's sprawling narrative, the middle-class filmmakers Meirelles and Lund[23] streamlined it into a familiar coming-of-age story, with Rocket as the narrator, his upward mobility as its framing device, and a frenetically mobile camera as the distinguishing feature of the seductive sensorium that is the *favela*. If in the novel, the "frequent and reductive designation of characters as 'the outlaw,' 'the criminal,' 'the brute,' 'the addict,' and so on reinforces … separation" between the detached, educated third-person narrator and the violent, uneducated, stereotyped *favela* residents,[24] then in the film this separation is recreated through the voice of Rocket, who is established early as aligned with the worldview of the

Undercity Fiction and the Crisis of Urbanization

middle classes and as someone whose morals prevent him from going through with acts of violence that are deemed normal in the *favela*. Thus, however much the relentless swish pans, jerky camera movement, and pulsating musical score suggest an intimate and embodied, insider's view, Rocket's voiceover returns to distance the viewer from the *favela*—in a manner more conducive to detached voyeurism than to engaged critique.

Like the novel, the film adaptation seals off the *favela* through its narrative techniques, along with its staging choices and visual style. The casting of actual *favela* residents has invited comparison to neorealism. But the rapid editing, abrasive camerawork, and dramatic angles that emblematize *City of God*'s "visual excess"[25] are nothing like the long takes and spare aesthetics of classic neorealist films like *Bicycle Thieves* or *Pather Panchali*. Unlike these neorealist films' focus on everydayness and on unexceptional protagonists, *City of God*'s emphasis lies in the excessive brutality of desensitized and dehumanized murderers and gangsters in the *favela*, from which only the exceptional Rocket can escape.

Rocket appears with his photographic camera in the very opening scene and, when confronted with the gun-toting gangster Lil Ze, he is presented with a choice of whether or not to integrate himself into *favela* culture. As camera and gun confront each other in this opening episode, the film articulates its central question: can the camera provide a ticket out of the gun-infested *favela*? Can the exceptional, artistic protagonist depart the culture of gun violence in the slums? After being subjected to episode after episode of brutal violence—interrupted only by occasional moments highlighting the residents' food, music, and religious practices—the viewer is set up to receive Rocket's final escape from the *favela* as a source of relief. In the film's final moments, he asserts his independence from its culture of violence when he takes photographs of the gangster Lil Ze's murder by the pre-teen Runts who become the new leaders

95

Beyond Alterity

of the drug business. Lil Ze's killing thus becomes Rocket's ticket to freedom from the *favela*. His photos of the incident appear on the front page of a local newspaper where he once worked as a delivery boy. The novel's bleak ending is thus replaced in the film by the promise of Rocket's maturation as an artist-entrepreneur and eventual escape from the *favela*. But this story of escape only reconfirms the hopelessness and disposability of the *rest* of the *favela* residents, who remain locked within its confines.

Sophia McClennen argues that the film's "slick aesthetic, morally reductive plot, and lack of context for City of God's poverty, violence, and drug culture ... are only part of its larger aesthetic project—[and] that, in fact, the commercially oriented features of the film are used strategically to expose a large audience to a film experience that combines pleasure with social critique through a very specific mode of montage and shot construction."[26] In her view, "Just placing the story of City of God on the big screen and opening up the injustices screened there to public debate has to be understood as a political act, ... that serves to destabilize the neoliberal practice of distracting the public from social inequities." In particular, "*City of God*'s focus on the way that the construction of housing projects for lower-class Brazilians instituted a politics of bare life where segments of the population were violently separated from civic society draws attention to social practices that border on apartheid."[27] I would argue, however, that at the same time that the film draws the public's attention to social inequities—including the problematic state-led apartheid practices that led to the formation of the *favela* in the 1960s—its visual aesthetics contribute to sealing off spaces of poverty and violence from the rest of the city in ways that both reflect and reinforce existing class and racial inequality in Brazil.

The scene close to the end of the film where the exceptional Rocket manages to sell his photographs to the local newspaper is one of the only times that the camera leaves the confines of the *favela*. Tellingly, the pace of the editing and camera movement slows down in this scene; the camera angles become less pronounced, the colors more muted, the contrast in lighting less dramatic. This shift in visual style also sets up a sharp contrast between the *favela*, with its largely dark-skinned working-class residents, and the world outside, which seems dominated by light-skinned professionalized workers. The film's stylistic choices do not merely register the racial and class divide between the *favela* and the world of the newspaper; they also reaffirm this divide. As Rocket makes his way out of the *favela* and enters into a sexual relationship with the female newspaper editor, the viewer is prompted to see the relatively prosperous outside world as simply another "culture"—one that is distinct from *favela* culture rather than produced by an overarching economic structure that necessarily produces poverty alongside wealth, and development alongside underdevelopment. This outside culture appears to be quite fair and professional—unlike the culture within the *favela*—as Rocket learns through his dealings with the journalists, who are helpful and also invested in compensating him for his photographs.

Throughout the film, the capitalist structures that produce the slum in the heart of the city—that create uneven development—remain unquestioned. Although the corrupt police and government are shown to be implicated in the *favela*'s culture of violence, capital and wealth accumulation remain invisible and therefore unimplicated. The only signs of this accumulation that are visible are the acts of exploitation carried out by the slum dwellers themselves, against others like them. We can therefore only witness, and perhaps enjoy the touristic ride through the *favela*, whose culture—lively, musical, yet consistently violent—appears to have been created by its residents themselves. This view, while occasionally recognizing the positive features of life in the *favela*, frames its poverty and chaos as inevitabilities. Furthermore, the senseless, pathological violence committed by gangsters makes it hard to imagine any kind of systemic solution to the "hell" that is the *favela*—leaving the "outside" world of legitimate capitalist activity to supply the only alternative. Given this, it is hard not to see the validity of Marta Peixoto's argument, that such representations of the *favela*, addressed to middle- and upper-class audiences, might in fact "increase the urban paranoia that segregates the classes and further erode the citizenship rights of those who already suffer race and class discrimination."[28]

Slum as Disease in *Q&A*

Vikas Swarup's *Q&A* is devoid of the deep cynicism that imbues both Lins's naturalist novel and Meirelles and Lund's sensational crime drama adaptation. The tone and worldview of Swarup's novel recall instead the picaresque, which, as Rob Nixon notes, emerged as a "countergenre" in sixteenth-century Spain and "a reminder that, for all the infusion into Spain of transatlantic imperial wealth, the great majority of Spaniards remained deeply poor." Today, Nixon adds, the *picaro* continues to possess "potency as a marginal literary figure, a seldom-heard voice, who belongs nonetheless to the statistical majority."[29] Indeed, a *picaro*-like protagonist often appears in what James Dawes calls the "escape plot" of contemporary human rights novels. These novels feature a "first-person narrator who comes from a socially marginal position, moving laterally from disaster to disaster through a world of moral chaos, rather than vertically through the organizing, socializing structures of the bildungsroman."[30] Although not quite a human rights novel, *Q&A* nonetheless features a socially marginalized protagonist whose movement "from disaster to disaster through a world of moral chaos" serves as a catalyst for introducing the reader to life in the "new" India. But ultimately, as I will show, the novel is pulled between the "countergenre" of the picaresque and the "organizing, socializing structures of the bildungsroman." This tension sets the stage for the novel's subsequent cinematic transformation into a familiar *Bildung* narrative of personal development and integration into the national community.

Much like the picaresque, *Q&A* is episodic and told from the perspective of a poor orphan, Ram Mohammad Thomas, whose name encompasses references to the three major religions of the Indian subcontinent—Hinduism, Islam, and Christianity. As he moves through the slums and *chawl*s (tenement buildings) of Delhi, Mumbai, and Agra, it is his *picaro*-like "quick-witted improvisation"[31] that allows him to survive and eventually to win a quiz show that makes him a billionaire. However, unlike the typical *picaro*, who is "governed by unruly appetites, potty-mouthed and scatologically obsessed,"[32] and speaks in a "disreputed vernacular,"[33] Ram has no "unruly appetites" and speaks in perfect English, a feature that complicates the novel's affinity to the picaresque, and aligns it with the *Bildungsroman*. Unlike the typical *picaro*, moreover, Ram stands apart from the rest of the poor for his exceptional moral integrity. If the picaresque's "comedic arc" is shaped in part by the *picaro*'s "quest for upward mobility,"[34] then Ram's participation in the quiz show is driven not by a desire for wealth, but only by a need to avenge his girlfriend's abuse by the game show host. This taming of the orphan protagonist's desires, appetites, and voice makes him function as a prototype of the entrepreneurial self, that Caren Irr aptly describes as "an already self-disciplined ascetic subject, well prepared for the demands of the marketplace and eager to advance within it on the terms laid by the system itself."[35] Indeed, it is Ram's character that prepares him for the "demands of the marketplace"; his lack of greed and unruly appetites makes him the "self-disciplined" subject who believes (in "terms laid by the system itself") that upward mobility comes from moral integrity and self-belief.

Robbery and theft are key motifs in the novel that contribute to establishing Ram as morally exceptional. For instance, when working as a servant for an Australian diplomat, Colonel Taylor, Ram emerges as the sole honest and reliable Indian servant. All of the others have a history of criminality and jail time, are dismissed from service for plotting to rob the diplomat's family, or are involved in sexual relations with the master's children. As a result, whereas the police treat Ram as a suspect in the robbery, his Australian employer is

Undercity Fiction and the Crisis of Urbanization

able to vouch for his innocence. Ram is neither greedy nor particularly sexual, all of which further proves that the rest of the poor are crooks who will do anything to get rich quickly.[36]

The criminality of the majority of the poor characters in Swarup's novel also brings into relief the exceptional artistic sensibilities of its protagonist. When he goes to Agra, Ram is so transfixed by the beauty of the Taj Mahal that he begins to forget his hunger and also that he has been robbed by *dacoits* of all his savings: "The loss of my fifty thousand rupees, the worries about where I will eat next, sleep next, the fear of being caught by the police, pale into significance against the purity of its perfection" (241). The Taj's "purity" contrasts sharply with the vivid descriptions of urban squalor and crime that dominate much of the novel. As Ram stands transfixed and "the Taj Mahal rises in all its beauty and splendor, shimmering in the afternoon haze" (242), the narrative appears to slow down and the episode provides relief from the grim material reality that it has been recording through Ram's peregrinations through poor and working-class areas. Ram's transfixed reaction on apprehending this historic monument confirms for the reader his ability to let beauty move him, despite his concerns about food and safety. This episode satisfies liberal fantasies about how aesthetics, like morality, can allow us to potentially transcend material constraints—a perspective that is conveyed in *City of God* as well, in Rocket's escape through a career in photography. In Swarup's novel, Ram's ability to be moved by aesthetics, despite his material constraints, suggests that it is one's inner life and mental capacities that are key to combating poverty.

Ram proves himself to be someone who although poor is able to reflect on poverty and to gain distance from the constraints of his material conditions through the powers of his mind. In one episode he introspects about "what it feels like to have no desires left because you have satisfied them all, smothered them with money even before they were born. Is an existence without desire very desirable? And is the poverty of desire better than rank poverty itself?" (258). This capacity to relativize his condition—to think of the "poverty of desire" as potentially equivalent to "rank poverty"—suggests his ability to rise above a narrow, self-serving materialism. Not only are the rich unable to do this, but the poor, too, like the servants Ram works with, who steal from their masters, are unable to have this sort of perspective. In performing this mental flexibility, Ram as narrator assuages the reader's liberal guilt about material poverty: this sort of poverty, he suggests, is comparable to the poverty of desire that the rich experience. The wealthy and poor alike must struggle to cultivate a rich inner life, rather than smother their desires with money. Ram's example thus conveys the idea that ultimately it is our *minds* that allow us freedom from the constraints imposed by having too little *or* too much.

The Mumbai slum, Dharavi—which the novel describes as "Asia's biggest slum" and where Ram lives for a while—emerges as the locus of urban crisis,

Beyond Alterity

whose effect can only be avoided through the kind of wit and mental agility that Ram displays. He describes the slum in his characteristic, educated voice:

> I live in a corner of Mumbai called Dharavi, in a cramped hundred-square-foot shack which has no natural light or ventilation, with a corrugated metal sheet serving as the roof over my head. It vibrates violently whenever a train passes overhead. There is no running water and no sanitation. This is all I can afford. But I am not alone in Dharavi. There are a million people like me, packed in a two-hundred-hectare triangle of swampy urban wasteland, where we live like animals and die like insects. Destitute migrants from all over the country jostle with each other for their own handful of sky in Asia's biggest slum. There are daily squabbles—over inches of space, over a bucket of water—which at times turn deadly. Dharavi's residents come from the dusty backwaters of Bihar and UP and Tamil Nadu and Gujarat. They came to Mumbai, the city of gold, with dreams in their hearts of striking it rich and living upper-middle-class lives. But that gold turned to lead a long time ago, leaving behind rusted hearts and gangrenous minds. Like my own. (133)

Although the narrator claims to be like the other residents with their "rusted hearts and gangrenous minds," his ethnographic description of the city and its slums sets him apart—much like the narrator of Lins's novel—and establishes him as exceptional. This manner of narrating slum life has signaled the novel's inauthenticity to critics like Chinmoy Banerjee, for "It is not likely that someone in [the protagonist's] situation would have access to the levels of language and information that he displays" about the slum's history and geography.[37] On the other hand, others like Snehal Shinghavi have read the passage as emblematic of the novel's use of "info-dumping"—a strategy in science fiction where "a narrator must unload a large amount of alien facts because the life-world in question is outside the ken of the reader."[38] Indeed, whether or not Ram's voice is authentic, what is interesting about this "info-dumping" is how it confirms Ram's position as a contemplative outsider to the "life-world" of the slum—one who has more in common with the implied middle-class reader than with the "destitute migrants" he describes. Although he claims to share an affinity with the other slum dwellers by pointing to how his mind, too, has turned "gangrenous," his detachment when describing the "daily squabbles" over inches of space or buckets of water suggests that he is a spectator here. Later, he speaks of Dharavi as a "grim landscape of urban squalor" (133), "landscape" giving the impression of a static view from above and from a distance, rather than from inside and through engagement with inhabitants of the space. Even when providing imagistic descriptions of "Its stinking, excrement-lined communal latrines" or its "Mounds of filthy garbage … from which ragpickers still manage to find something useful" (133–134), the narrator appears to be neither ragpicker nor starving resident of Dharavi, but rather an outsider-observer and thinker.

From this position of detached observation of Dharavi's static curiosities, Ram then gestures towards the causes underlying its poverty:

Undercity Fiction and the Crisis of Urbanization

> Amid the modern skyscrapers and neon-lit shopping complexes of Mumbai, Dharavi sits like a cancerous lump in the heart of the city. And the city refuses to recognize it. So it has outlawed it. All the houses in Dharavi are "illegal constructions", liable to be demolished at any time. But when the residents are struggling simply to survive, they don't care. So they live in illegal houses and use illegal electricity, drink illegal water and watch illegal cable TV. They work in Dharavi's numerous illegal factories and illegal shops, and even travel illegally—without ticket—on the local trains that pass directly through the colony. (134)

Here the city's refusal to "recognize" Dharavi as a "cancerous lump" becomes a way of critiquing the ruling class's denial about the "disease" (of poverty) that afflicts the city. Making the slum "illegal"—the narrator astutely suggests—justifies this refusal to "recognize" the slum and to see the slum dwellers as full human beings. At the same time, by also describing the slum as a "cancerous lump in the heart" of the modern city, the narrator mirrors the ruling class's view of slums as the *locus* of urban "disease"—something that, if removed, could allow for a life free of disease—thereby mistaking the symptom for the cause.

As in Lins's novel and its film adaptation, the narration does not merely register the class-based spatial segregation between the slum and the world outside it but also reinforces this segregation. The slum is separated out as the cancerous lump that needs to be recognized for what it is, in order to restore wellness to the city as a whole. Similarly, while its description of the lively, entrepreneurial culture of Dharavi—with its numerous factories and shops—challenges the government's dismissal of slums as unproductive, illegal constructions, what is nonetheless glossed over are the dynamics of the legal forms of exploitation of slum dwellers who do the actual work of building "modern skyscrapers and neon-lit shopping complexes," and whose economic precarity compels them to work for little pay. In other words, the positioning of the slum as the locus of urban disease and the site of illegal economic activity erases the broader context of legally sanctioned exploitation of workers, many of whom are also slum dwellers. Furthermore, the ethnographic narration positions the implied middle-class reader as a distanced bystander who can, at best, learn to passively "recognize" the slum as a problem rather than question the exploitative economic system that produces and perpetuates it. On the whole, while the narration unmasks social inequality, it locates urban "disease" within the slum rather than the broader economic system. It is not surprising, then, that at the same time that it produces a sympathetic picture of internal migrants who come to the slums with their dreams and aspirations, Swarup's novel also reinforces longstanding stereotypes of slum dwellers as thieves and prostitutes.[39]

In the end, his mental flexibility enables Ram's victory on *Who Will Win a Billion*. In Swarup's novel this game show is presented as produced by a corrupt American-owned corporation New Age Telemedia, whose US and

101

Indian producers are both perfectly comfortable with torturing Ram and denying him his earnings, having never anticipated that they would have to pay anyone the full prize money. Ram manages in the end to outwit the deceitful game show host as well as the corrupt policemen who are loyal to him. In the novel's final episode, as billionaire Ram walks along Mumbai's Marine Drive with his lawyer, Smita, his final words are, "luck comes from within" (318)—implying that good luck comes not from something in the external world, but rather from the individual drawing on his or her inner resources. Moreover, Ram's generous actions after winning the show—his freeing of crippled children who are being used as beggars, and his secret production of films to employ his actor friend Salim—confirm for the middle-class reader his innate generosity and his readiness to be the sort of rich person who is both wealthy and moral. In short, Ram's example serves to affirm key mythologies about slums and urban poverty—that the slum is the locus of urban disorder and disease, that the plight of the poor is at least partially the result of their own criminality, and therefore the best way out of poverty is through acts of individual ingenuity and the cultivation of inner resources. Although the novel engages in sensitizing the reader to the conditions of the urban poor, and also in critiquing the corruption of elites, its approach to explaining and addressing poverty is classically neoliberal, with mental flexibility and moral uprightness posited as the ultimate solutions.

Slumdog Millionaire's Narrative of Capitalist Development

Adapted from *Q&A* by Simon Beaufoy, the film *Slumdog Millionaire* takes the episodic, picaresque form of the novel and transforms it into a more familiar narrative of personal development that ends up glossing over some of the more interesting aspects of Swarup's critique of urban poverty. The film builds on the commercial success of a popular category of representations of Mumbai—sometimes known as Bombay Noir—that came to prominence in the early twenty-first century, and in which the slum or working-class *chawl* functions as a key site for generating both drama and social commentary. These representations have traveled widely across media as well as genre boundaries.[40] For instance, Suketu Mehta's bestselling nonfiction book *Maximum City: Bombay Lost and Found* (2004)—particularly its description of Mumbai's criminal underworld—informed Danny Boyle's direction of *Slumdog*.[41] Similarly, Katherine Boo's *Behind the Beautiful Forevers* was adapted for the London stage in 2014 by British playwright David Hare. This adaptation, in turn, built on the theatrical success of British composer Andrew Lloyd Weber's *Bombay Dreams*, a Broadway musical about Mumbai slum dwellers that drew on Bollywood costumes and conventions and played to large audiences in London (2002–2004) and New York (2004–2005)—cities themselves with growing disparity between rich and poor.

Although many Indian commentators have criticized *Slumdog* for providing a negative portrait of India,[42] the film, in fact, ultimately reinforces official narratives of a new, transformed, globalizing nation in which the embrace of free-market capitalism promises upward mobility for all. Ram Mohammad Thomas's character in *Q&A* is split in the film into Jamal—a quick-witted, English-speaking Muslim boy from the slums who wins the Indian version of *Who Wants to Be a Millionaire*—and his brother, Salim, who ends up joining the criminal underworld. British-South Asian actor, Dev Patel, who plays Jamal with a British accent, makes Jamal's character palatable to both the Indian and British viewer (who might most likely be familiar with the actual TV show of the same name that originated in Britain and was adapted in India as *Kaun Banega Crorepati*). On the whole, the film goes further than Swarup's novel in sanitizing the *picaro* and transforming him into a protagonist worthy of transformation from slumboy to citizen.

Tanushree Ghosh calls attention to the many parallels between *Slumdog* and *Oliver Twist* (1838), Charles Dickens's *Bildungsroman* about the education and maturation of an orphan boy who finds himself involved in a gang of criminals and pickpockets in London's East End. Oliver, much like Jamal, "is distinguished from his lower-class counterparts by his use of standard English, untainted by the use of urban jargon as opposed to the use of Cockney speech variation by various lower-class characters, such as the Artful Dodger and other members of Fagin's gang."[43] Both director Danny Boyle and scriptwriter Simon Beaufoy acknowledge the influence of Dickens's nineteenth-century social-problem novels on the film.[44] But their Dickensian narrative—filmed in Dharavi itself—presents the slum as primarily a wasteland of trash and excrement. In Boyle's film the slum stands as the ultimate symbol— or, as Ananya Roy puts it, "metonym"—of Third World urban poverty and degradation.[45] *Q&A*'s depictions of community as well as entrepreneurial activity in the slums do not make their way into the film. The filmic slum is instead constructed as a site of violence and the relentless abuse of children like Jamal (which recalls Oliver's abuse in Dickens's novel). If Swarup's fiction isolates the slum as "cancerous lump," then Boyle's work goes further, by constructing it as a self-contained world of criminality, abuse, and chaos that is strongly reminiscent of the representation of City of God in both Lins's novel and its filmic adaptation.

The chaos and separateness of slum life is heightened by *Slumdog*'s visual style—also reminiscent of the film *City of God*, with its rapid-cutting, unstable mobile camera, extreme close-ups and canted angles, and pulsating soundtrack that makes slum dwellers curiosities. Early in *Slumdog* we watch Jamal and Salim as children being chased by a policeman. Handheld camerawork, rapid editing, oscillation between high- and low-angled shots, contrasts between harsh sunlight and the darkness of slum interiors, loud percussive music, and the lyrics of South-Asian-British rapper MIA, combine to convey the chaotic energy of the boys' escape from the disorder of the slum's vast garbage-strewn areas, waterways, and narrow, crowded streets. In the midst of this chase

Beyond Alterity

sequence, a momentarily stable camera pulls back to reveal a series of wide, top-angle shots of the slum that generalize the disorder, suggesting to the viewer that it is emblematic of the slum as a whole, and potentially a metonym for India as well. Following this wide view, the camera continues to be unstable and the close views of slum life are from canted camera angles that confirm its disorder. In a later scene in which Jamal and Salim witness their mother's killing during the anti-Muslim violence of 1992–1993, the patterns established in the opening chase sequence are reproduced. Cumulatively, and in conjunction with the film's frequent cutting between past and present, these techniques conjure a world of frenetic energy but also spectacular disorder.

Jamal and Salim live largely in Mumbai, except for a brief period in Agra, when—as teenagers who are able, magically, to speak English—they survive by stealing and pretending to be tourist guides at the Taj Mahal. The lyrics of the song on the soundtrack, "All I want to do is take your money" (from MIA's "Paper Planes") confers on the boys the transnational identity of hustlers who thrive through illegal activities. Nandini Chandra points out that in this depiction of the poor,

> [t]hey are seen as gaining from rather than giving to the system, sabotaging, picking up the leftovers, staying in empty hotel rooms, stealing from it. Their labor is forever in the background. What is in the foreground is the readymade wealth they are continually grabbing. Wealth is seen not as something created by labor but as already always there to be accessed—like the twenty million to be won for the answering of ten questions, a clear repudiation of the true dynamics of labor and class.[46]

Further contributing towards this masking of labor's role in wealth creation is the portrayal of Salim as a gangster. While Jamal works in a restaurant and later as a *chaiwallah* who brings tea to the middle-class employees of a call center, Salim joins an underworld gang and gets used to a life of "grabbing" and killing. Salim emblematizes the potential in the poor to be criminals and killers and thereby reinforces Jamal's status as an exception. This view of the urban poor not only repudiates "the true dynamics of labor and class" but also masks the economic violence inherent in legitimate forms of capitalism.

As in the film version of *City of God*, legitimate forms of capitalism are invisible in *Slumdog*, and when they do come into view, they appear to be modernizing and civilizing agents. When Jamal and Salim return from Agra and find that a globalized, corporatized Bombay has been renamed Mumbai, the pace of the editing appears less frenetic than in the slum scenes of the first third of the film. Similarly, when Jamal goes looking for his love interest, Latika, the city appears notably less chaotic, the streets more navigable. Such stylistic choices present the city transformed by economic liberalization as a superior version of the slum-dominated habitat of the early parts of the film. The film returns to the extreme close-ups and unstable, moving camera only in the sequence in which Salim frees Latika from the gangster Maman—an episode that leads to Salim's incorporation into the criminal underworld. In other words, stylistic excess is reserved for scenes featuring the underworld, thereby containing criminality and violence within this world of illegitimate capitalism. Years later, when an adult Jamal reconnects with Salim and follows him in an attempt to find Latika, the city streets once again seem orderly (even if the omnipresence of buildings under construction give it a ghostly look). Even the crowds at the Victoria Terminus station where Jamal waits for Latika appear orderly, enabling the lovers to find each other. Finally, in the sequence towards the end of the film that crosscuts between Latika driving into the city and Jamal being driven to the quiz show, the crowds and car traffic make Mumbai seem crowded, yet nowhere as chaotic as in the early sequences set in the slums. This is no longer complete anarchy, but rather more manageable urban chaos, giving the impression that the economic liberalization that propelled the transformation of Bombay into Mumbai has brought with it progress and modernization. In the process, the violence and anarchy that seemed to be everywhere in the film's first third are effectively restricted to the realm of the criminal underworld, which—like in *City of God*—is shown to be enmeshed with a corrupt police.

When the brothers reconnect as adults, it is on a construction site—in a scene that clearly spells out the film's attitude towards the "new" corporate/globalized Mumbai. As Salim and Jamal regard the surroundings from atop a building in construction, the camera circles around them, making visible a vast landscape of emerging skyscrapers. Salim exclaims, "Can you believe, we used to live right there, man. Now it's all business. India is at the center of the world now, *bhai*. And I am at the center of the center." This picture of the city's subordination to the corrupt underworld—to which Salim belongs—complicates official narratives about modernizing Mumbai. And yet, the shots of the construction site—cleansed of all signs of the anarchic slum and replaced by skyscrapers- in-formation—give credence to the view that the transition from Bombay to Mumbai spells progress, and that it may even be part of an *inevitable* transformation of the Third-World city of "hidden"

Beyond Alterity

and "messy" urbanization to a "world-class city" of high-rises and private development.

Furthermore, by attributing corruption in the globalizing city primarily to the police and criminal underworld, the film erases *Q&A*'s references to corporate corruption. In the novel, the quiz show host participates in the practices of a corrupt multinational US corporation that owns the show and tries to prevent Jamal from getting his prize; by contrast in *Slumdog*, the quiz show host, Prem, is simply personally corrupt: he is a former slum dweller who does not wish another slum dweller to advance economically. The American corporate organizers of the quiz show, unlike Prem, seem excited about Jamal's victory, and are not bothered by the prospect of having to pay him the money he wins. If the novel suggests that the American company is involved in deception and stealing from the poor, in the film the company is not complicit in any wrongdoing. Jonathan Cavallero quotes Simon Beaufoy as saying that his team had to be very careful to *not* make the quiz show appear corrupt because "Celador, the British company that produced *Slumdog*, was the original producer of *Who Wants to be a Millionaire*. Since the show's set, its title, and its format were recognizable to many westerners, the producers calculated that mobilizing these aspects of the program would increase the film's marketability to western viewers."[47] In the process, the film not only erases the novel's critique of corporate corruption but also fuels narratives produced by corporations like Celador about how a game show can be a ticket out of poverty.

In the end, Jamal's moral triumph over Prem, as well as the corrupt police who torture him on Prem's behalf, allows him to win the show and be transformed from slumboy to citizen of the "new," globalized India. The corporate sector and capitalist globalization more generally emerge not as obstacles to but rather as harbingers of progressive social change. When at the end of the film crowds collect all over the country to watch the final, decisive episode of the game show, the country appears united, as everyone—from middle-class call center workers to slum residents—tunes in to watch Jamal win. Successive shots show crowds applauding him in a variety of class contexts—from small, dark tenement rooms to brightly lit shops where multiple TV sets simultaneously broadcast his victory. Such juxtaposition makes clear that Jamal's participation in the televised game show has united Indians across class lines. For much of the film, the world of the working classes and the poor is presented as fraught with violence and, as in most Danny Boyle-directed films, as "profoundly atomist."[48] But by the end of *Slumdog*'s *Bildung* narrative, the viewer is left with the impression that capitalism has facilitated societal unification and regeneration.

The final scenes present the promise of a new, technologically connected, global India that seems to be beginning to break down class and other social divisions. Globalized capitalism, and its mediascapes, the film suggests, have transformed India's culture into a less brutal place. Jamal's win, in other words, is positioned as not just an individual's triumph. With everyone celebrating,

Undercity Fiction and the Crisis of Urbanization

these final scenes show *also* how a more mature, globally oriented capitalism can unite Indians and make citizens of India's poor. Jamal's maturation, in other words, parallels the maturation of Indian capitalism, and the slumboy's full incorporation into the body politic provides proof of the arrival of "new" India.

***

If cities are being increasingly built in the image and interest of private capital, then the danger of popular undercity narratives like *Slumdog Millionaire* and *City of God* lies in their further marginalization of the perspectives of the poor and working classes even as they attempt to give voice to the stories of these marginalized groups. The "abrasive visual style" of these films impedes empathetic identification with the majority of the poor characters, except for Rocket and Jamal. Put differently, the rest of the *favela* and slum dwellers appear to be, in Evan Watkin's words, "relics, throwaways, isolated groups of the population who haven't moved with the times, and who now litter the social landscape and require the moral attention of cleanup crews, the containing apparatus of police and prisons, the financial drain of 'safety nets,' the immense maintenance bureaucracies of the state."[49] While Watkins is channeling here a master narrative emergent in the United States during the 1980s and 1990s, his words could just as easily be used to encapsulate the worldview of *Slumdog* and *City of God*. There is nothing natural about "throwaways," Watkins argues, even though they are framed as resulting from naturally existing inequalities. In the US context, they were produced by policies that began with the Reagan administration but continued to be hegemonic through the Clinton era. As Watkins puts it, "Throwaway populations are not the survival of the unfit, the waste of change. They are produced by and indispensable to present social organization."[50] Extending his analysis to *Slumdog* and *City of God*, we might say that these films' representational strategies—especially the exceptionalizing of their protagonists—end up casting the majority of poor people as "unfit," which only masks how the poor are in fact "produced by and indispensable to" (neoliberal) capitalism.

Furthermore, through their representational strategies and styles, films like *Slumdog* might, even if unwittingly, supply fodder for the solutions proposed by neoliberal policymakers. The World Bank proposes that the solution to the problem of "slums and sprawl" lies in governments changing their titling and registration systems, to make it easier for "private developers ... to acquire and assemble multiple parcels of land for residential development" and for financial institutions "to finance land development or to accept land as collateral."[51] Thus, the proposed solution is private developers taking over public land on which slums have developed, with the implication that private redevelopment projects will ultimately benefit everyone, capitalists and relocated slum dwellers alike. Similar solutions have been recommended by local think tanks in India like Mumbai First, whose Vision Mumbai proposal (the product of a McKinsey & Co. study) has been supported by the Maharashtra state government.[52] To make these proposals, both Mumbai First and the World Bank elide the charged nature of class conflict in present-day Mumbai, including over the takeover of public land by real estate developers. In the slum of Dharavi, for instance, longstanding residents have for more than a decade been pushing back against developers, who, they argue, are getting rich at their expense—a valid assumption given how little the residents have been involved in the planning process, and also how many of them have already been deemed ineligible by the government for rehousing.[53]

Films like *Slumdog*, with their naturalization of the transition from Bombay to Mumbai, suggest that there might be no alternative to the sort of capitalist redevelopment proposed by policymakers. What this all goes to show is that challenging poverty through cultural representation requires much more than making the living conditions of the poor visible to middle- and upper-class audiences. What is also needed is attention to the role of legally sanctioned capitalism in creating poverty—in order to dismantle the assumption that the poor are either criminals (who have created their own fate) or else relics of a disease-producing undercity who occasionally, though ultimately unthreateningly, interrupt the lives of those occupying the heart of the city.

CHAPTER 5

Fixity Amid Flux: Literary Fiction and Rural Dispossession

A lot of my work is set in the rural areas, because they retain that magic, whereas the urban areas have lost it to Westernization.

—Zakes Mda[1]

[T]he quality of one's interaction with the fishermen—there is something so lovely in it, something so beautiful about the texture.
—Amitav Ghosh[2]

The "undercity" fiction described in the previous chapter speaks to some of the provocative contradictions animating popular representations of the poor in the era of neoliberalism. This chapter suggests that even the more politically and stylistically sophisticated genre of "literary" fiction has not simply resisted the neoliberal script and its associated narratives of personal and national emergence. I show how critically acclaimed novels like Amitav Ghosh's *The Hungry Tide* (2004) and Zakes Mda's *The Heart of Redness* (2000) attune to neoliberalization's impact on rural India and South Africa, but nonetheless remain tethered to core features of the neoliberal imagination. Ghosh and Mda are celebrated writers whose reputations have grown in tandem with the increased circulation of global South literatures—especially English-language literatures—in the neoliberal period. *The Hungry Tide* and *The Heart of Redness* were both published by major multinational presses operating in the authors' countries of origin—HarperCollins India and Oxford University Press of South Africa, respectively. Attending to the striking parallels between these texts, together with the global context in which they have been produced and distributed, helps to "dispel notions of [nationalist] exceptionalism," as Isabel Hofmeyr and Michelle Williams put it, and to "look to local, national, *and* global processes and forces shaping" politics and culture in the contemporary South.[3]

Beyond Alterity

Once part of the British Empire, India and South Africa are now leading multilingual, multiethnic democracies as well as regional hegemons that constitute, along with Brazil, Russia, and China, the so-called BRICS alliance of emerging economies. Although spurred on by distinct circumstances, both regional powers pronounced themselves "new" nations in the 1990s. In South Africa this discourse of newness referenced primarily its political transition from apartheid to democracy, although here, too—as in India—the end of the Cold War had catalyzed a turn towards increasing neoliberalization and globalization of the economy. Indeed, the less publicized aspect of South Africa's political transition is the ANC-led government's abandonment of its promise to redistribute wealth by nationalizing mines, banks, and monopolies and its embrace instead of privatization, deregulation, and financialization. Today, South Africa, like India, has some of the highest levels of income and wealth inequality in the world, despite the rise over the last decades of a sizeable and increasingly influential middle class.[4] Across these contexts, elites professed that neoliberal policies would bring about greater efficiency in the development of national infrastructures and in the dissemination of essential services to all sections of the population. In actuality, these policies have strengthened the hold of big business while further dispossessing impoverished and historically marginalized groups.

The Hungry Tide illuminates India's growing class divide in the neoliberal period, and it does this specifically through a "network narrative," a form that gained prominence in the 1980s and 1990s with the commercial success of novels like David Mitchell's *Ghostwritten* (1999), films like *Babel* (dir. Alejandro González Iñárritu, 2006), and a variety of video games and digital media focused explicitly on capitalist globalization. As Patrick Jagoda explains, "The sense of decentralization inherent in network form ... served as a model for the fundamental techniques of post-Fordism, including flexible production, affective labor, and the centrality of information technology."[5] *The Hungry Tide* resembles texts like *Ghostwritten* and *Babel*, in that it features a decentralized narrative with individual chapters alternating in a regular and predictable manner between the perspectives of three primary narrative focalizers. The result—to use Rita Barnard's description of *Ghostwritten*—is "a kind of synthetic or sutured omniscience that transcends any single individual's experience."[6] But if *Ghostwritten* and *Babel* feature connections forged primarily across spatial boundaries, *The Hungry Tide* connects characters across temporal moments as well—and this is where it most clearly parallels Mda's *The Heart of Redness*.

The Hungry Tide moves between the 1970s and early 2000s, and in each of these moments stages interactions between rural and metropolitan subjects. Through movements in time and across perspectives, the novel reveals the effects of violence inflicted in the name of environmental conservation on two generations of characters that converge in the rural Sundarbans.[7] *The Heart of Redness* is less neatly patterned, its form moving more fluidly between rural and metropolitan perspectives and also between the styles

Fixity Amid Flux: Literary Fiction and Rural Dispossession

of conventional and magical realism. The novel's layered form ultimately calls attention to parallel forms of dispossession taking place in the eras of colonialism and neoliberalism within the rural Eastern Cape, South Africa's poorest province. But despite its less structured network form, *The Heart of Redness* nevertheless shares with *The Hungry Tide* a common "event frame"[8]— the return of a diasporic, highly educated, and entrepreneurial subject from the United States—which launches its reckoning with histories of violence and their lingering effects on rural populations. In both novels, moreover, folklore plays a crucial role in the staging of historical recovery—even if in *The Heart of Redness* this element is integrated into the novel's form through techniques of magical realism (that blur the lines between past and present and oral and literary modes of storytelling), whereas in *The Hungry Tide* folklore appears primarily through translation by the novel's metropolitan characters and key focalizers. The invoking—even archiving—of regional folklore in these novels speaks to the authors' attempts at defending the local and the indigenous within the context of global capital's deepening penetration into rural ecologies.

Ghosh's and Mda's complex network narratives bring to mind the Warwick Research Collective's (WReC) characterization of "world literature" from the (semi-)periphery—as particularly capable of registering through both form and content a capitalist world-system that is singular, yet highly unequal. Drawing on Leon Trotsky, the WReC notes that capitalism's "combined and unequal development" results in "a contradictory 'amalgam of archaic with more contemporary forms'—an urban proletariat working in technologically advanced industries existing side by side with a rural population engaged in subsistence farming; industrial plants built alongside 'villages of wood and straw'; and peasants 'thrown into the factory cauldron snatched directly from the plow.'"[9] Given that the "shock" of combined and uneven development is most starkly visible in the peripheries and semi-peripheries of the modern capitalist world-system, the WReC suggests that literature from these regions is more likely to register—"with particular intensity and resonance"—the impact of combined unevenness. With their attentiveness to the effects of an extreme rural-urban divide and the coexistence of new and "archaic or residual" modes of living in India and South Africa, Ghosh's and Mda's novels exemplify the sort of sensitivity that the WReC believes is characteristic of peripheral and semi-peripheral literatures. This is borne out in how these novels convey—in form and content—what the WReC describes as "the palimpsestic, combinatory and contradictory 'order' of peripheral experience" as well as the "temporal and spatial dislocations and abrupt juxtapositions of different modes of life engendered by imperial conquest, or the violent reorganisation of social relations engendered by cyclical crisis."[10] Indeed, the novels' oscillations between perspectives and moments in time, and their merging of literary with oral storytelling, all contribute towards imaginatively concretizing the "palimpsestic, combinatory and contradictory 'order' of peripheral experience" that Trotsky and the WReC describe.

Yet, even as these novels' hybrid forms capture the palimpsestic nature of uneven development, they also, as I will show, are underwritten by a countervailing, stabilizing force that seeks to contain and preserve "archaic and residual" modes of living, and not simply reveal the coexistence of these modes of living in contemporary times. I argue that these novels are marked by a palpable tension between fluidity and fixity—and between processes of transformation on the one hand and idealization on the other. As a result, the decentralized form produced through careful oscillation between perspectives, time periods, and modes of storytelling, gets gradually funneled into a linear *Bildung* plot in which the diasporic characters, having gone through an alternative education following eye-opening encounters with peasants, become ethical enterprising subjects. Ultimately both of these novels invoke the neoliberal script and its associated plots of personal development to give coherence to their layered registration of uneven development. They both conclude with diasporic subjects committing to staying on in rural areas (rather than returning to the United States), and to using their newly acquired indigenous knowledge to help run non-governmental and locally based organizations and cooperatives. Through these diasporic protagonists *The Hungry Tide* and *The Heart of Redness* convey hope that the formally educated and Westernized middle classes, when less alienated from their roots, will help bridge the divide between urban and rural, and global and local, within the "new" economies of India and South Africa. Consequently, these novels' portraits of rural poverty and dispossession become backdrops for staging—and resolving to a certain extent—the identity crisis of dislocated metropolitans looking for a sense of belonging amidst the flux of capitalist globalization.

The diasporic metropolitans also become the chosen translators and commodifiers of "archival and residual" knowledge which the peasant characters transfer to them. Owing partly to this transfer of knowledge, the metropolitan characters evolve, whereas the peasants are static representatives of a disappearing way of life. In both novels, the peasants' fixity stands in marked contrast to the fluid and evolving subjectivities of the metropolitans. Moreover, whereas the metropolitan characters' internal transformations imply a view of human subjectivity as fluid and produced continually via interaction with others, peasant characters like Fokir in *The Hungry Tide* and Qukezwa in *The Heart of Redness* suggest an attachment to notions of authenticity and immutability. By the end of both novels, the peasant characters' primary function appears to be that of facilitating the informal education and moral transformation of previously self-centered and rootless metropolitans. Thus, an irony emerges: at the same time that these novels' complex forms expose the unevenness of capitalist development, the idealized peasant characters—and the transfer of knowledge and agency that they enable—also contribute to reinforcing the marginalized status of the peasantry that results from this kind of development. The globally mobile urban middle classes emerge as key political agitators, capable of galvanizing and also representing rural struggles to a metropolitan audience. In

Fixity Amid Flux: Literary Fiction and Rural Dispossession

what follows, I explore some of the causes and implications of these narrative choices that shape Ghosh's and Mda's responses to rural transformation and dispossession in contemporary India and South Africa. And I propose that the striking thematic and structural parallels between these novels are helpful for illuminating both the diagnostic potential and the political contradictions of a contemporary literary imagination of the rural.

Plotting Interconnectedness in *The Hungry Tide*

Amitav Ghosh first gained prominence in the 1980s with his critically acclaimed novel *The Shadow Lines* (1988). An emblematic example of what Priya Joshi calls the "nationsroman,"[11] *The Shadow Lines* engages the lingering psychic effects of the violence of Bengal's partition along national lines. Like *The Shadow Lines*, *The Hungry Tide* comments on the disastrous consequences of boundary making. Here, though, Ghosh's canvas is broader, and the novel reveals how boundaries destroy not only because of the parochialism of the nation-state—and its perpetuation of communal violence—but also its myopic agenda of development that ignores nature's patterns as well as the vital and fluid relationship of humans with their surroundings. Moreover, unlike *The Shadow Lines*'s mostly urban settings, *The Hungry Tide* unfolds in a rural context—in the Sundarbans archipelago, located off the northeast coast of India.

Roshan Shahani notes that, "In the years preceding independence and in the euphoric decade that followed, as the young nation was consolidating itself, the need for 'Indianness', of tradition, found expression through a valorization of the Indian peasant and of the Indian ruralscape." Thus, some of the quintessential early Indian English novels—for instance, Mulk Raj Anand's *The Untouchable* (1935) and Raja Rao's *Kanthapura* (1938)—are set in villages. Since the 1980s, however, writers have tended to gravitate towards "urbanity and ... metropolitan perceptions and issues," and these "metropolitan concerns of literary productions can be ascribed to the rapid growth of an urban middle-class readership."[12] *The Hungry Tide* departs from the "metropolitan concerns" of much post-1980s Indian fiction—even if it, too, addresses primarily a urban middle-class readership through its staging of interactions between two generations of rural and urban subjects.

The novel was published in 2004, amidst euphoric celebration of India's "new" economy on the one hand and news of growing rural poverty on the other. Following economic liberalization in the 1990s, the Indian government increasingly withdrew support for agriculture, precipitating an ongoing agrarian crisis. C.P. Chandrashekhar and Jayati Ghosh note that the prevailing "presumption was that freeing agricultural markets and liberalising external trade in agricultural commodities would provide price incentives leading to enhanced investment and output in that sector."[13] The government also withdrew support from public infrastructure and energy investments in rural areas. If in the post-independence period successive regimes had failed to carry

Beyond Alterity

out progressive land redistribution, then in the post-liberalization period land reform was nowhere on the agenda. Instead, the government started playing a prominent role in facilitating the transfer of rural land to powerful private entities, including for the establishment of Special Economic Zones.[14]

As is now well known, neoliberal policies have led to further impoverishment and hollowing out of the village economy. Over the last decade and a half, expenditure on agriculture as a percentage of the GDP has been less than 1 percent, even though the population dependent on the agricultural sector "has declined little and faces falling per head real income."[15] Many have abandoned agriculture and been forced to seek low-wage nonagricultural employment within the village or the city, adding to the ever-growing, underpaid, and precarious "informal" labor force. For those still dependent on agriculture, landholdings have been subdivided and reduced in size; the entry of transnational producers of genetically modified seeds has increased the cost of agricultural inputs; and farmers have been prompted to shift cropping patterns, often at the cost of their own food security. In this climate, many, especially poor farmers, have committed suicide.[16]

These details are not part of the plot of *The Hungry Tide*, though they constitute the context for its emergence. The novel instead invests in recovering a forgotten episode of dispossession that took place in the Sundarbans during the 1970s. One of the novel's key characters, Kusum, is killed in 1979—in the novel's recreation of an actual state-sanctioned massacre of refugee settlers carried out in the name of tiger conservation on the island of Morichjhapi.[17] A Dalit or low-caste refugee from Bangladesh, Kusum was being forced by state authorities to resettle in a dry area of central India, despite her wish to stay on in the Sundarbans because of her longstanding ties to the ecology and culture of the region that she and other locals lovingly refer to as the "tide country." Kusum's death at the hands of a casteist police force exposes the human costs of conservation. Through her story Ghosh uncovers a tragic episode of state violence and critiques an environmentalist politics that assumes human welfare to be irrelevant to the project of preserving "Nature." Kusum's death in 1979 impacts directly and indirectly several of the novels' characters. These include her son, Fokir, who grows up to become a fisherman with strong ties to the tide country; her Marxist friend, Nirmal, who hails from Calcutta but has spent most of his life in the Sundarbans; and Nirmal's Delhi-based nephew, Kanai, who owns a small translation business and comes to the Sundarbans in the early 2000s, following his uncle's demise, at the same time as Piya, an Indian-American marine biologist. Kusum thus comes to function as a crucial node within the novel's complex network narrative.

The key focalizers of this network narrative are the metropolitan characters—Nirmal, Kanai, and Piya—whose shifting internal states are revealed either through their own accounts or through an omniscient third-person narrator's channeling of their points of view. Thus, we learn how Nirmal's Marxism and faith in the postcolonial state are altered by his contact

Fixity Amid Flux: Literary Fiction and Rural Dispossession

with Kusum in the 1970s. Years later, Kusum's son Fokir acts as catalyst for the internal transformation of the next generation of metropolitans, Piya and Kanai. While Piya's collaboration with Fokir makes her socially conscious and teaches her to bring the concerns of peasants into her biocentric environmental activism, the elitist Kanai's interactions with Fokir prompt him to reevaluate his privilege. Together, the transformations experienced by Nirmal, Kanai, and Piya convey Ghosh's vision of a revolutionary environmental politics—one fueled by a vision of human connection and collaboration across class and cultural divides.

As this narrative unfolds, surprising affinities develop between several of the characters, and particularly between Nirmal, writing in the 1970s, and Piya in the early 2000s. In his diary entries Nirmal, a Marxist humanist and aspiring writer, documents his growing conviction that the islands' hybrid geography is interlinked with its inhabitants' syncretic belief system (that combines Muslim and Hindu influences) and folklore (that combines Arabic and Bangla legend). He concludes that, "the mudbanks of the tide country are shaped not only by rivers of silt, but also by rivers of language … Flowing into each other they create a proliferation of small worlds that hang suspended in the flow" (247).[18] Many years later, and in very similar language, the cetologist Piya attends to the region's incredible biodiversity and takes note of the "proliferation" of balloon-like "micro- environments … suspended in the water" that "had their own patterns of flow" (125). Through the parallels between Nirmal's and Piya's observations, Ghosh unsettles the opposition between humanism and natural science and shows how both of these perspectives deem the proliferation of "small [linguistic cultural] words" and "micro-environments" to be essential for global hybridity and flow.

Beyond charting convergences in their worldview, *The Hungry Tide* parallels Nirmal's and Piya's trajectories through the unconventional romantic attachments they each develop—to Kusum and Fokir, respectively. In both cases of inter-class attachments, a shared structure of feeling becomes the basis for intersubjective identification, solidarity, and love. A central episode in Nirmal's diary stems from his realization that the police was evicting Kusum and other refugees from Morichjhapi. Nirmal hears from Kusum how the police would bombard the settlers' housing with announcements that "[t]his island has to be saved for its trees, it has to be saved for its animals, it is part of a reserve forest, it belongs to a project to save tigers, which is paid for by people from all around the world" (261). Kusum wonders how their living in Morichjhapi could possibly be a crime when this was how "humans have always lived—by fishing, by clearing land and by planting the soil" (262). As he comes to sympathize with Kusum's perspective, Nirmal also begins to see his personal struggle for belonging mirrored in the settlers' struggle against displacement. Originally from Calcutta, he felt only a tenuous sense of belonging to his new home in the Sundarbans. Thus, when he hears the protesters cry, "Who are we? We are the dispossessed," Nirmal wonders:

Beyond Alterity

> Who, indeed, are we? Where do we belong? And as I listened to the sound of those syllables, it was as if I were hearing the deepest uncertainties of my heart being spoken to the rivers and the tides. Who was I? Where did I belong? In Kolkata or in the tide country? In India or across the border? In prose or in poetry? (254)

Nirmal is able to identify with the refugee settlers because of his own lifelong struggle to belong and to find an effective political and artistic voice. Moreover, although a lifelong Marxist, he had never been part of any collective struggle and had only ever dreamed of revolution. His romantic attachment to Kusum develops in part out of a feeling that what he is witnessing with the peasant settlers' mobilizations in Morichjhapi is revolution in action.

Years later, Piya similarly identifies with Kusum's son, Fokir. In this case, what connects them is their shared passion for living a life "far from the familiar" (126). The narrative voice registers the Indian-American marine biologist's puzzlement over her ability to feel so intimately connected to this rural Bengali fisherman:

> But that it had proved possible for two such different people to pursue their own ends simultaneously—people who could not exchange a word with each other and had no idea of what was going on in one another's heads—was far more than surprising: it seemed almost miraculous. And nor was she the only one to remark on this: once when her glance happened accidentally to cross Fokir's, she saw something in his expression that told her that he too was amazed by the seamless intertwining of their pleasures and their purposes. (141)

Piya's imagining of a hidden affinity with Fokir is reinforced when she realizes that they share the experience of having lost their mothers at an early age. She senses in Fokir a familiar melancholia, and this allows her to connect to him despite class and cultural difference and a lack of verbal communication.

In its emphasis on revealing the interconnectedness of social and ecological concerns, as well as affinities in consciousness forged across class and cultural divides, Ghosh's novel shares the tendency of some network theory and ecological discourse to suggest that, ultimately, "everything is connected with everything else."[19] Nirmal most clearly embodies this belief, and his perspective is privileged early in the novel. Kanai describes his uncle as a "historical materialist" (282) for whom "everything which existed was interconnected: the trees, the sky, the weather, people, poetry, science, nature. He hunted down facts in the way a magpie collects shiny things. Yet when he strung them all together, somehow they did become stories—of a kind" (282–283). Nirmal's fascination with interconnected particularities resonates powerfully with the novel's practice of connecting characters' lives to one another, while also hunting down and stringing together fragments of folktales and stories related to the goddess Bonbibi that emanate from the islands.[20] Although the novel occasionally reveals the limits of Nirmal's thinking, it nevertheless validates his drive to accumulate ethnographic and geographical information about the islands, and to demonstrate connections across temporal, cultural, and socio-economic boundaries.

The parallel between Nirmal's and Piya's trajectories is, then, but one moment in the novel's sustained effort at plotting interconnectedness. However, this sustained tracing of networks and interconnected subjectivities finds its limit in the peasant characters, Kusum and Fokir. Whereas the metropolitans' internal transformations and ethical development supply the dynamism that propels the plot's forward movement, the peasants who trigger and catalyze these transformations remain themselves relatively fixed and unchanging. Fokir in particular functions as an anchor of sorts. Patrick Jagoda notes that "a network is never a static structure" and depends "on an active flow among interlinked vertices."[21] Fokir's fixity interrupts this flow.

The Authentic Peasant

Piya comes to rely on Fokir's vast knowledge of the river for her cetological research. As she develops amorous feelings for him, her interest in protecting the *Oracella* appears to her indistinguishable from this local fisherman's interest in the endangered species. She also romanticizes his decision to remain a fisherman despite the increasing difficulty of his way of life. Her witnessing of Fokir's participation in the killing of a tiger is, however, a turning point in her consciousness. She had assumed that because of their shared love of the natural world Fokir would be opposed to the killing, not recognizing the threat the tiger population poses to local inhabitants, nor how its preservation by conservation groups had led to the death of Fokir's mother in 1979. Eventually, Piya comes to appreciate Fokir's history and begins to notice the extent to which his values and mode of relating to the natural environment are different from hers. Kanai, playing the relatively rooted and more knowledgeable local cosmopolitan, pushes Piya to reevaluate her thinking following the tiger killing:

> "[I]t was people like you," said Kanai, "who made a push to protect the wildlife here, without regard for the human costs. And I'm complicit because people like me—Indians of my class, that is—have chosen to hide these costs, basically in order to curry favour with their Western patrons. It's not hard to ignore the people who're dying—after all they are the poorest of the poor. But just ask yourself whether this would be allowed to happen anywhere else? There are more tigers living in America, in captivity, than there are in all of India—what do you think would happen if they started killing human beings?" (301)[22]

Despite his urban arrogance, Kanai is shown to possess greater awareness than Piya of how class and transnational power relations inform the project of tiger conservation and disproportionately impact the "poorest of the poor." Over time, she begins to see that he is right.

Beyond Alterity

Her growing bond with Fokir eventually propels a change in Piya's Western, purely science-driven environmental activism. After his death in a cyclone, Fokir's prior transfer of local geographical knowledge and data—which Piya saves in her GPS device—becomes a crucial factor in shaping her decision to stay behind in the Sundarbans. In the novel's epilogue, Piya declares her intention to continue her cetological research but this time "in consultation with the fishermen" and close collaboration with the local community. "I don't want to do the kind of work that places the burden of conservation on those who can least afford it," she announces (397). Fokir, in other words, plays a vital role in enabling a socially responsible environmentalist politics to take root in the Sundarbans.

Following Fokir's death Piya emerges as an ethical entrepreneurial subject who uses her resourcefulness—often remarked upon in the novel—to raise money on the Internet for Fokir's family, and to secure donations from conservation groups for the continuation of cetological research. The novel's final scene plays out an exchange between Piya and Nilima, Nirmal's wife who has long run a non-governmental organization in the Sundarbans. Nilima is presented as someone who, from Kanai's perspective, "had made great sacrifices in the public interest, ... [and] who was a throwback to an earlier era when people of means and education were less narrow, less selfish than now" (21). By the end of the novel, Piya, too, is made less narrow and selfish; and this is made clear when she decides to partner with Nilima so that she can have the support of a local organization as she carries out her work on the islands. She also declares to Nilima her intention of hiring Fokir's enterprising wife, Moyna, who she imagines would welcome the opportunity for "an additional source of income" (397). The novel ends with the promise of a mutually beneficial arrangement between three entrepreneurial women from diverse class contexts and backgrounds.

Meanwhile, Kanai, the small businessman, undergoes a parallel shift in consciousness. Early on in the novel he is described as "the founder and chief executive of a small but thriving [translation] business ... that specialized in serving the expatriate communities of New Delhi: foreign diplomats, aid workers, charitable organizations, multinational companies and the like" (20). This translator-entrepreneur is portrayed as smug and self-satisfied, and there is some irony in the omniscient narrator's descriptions of Kanai's life. But the businessman is forced to change when Fokir dares him to go to an island where he had earlier spotted tiger prints. The narrator remarks that, "it was as though in stepping on the island, the authority of their positions had been suddenly reversed" (325). Kanai finds himself helpless and angry to be at Fokir's mercy. However, his anger then prompts him to see himself through the latter's perspective, and Kanai realizes the ways in which he is attached to a social class and thereby to a history of oppression that has not only dehumanized men like Fokir but also destroyed the Sundarbans' ecological balance. This exchange with Fokir triggers in Kanai a moral transformation. The novel's epilogue suggests that Kanai has decided to move closer to the

Fixity Amid Flux: Literary Fiction and Rural Dispossession

Sundarbans—from Delhi to Calcutta—after "restructuring his company so that he can take some time off." He aims to "write the story of Nirmal's notebook—how it came into his hands, what was in it, and how it was lost" (399). Thus, the small businessman and translator is transformed into a potential artist and writer whose plan to write the "story of Nirmal's notebook" brings to mind the novel's project itself.[23]

Piya's and Kanai's processes of ethical maturation are enabled and supported by "gifts" of indigenous knowledge and folklore. As mentioned, Fokir leaves vital data representing "decades of work and volumes of knowledge" on Piya's GPS. This data then becomes the "foundation of [Piya's] own project," which she decides to name after him (398). Meanwhile, Kanai, as part of his effort to impress Piya, translates the local Bon Bibi legend that Fokir sang. When Piya is on the boat with Fokir, she hears the fisherman sing a song that is later revealed to be the story of Bon Bibi. This song plays a vital part in the love triangle that forms between Piya, Fokir, and Kanai. Once he realizes his inability to win Piya's heart, the chastened Kanai gives her the parting gift of a written version of the song she heard and was haunted by but could not understand. In the letter that accompanies his gift, Kanai writes: "this was the story which gave this land its life ... This is my gift to you, this story that is also a song, these words that are a part of Fokir" (354). Gifts like the song that Kanai translates for Piya, or the data that Fokir leaves behind before his death, contribute to preserving local cultural knowledge and scientific data—which then fuel Kanai's writing and Piya's research. In other words, Piya's and Kanai's independent projects are enabled in part by a transfer of knowledge and expertise from idealized, authentic, dead peasants to surviving metropolitans.

Since the metropolitan subjects do not claim ownership over the knowledge they receive, it is possible to see these gifts as part of Ghosh's vision of a politics of solidarity and collaboration across class and geographical divides. As Neil Lazarus argues, Ghosh is aware of the danger of appropriation and therefore does not give us "unmediated access" to Fokir's thoughts and knowledge; and still, the novel conveys the possibility for "deep-seated affinity and community, across and athwart the social division of labour."[24] Ashley Dawson also finds the novel's emphasis on cross-class connection noteworthy and sees it as complementing the solidarity-building work of rural landless people's movements: "if contemporary landless people's movements are advancing radical democratic strategies that hinge on the rejection of authoritarian social relations, *The Hungry Tide* deploys narrative to involve its readers in a complementary process of empathy and affiliation with the marginalized."[25] Lazarus and Dawson are right to underscore Ghosh's investment in political possibilities born out of cross-class and empathy-based affiliation. However, the construction of *The Hungry Tide*'s primary rural character as an unchanging peasant complicates its politics of solidarity and interconnectedness. In fact, Fokir is constructed much like the "timeless and unchanging" villager that, as Dipankar Gupta notes, remains a persistent trope within imaginings of rural life in India.[26]

Beyond Alterity

While Fokir acts as catalyst for the transformations of Piya and Kanai, he is himself a figure of fixity. He is depicted as closely intertwined with his natural environment. Observing him as a child, Horen says that "the river is in his veins" (245). Piya echoes this sentiment years later when she notes of the adult Fokir that "It's like he's always watching the water—even without being aware of it. I've worked with many experienced fishermen before but I've never met anyone with such an incredible instinct: it's as if he can see right into the river's heart" (267). Over the course of their evolving relationship, Piya learns to rely on Fokir's instinctive and embodied wisdom. She also reflects more generally on humans' connection to the natural world while observing him. For instance, when watching him fish, while dolphins celebrate a "catch of their own," Piya is "awestruck." She wonders: "Did there exist any more remarkable instance of symbiosis between human beings and a population of wild animals?" (169). Through the globally mobile Piya's marveling at Fokir's intimacy and affinity with local wildlife, the novel, too, marvels at his manifestation of the "symbiosis" between human beings and nonhuman nature.

Fokir's stable connection to nonhuman nature is part of his overall construction as an innocent who represents a refreshing alternative to the materialism and flux of modern life. Through much of the narrative, he rarely speaks but often sings verses from the Bon Bibi legend. From Nirmal's diary, we gather that the legend is "all in his head," as Kusum told him the story so many times as a child "that these words have become a part of him" (248). Piya appreciates her wordless exchanges with the adult Fokir. Kanai, too, is struck by Fokir's innocence, especially in a moment when the peasant declares that he sees his mother everywhere: "The phrasing of this was simple to the point of being childlike," Kanai reflects (319). Kanai tries to understand why the worldly, literate, and enterprising Moyna would choose to be married to this illiterate and "unformed" man who insists on continuing his life as a fisherman, despite the impossibility of making a living in this manner. Although Moyna occasionally pushes back against Kanai's framing of her motives and desires, and although the reader learns to take with a grain of salt the metropolitan businessman's patronizing, "egalitarian, liberal, [and] meritocratic" perceptions (219), his view of Fokir's childlike innocence is nevertheless left unchallenged.[27]

This representation—that treats the peasant as bearing an organic and stable connection to the natural world—resonates with framings of indigenous inhabitants within strains of environmentalist discourse. These framings have elicited critique from postcolonial environmentalists. Ramachandra Guha, for instance, criticizes the trend in American environmentalism known as "deep ecology," particularly its problematic commitment to an "unspoilt wilderness" as well as its construction of "primal" peoples from Eastern cultures as the bearers of deep ecological knowledge. Guha notes that

> [m]any agricultural communities do have a sophisticated knowledge of the natural environment that may be equal (and sometimes surpass) codified

"scientific" knowledge; yet, the elaboration of such traditional ecological knowledge (in both material and spiritual contexts) can hardly be said to rest on a mystical affinity with nature of a deep ecological kind.[28]

Through its deliberate paralleling of Piya's and Nirmal's perspectives as well as its critique of Piya's disregard for human and social dynamics, *The Hungry Tide* challenges the sort of biocentric environmentalism popularized by trends like deep ecology. Yet, even as it opposes Piya's narrow defense of conservation on deep ecological grounds, the novel—at least in its construction of Fokir—is also informed by deep ecology's view of peasant communities as possessing prescientific knowledge and a "mystical affinity with nature." In fact, the novel's framing of Fokir's subjectivity as fixed and especially connected to Nature and to traditional ecological knowledge, weakens its historically attuned critique of the politics of conservation and dispossession in rural India.

A few instances in the novel suggest that Fokir is doubly displaced: first, because he is the child of refugees, and second because of the fish and prawn farming industry whose large-scale operations are changing the river's ecology and making his way of life increasingly unsustainable. At one point, Moyna speaks of the new nylon nets used by the big fishing companies to catch tiger prawns: "The nets are so fine," she says, "that they catch the eggs of all the other fish as well." This new equipment thus depletes the diversity of the river's marine life, while enriching the "traders [who] had paid off the politicians" (134). Moyna fears that with the new nets all the fish could be gone in 15 years and Fokir would be rendered disposable. Fokir's condition, as implied in these moments, testifies to what Rob Nixon describes as a

> more radical notion of displacement, one that, instead of referring solely to the movement of people from their places of belonging, refers rather to the loss of the land and resources beneath them, a loss that leaves communities stranded in a place stripped of the very characteristics that made it inhabitable ... Such a threat entails being simultaneously immobilized and moved out of one's living knowledge as one's place loses its life-sustaining features. What does it mean for people declared disposable by some "new" economy to find themselves existing out of place in place, as against the odds, they seek to slow the ecological assaults on inhabitable possibility?[29]

In some of its most interesting moments—such as when Fokir resists his wife's attempts to persuade him to abandon fishing and turn to more lucrative work—*The Hungry Tide* captures the contemporary peasant fisherman's experience of alienation, or of "existing out of place in place" within the "new" economies of contemporary globalization. However, these brief moments that place Fokir in a changing context of uneven development are overwhelmed by the novel's dominant tendency to represent him as an innocent who possesses a mystical and stable connection to the natural world. Fokir's death at the novel's end forecloses possibilities for fleshing out the peasant's experience.

Beyond Alterity

Victor Li argues that Fokir is constructed like the idealized subaltern of much of subaltern studies theory, who dies so that the subaltern ideal can be preserved. In the process, Li argues, "The complexities of subaltern existence fall away before the novel's project of aesthetic idealization in which a chosen subaltern, especially in death, becomes for the reader a symbol of utopian desire and hope."[30] Building on both Li and Nixon, I would add that what "fall[s] away before the novel's project of aesthetic idealization" is deeper engagement with the causes and consequences of the dispossession that, as the novel fleetingly suggests, characterizes the "new" rural economy of the Sundarbans and shapes Fokir's subjectivity. Ghosh's construction of Fokir as a figure of fixity obscures insight into how destabilizing economic forces shape the subjectivities of rural populations in the present. Not surprisingly, this construction also denies rural characters the agency to respond, except on a symbolic level, to these economic forces and the uneven development they produce.

Transformation and Idealization in *The Heart of Redness*

A similar tension between transformation and idealization pervades *The Heart of Redness*, Zakes Mda's critically acclaimed novel set in South Africa's Eastern Cape. Mda—much like Camagu, the metropolitan protagonist of *The Heart of Redness*—returned to South Africa in the aftermath of apartheid, after years spent in exile in the United States. In the 1980s, he was already well regarded as a playwright. In the 1990s, Mda turned to writing novels as well, and he is now one of South Africa's most celebrated and globally recognized novelists.[31] His first novel, *Ways of Dying* (1995), was set almost entirely in post-apartheid Johannesburg. *The Heart of Redness* (2000), by contrast, begins in this urban setting but then moves to the rural Eastern Cape, which, as David Bell notes, "is a place of historical resonance in the violent history of South Africa being the home of the AmaXhosa who bore the brunt of British colonial expansion in the early nineteenth century. It is also the area which saw the first hearings of the Truth and Reconciliation Commission (TRC) in 1996 following the end of apartheid, and it is a region marked by severe rural poverty."[32] In its portrayal of a fictionalized Eastern Cape village, Qolorha-by-Sea, *The Heart of Redness* stages a struggle between pro-development supporters of casino construction and traditionalists who fear that the gambling industry will destroy local ecology and further impoverish the village population. Interestingly, the novel frames these contemporary debates about tourism-led development as the continuation of a colonial-era conflict between so-called Believers and Unbelievers that culminated in the Xhosa Cattle Killing of 1856–1857.[33] By linking these moments, the novel prompts the reader to look at contemporary concerns afresh, and from a historically informed perspective.

To engage with the novel in depth, we need first to attend to the particularities of South Africa's neoliberal transformation and to Mda's relationship to the "new" South Africa. It is important to note that the neoliberal turn in South Africa occurred within the context of a declining apartheid regime. Since 1948, the government had legalized and consolidated a system of racial segregation in service of white elites—a brutal and virulent form of accumulation by dispossession.[34] By the 1980s, however, as Patrick Bond points out, the apartheid system was reaching its limits, with deepening "recession, intensifying sanctions, growing worker militancy and international competition" putting pressure on the economy. These conditions compelled the ruling National Party to begin the processes of democratization and economic liberalization.[35] Thus, in the late 1980s, the National Party began to negotiate a compromise with the African National Congress (ANC), which had for several decades led the anti-apartheid struggle under conditions of brutal political repression. This political compromise paved the way for the first multiracial election in 1994, in which the ANC and its political allies proved victorious, with Nelson Mandela elected president of a democratic South Africa. In national as well as international discourse South Africa came to be celebrated as a radically transformed polity. The establishment of the monumental TRC in 1996 furthered this image and led to the proliferation of oral, written, and audiovisual narratives about South Africans' direct confrontation with apartheid's traumas.[36] In particular, stories of personal confession, expiation, and interpersonal reconciliation made visible the ways in which South Africa's transition was not simply political in nature but cultural and emotional as well. Storytelling provided South Africans a chance to reckon collectively with the brutality of apartheid and its aftereffects. Simultaneously, this storytelling's commodified forms contributed to promoting the post-apartheid nation as a new "human rights culture" and hence a legitimate space to do business after years of economic sanctions.[37]

The discourse of "new" South Africa at once attests to the significance of its political and cultural transformation and potentially obscures the lingering hold of apartheid elites on the post-apartheid government and its policies. Whereas the ANC had long advocated for the nationalization of white-owned mines, banks, and business monopolies, it was compelled to forego this goal once confronted with the reality of having to compromise with the former apartheid government and its business allies within an international climate marked by the decline of the Eastern Bloc and the globalization of neoliberal capitalism. By 1996, nationalization was abandoned as a goal and the post-apartheid government continued down the neoliberal path set by its predecessor. In this manner, processes of economic liberalization and privatization went hand in hand with South Africa's political transition from apartheid to liberal democracy.[38] As in India, neoliberal policies have exacerbated poverty and economic inequality in South Africa, owing in part to the privatization of basic services including water and electricity[39] and to the increase in non-secure, contingent employment as well as unemployment.[40] In South Africa deepening economic inequality has also been accompanied by reinforcement of the racial divide—and this, despite rising living standards for a black middle class and elite in the post-apartheid period.[41]

Beyond Alterity

Published six years after South Africa's first multiracial election, Mda's *The Heart of Redness* expresses an overall disenchantment with the elite nature of the nation's political transition. In particular, the novel critiques the hollowness of official discourses of "black empowerment" that, as the protagonist Camagu discovers, privilege a few at the expense of the many. Simultaneously, it sheds light on the plight of those living in the countryside, as uneven development from the colonial and apartheid eras is reinforced in the post-apartheid period because of continued lack of access to cultivable land, combined with a dearth of alternative employment opportunities. In a passage where temporality is left ambiguous, the omniscient third-person narrator speaks of "pacified men ... crammed into tiny pacified villages. Their pacified fields have become rich settler farmlands" (272).[42] The reader is prompted here, as elsewhere in the novel, to see the present as marked by a return of colonial-era modes of "pacification" as, once again, "settlers" assume control over existing farmland.

As in India, lack of access to cultivable land leaves villagers in present-day South Africa with little choice but to migrate to cities and join the highly precarious workforce, or to work in dangerous mines,[43] or to depend on paltry, nonagricultural sources of income—including from tourism. Mda's novel reflects some of these realities of post-apartheid South Africa. Early in the novel we learn that an elderly character called NoPetticoat supplements the inadequate government pension she receives by working as a babysitter at the Blue Flamingo Hotel (6). Some of the younger women, meanwhile, perform sex work for "red-blooded male tourists" living at the hotel (6); and tourists visiting the village leave their children with "part-time nannies while they walk or ride all over the valley, or swim in the rough sea" (6). The Blue Flamingo Hotel comes to emblematize the problems with a culture of tourism that profits off of the commodification of local populations and exoticization of village culture for wealthy metropolitans.

Mda's novel is pointed, even scathing, in its critique of business and corporate culture in post-apartheid South Africa. We learn through Camagu's experience that "the [white-dominated] corporate world did not want qualified blacks. They preferred the inexperienced ones who were only too happy to be placed in some glass affirmative-action office where they were displayed as paragons of empowerment. No one cared if they ever got to grips with their jobs or not." But "The beautiful [Black] men and women in glass displays did not like the Camagus of this world [either]. They were a threat to their luxury German sedans, housing allowances, and expense accounts" (30). This critique of the faux-progressivism of corporate culture is part of the novel's commentary on continuities between past and present forms of racial and economic exclusion. Apartheid's racialism appears to linger on in the corporate world's intolerance for "qualified blacks," just as British colonialism's "pacification" of rural populations in the nineteenth century is mirrored by settler farming and tourism's domination of the rural economy in the twentieth century.

This kind of interplay in Mda's novel between past and present sets it apart from *The Hungry Tide*, where the state-sanctioned dispossession of the

1970s is vividly explored, but the present forms of dispossession—by both state and business elites—remain tangential, especially in contrast to the overwhelming force of Nature that results in Fokir's death. In fact, whereas Ghosh's 2004 nonfiction piece, "Folly in the Sundarbans," pointedly attacks a proposal put forth by the Indian business conglomerate Sahara Pariwar to make a beach resort and "eco-village" in the Sundarbans, this sort of corporate presence and its methods of accumulation by dispossession are imperceptible in the rural environment recreated in *The Hungry Tide*.[44] In Mda's novel, on the other hand, corporate tourism is a major player in the staged interactions between past and present, and it is framed as bringing back the longstanding conflict between so-called Believers and Unbelievers. The narrative voice moves fluidly in channeling perspectives from both sides of this historical divide. If in the past this divide arose in response to British colonialism, then its present form responds to tourism, with Unbelievers like Xoliwa Ximiya and her father, Bhonco, supporting casino construction in the Eastern Cape, and Believers like Qukezwa and her father, Zim, fearing that the gambling industry will destroy the local ecology and enrich developers at the expense of the local population. Camagu's arrival in Qolorha occasions an exploration of this ideological conflict and provides a reminder of its historical antecedents.

Like the America-returned Piya in *The Hungry Tide*, Camagu is highly educated. He has a doctoral degree in communication and economic development from a US university and has worked in "the communications department of an international development agency in New York," in addition to doing consulting work for UNESCO in Paris, for the Food and Agricultural Organization in Rome, and for the International Telecommunications Union (29).[45] Just as Piya learns to alter her Western environmentalist perspective as a result of her growing attachment to Fokir, the highly cosmopolitan and America-returned Camagu learns—in large part through his debates with the peasant woman Qukezwa—to recognize the problems with a form of development that shows no concern for local ecologies. Similarly, if Fokir introduces Piya to the secrets of marine life in the Sundarbans, Qukezwa teaches Camagu about how the introduction of foreign species can harm indigenous plants and wildlife and destroy the ecological balance. When Camagu chides her for chopping down "nice plants"—just as Piya judges Fokir for his participation in tiger killings—Qukezwa tells the America-returned protagonist that these are "not nice for indigenous plants":

> These flowers that you like so much will eventually become berries. Each berry is a prospective plant that will kill the plants of my forefathers. And this plant is poisonous to animals too, although its berries are not. Birds eat the berries without any harm, and spread these terrible plants with their droppings. (90)

Qukezwa possesses a lived and holistic understanding of the ecology of Qolorha—which, for all his education, Camagu lacks, and which is also sorely lacking in the developers' vision to build a gambling complex in the village.[46]

Beyond Alterity

Unlike the taciturn Fokir, Qukezwa has an "acerbic tongue" (101) and she bravely flirts with Camagu during their first meeting. Qukezwa also, unlike Fokir, clearly articulates her thoughts and feelings about the corporate forces threatening Qolorha's ecology and economy in the present. She openly confronts Camagu about how casino building in Qolorha would negatively impact the village population. "The whole sea will belong to tourists and their boats and their water sports. Those women will no longer harvest the sea for their own food and to sell at the Blue Flamingo. Water sports will take over our sea!" she warns (103), while also pointing out that the villagers will not even have the skills to take on the few jobs that tourism might bring to the area. If Fokir is the mild, unthreatening, and silently suffering peasant, then Qukezwa is fierce, thoughtful, and argumentative—leading Pillay and Addison to describe her as a "Gramscian organic intellectual."[47] In other words, Camagu's contact with her allows him to obtain more than mere bookish knowledge about what is needed for sustainable rural development.

Aligned with Qukezwa's perspective, *The Heart of Redness* at first maintains a critical and ironic distance from the US-educated Camagu, who is also portrayed as an excessive drinker, womanizer, and a predatory man akin to a slave master (28). As his encounters with Qukezwa lead him to develop greater ecological and cultural sensitivity, his perspective becomes increasingly reliable. Put differently, the gap between the omniscient voice and Camagu's perspective narrows through the course of the narrative. We detect this narrowing in a passage where—channeling Qukezwa's impressions—he challenges the developers' claim that the gambling resort and casino are of national importance: "It is of national importance only to your company and shareholders, not to these people!" (200), he exclaims:

> You talk of all these rides and all these wonderful things, ... but for whose benefit are they? What will these villagers who are sitting here get from all these things? Will their children ride on those merry-go-rounds and roller coasters? On those cable cars and boats? Of course not! They will not have any money to pay for these things. These things will be enjoyed only by rich people who will come here and pollute our rivers and our ocean. (200)

A few paragraphs later, and in similar language to Camagu's, the omniscient narrator comments on how "The developers seem to have forgotten about the rest of the people as they argue about the profitability of creating a beautiful English countryside versus that of constructing a crime-free time-share paradise" (203). Thus, Camagu's voice becomes indistinguishable from the omniscient narrative voice by the novel's end—especially as he takes on the role of mediator between the Believers and Unbelievers and between corporatism and environmentalism.

Camagu comes to oppose the Unbelievers' plan to develop Qolorha into a casino and theme park. However, rather than dismiss this plan entirely he advocates instead for an environmentally sound tourism project that uses as part of its attractions the indigenous plant life that Believers like Qukezwa defend. In developing this alternative plan that serves as a compromise of sorts between the opposing sides, Camagu once again resembles Piya, who chooses in the end to serve as pragmatic mediator between the global and the local. Piya, while accepting support from Western environmental groups, commits to a form of conservation that takes local perspectives into account. In a similar manner, Camagu's model of tourism-fueled development recognizes the pressures of globalization but nevertheless prioritizes local ecology and culture.

But Camagu emerges as more pragmatic than Piya or even the small businessman Kanai, owing to his ability to unite in his view of development the roles of government and private enterprise. In this regard, the novel performs a slightly different iteration of the neoliberal script than *The Hungry Tide*. If Ghosh's novel suggests that the government is to be bypassed—given its record of (classist and casteist) violence against the poor—then Mda's novel suggests that the government, despite its entanglement with corporate elites, needs to be pushed to be more responsive to the concerns of ordinary people. In contrast to the metropolitans of *The Hungry Tide*, who work entirely on their own and align themselves only with non-governmental organizations, Camagu makes the case for combining government intervention with private efforts. For instance, he argues that "Electricity must come to the village … but not because of the gambling city … The government must bring electricity here because the village needs it. It is the policy of the government now to electrify even the most remote villages" (239). Through his advocacy, which the reader grows to trust, the novel presents the government as an unreliable force because of its alliances with corporate elites, but one that is nonetheless crucial for ensuring the welfare of vulnerable populations.

At the same time, Camagu invests in a private tourism project designed to give villagers greater autonomy over their lives. Hence, he forms a cooperative with women who harvest the sea for shellfish and supply traditional Xhosa skirts to the Johannesburg elite. "I do not own the cooperative society," he insists. "Its members own it" (240). For this tourist destination Camagu also argues for the necessity to strategically commodify traditional cultural practices, which are dismissed by the Unbelievers as signs of lack of civilization or "redness." A term emanating from the Xhosa custom of using red ochre to dye traditional skirts, this notion of "redness" resonates with "darkness" in Joseph Conrad's *Heart of Darkness*—a text Mda invokes through the title of his novel. Much as the colonizers in Conrad's novel dismiss Africa as "darkness," white people as well as the Unbelievers equate Qolorha with redness, or "unenlightenment" and lack of modernity (71). But Mda's novel—via Camagu— reframes redness as cultural richness, rather than unenlightenment. Camagu learns from Qukezwa that Qolorha was the birthplace of Nongqawuse, the girl who prophesied that if the Xhosa killed their cattle and destroyed their crops, their ancestors would rise from the dead and defeat the British. This millenarian prophesy led to widespread destruction and cattle killings, which eventually resulted in starvation and paved the way for the British to dominate the region. Through Qukezwa's influence, Camagu learns to view this story not as shame-inducing, but rather as part of the Xhosa people's anti-colonial struggle. Moreover, he begins to use Qolorha's historical significance as birthplace of Nongqawuse as a means of attracting tourists to his backpackers' hostel, which is built from natural materials found in the village, owned and operated by the villagers who come together to build the place (240), and invested in serving the "Authentic food of the amaXhosa" (239).

At the end, Camagu is successful in his efforts: the backpackers' hostel becomes a thriving, rustic holiday camp, and we learn that "The place now gives the Blue Flamingo Hotel tough competition. Tourists are attracted by the gigantic wild fig tree and the amahabohobo weaverbirds that have built a hanging city on its branches. And by the isiXhosa traditional costumes and beadwork that are created by the coop women" (273). Thus, Camagu's education in both indigenous plant life and culture become crucial to his organizing of an alternative, yet competitive, tourist destination. In the novel's final pages, he even makes a gesture of pragmatic reconciliation with his nearest competitor, John Dalton, owner of the rival cultural village at Qolorha. "We must all work together," he tells Dalton. "We need your business expertise at the [cooperative's] holiday camp" (277). On the whole, Camagu's mature social consciousness, combined with healthy pragmatism, model for the implied metropolitan reader of Mda's novel how a progressive form of entrepreneurialism—one that mediates between capitalist globalization and the villagers' needs—can help shift stubborn realities of rural underdevelopment.

Interestingly, though, as Camagu grows through Qukezwa's influence into a mediator between the Believers and Unbelievers as well as a principled and pragmatic entrepreneur who preserves Qolorha's indigenous plants and birds, Qukezwa herself, despite her feistiness, remains static—much like Fokir in *The Hungry Tide*. Also like Fokir, Qukezwa's singing of folksongs plays a crucial role in portraying her as bearing a stable connection to Nature. Early in Mda's novel we learn that folklore elicits in Camagu a palpable sense of longing for the village life he knew as a child but had to abandon when his family was forcibly displaced during apartheid. The villagers' singing and dancing reconnect him with his past and counteract the alienation he feels from his displacement—both from village to city and from South Africa to the United States. Furthermore, song and dance functions as a vital force that attracts him to Qukezwa. Qukezwa's split-tone singing resonates with Fokir's singing of the Bon Bibi legend (which Kanai translates for Piya); except that in *The Heart of Redness*, this singing elicits not just wonder and curiosity but also sexual desire in the metropolitan subject. When Qukezwa rides bareback and reinless on the horse Gxagxa and sings, whistles, and plays an isiXhosa instrument (151), Camagu has an involuntary bodily response: her split-tone singing leaves him "spellbound" and aroused to a state of orgasm. Because much of the narrative is focalized through Camagu's perspective, Qukezwa emerges in these episodes as simultaneously object of desire and "guardian

Fixity Amid Flux: Literary Fiction and Rural Dispossession

of a dying tradition," as he puts it (152). Further, her singing catalyzes their virtual coupling. Shortly after her singing takes him to orgasmic ecstasy, Qukezwa bears a child through immaculate conception (an exemplary instance of magical realism in the novel), and she and Camagu end up getting married.

Although Qukezwa is unpredictable, fierce, and far less idealized than Fokir, her construction seems nonetheless to be informed by a "deep ecological" perspective. This perspective is especially pronounced in the scenes and moments in which she displays (what Guha calls) "mystical affinity with nature." These include her split-tone singing that resounds through the natural geography, her bareback horse riding on moonlit nights, her half-naked swimming in the lagoon, and, most of all, her magical fertility, which allows her to give birth after an act of immaculate conception. While Fokir dies in the end, and Qukezwa gives birth, both of these characters are modeled around similar, conservative tropes—of "authentic peasant" and "natural woman," respectively. As embodiments of these tropes, Fokir's and Qukezwa's primary function is to propel the dynamic evolution of the metropolitans into ethical entrepreneurial subjects who ultimately take to raising money to address the villagers' needs or to organizing rural cooperatives.

In fact, in the final pages of *Heart of Redness*, Qukezwa fades into the background. When Camagu "haggles" with Zim and the elders (241) over the terms of his marriage with her, Qukezwa assumes the requisite posture of shyness. Camagu is the one with significant agency and power, as he arranges all the necessary customs and sacrifices for the marriage and continues simultaneously to do his mediating work and his development of eco-friendly tourism. In the novel's evocative final chapter, the omniscient narrator's descriptions of Qukezwa singing make her an otherworldly mythic figure, simultaneously the peasant woman Camagu met *and* the nineteenth-century ancestor after whom she was named. "She sings in soft pastel colors, this Qukezwa," the narrator tells us in a new, rhythmic, and lyrical voice that is reminiscent of oral storytelling:

> She sings in many voices, as Heitsi plays on the sand ... She sings in glaring colors. In violent colors. Colors of gore. Colors of today and of yesterday. Dreamy colors. Colors that paint nightmares on barren landscapes. She haunts yesterday's reefs and ridges with redness. (271)

Qukezwa's singing—described as a richly colored landscape—transcends time and is used to suggest the continuity of Xhosa tradition. While this tradition appears here as filled not just with "dreamy colors" but also "violent colors" and "colors of gore," the lyricism of this passage serves to freeze Qukezwa into a symbol—"guardian of a dying tradition."[48] In a world where—as the narrator prosaically declares—"the gambling complex shall [ultimately] come into being" (277), tradition is preserved with and through the maternal Qukezwa.

Beyond Alterity

Fixity Amid Flux

What is at stake in the construction of characters like Qukezwa and Fokir as guardians of tradition and points of stillness in a changing world? Ghosh gives us some clues in an interview conducted during the Pordenonelegge literary festival:

> What I liked most about writing *The Hungry Tide* was just spending time in the Sundarbans. With those people it was so beautiful to hear the language around me all the time and to hear the songs. It was such a wonderful thing to experience the simplicity of that life, because people like me, in Bengal, we all come from a peasant background. And I certainly feel a very deep sense of connection with that sort of life … If I was to write ten books like *The Hungry Tide*, it would never do justice to the absolute magic of being there at night with the tide changing, under the moon, and to hear the tiger nearby. And you know, the quality of one's interaction with the fishermen—there is something so lovely in it, something so beautiful about the texture. I suppose you can experience that if you go to some rural part of Italy. It is something you cannot experience as a tourist. It is because I am Bengali, because I am of a certain age that they can interact like that with me. With that sort of simplicity and openness and a kind of trust.[49]

In this interview Ghosh emerges as a global citizen—a former professor who, like Kanai and Piya, lives in New Delhi and the United States—and a socially and environmentally conscious writer who finds an audience even in non-English speaking contexts like Italy. Ghosh's description of the "magic" of being in the Sundarbans, with "those people," and of "hear[ing] the language around [him] all the time," illuminates his separation from the rural and desire to reconnect with what he sees as his "peasant background." It is interesting that he should attribute the "lovely" quality and "texture" of his interaction with the Sundarbans fishermen to his being a Bengali "of a certain age." Ghosh suggests here that the fishermen are able to relate to him "With that sort of simplicity and openness and a kind of trust" because he is Bengali and also because he belongs to a generation that still desires connection with its peasant roots. Ghosh's words imply an awareness of change as well as loss. One senses that an open, trusting relationship between fishermen and urban men like him is precious to him in part because he sees it as at risk of being challenged or eroded in a world where metropolitans interact with the rural largely as tourists.

The Hungry Tide registers a similar awareness of change as well as attentiveness to the various dimensions of loss incurred as a result of ongoing processes of rural transformation and dispossession. This sense of loss animates episodes such as that in which Piya hears Fokir sing the legend of Bon Bibi on the boat with him at night. Nirmal narrates his account of Morichjhapi out of a fear of the skillfulness of "the tide country … in silting over its past" (69). His urge to narrate his account of Morichjhapi emerges from his need to leave behind a "trace, some hold upon the memory of the world" (69). The construction of Fokir as the "authentic peasant" expresses a related fear—of rural ecologies and cultures being eclipsed by the forces of capitalist globalization and tourism, and hence the desire to (like Nirmal) place "some hold upon the memory of the world."

Like Ghosh, Mda has spoken of the "magic" of rural areas—and has attributed to this magic his choice of magical realism as a literary mode: "I wrote in [the mode of magical realism] from an early age," he notes, "because I am a product of a magical culture. In my culture the magical is not disconcerting ... The unreal happens as part of reality. A lot of my work is set in the rural areas, because they retain that magic, whereas the urban areas have lost it to Westernization."[50] Mda's characterization of Qukezwa registers this desire to preserve the "magic" of rural South African life that has been lost in the urban areas. This character therefore merges an ecofeminist perspective with a conservative desire for a timeless maternal figure that embodies and acts as guardian of tradition.[51] Put differently, Qukezwa's construction as married woman, mother, and folk singer who inspires urbanites like Camagu—and, perhaps, the reader as well—to connect with lost "magic" registers the novel's desire to preserve "archaic and residual" elements of village life at a moment when rural ecologies and cultures are in flux as a result of neoliberal practices of accumulation by dispossession.

My point is not to insist that Fokir or Qukezwa ought to have been constructed as rebellious peasant leaders, or as evolving entrepreneurial subjects in their own right. Rather it is to note how, even as *The Hungry Tide* and *The Heart of Redness* seek to bridge the rural-urban divide with their network narratives, they construct figures of fixity that preserve a stable ideal of peasant life and maintain the invisibilizing and marginalizing of rural populations in the present. Furthermore, Qukezwa's "gifts" of indigenous knowledge, and the "gifts" of data and folklore that Fokir leaves behind for Piya and Kanai, enable a transfer of resources and agency from the rural to the evolving metropolitan characters. This view of the world is hard to reconcile with the considerable grassroots organizing by rural populations, or what Nixon, building on Ramachandra Guha, calls the "environmentalism of the poor" that has grown "particularly (though not exclusively) across the so-called global South" in response to an "intensified assault on resources" by neoliberal capital.[52] Eclipsing the scale and character of these present-day struggles, Mda's and Ghosh's novels contribute towards a liberal political imagination in which social change emanates largely from the moral transformation of the professionalized urban middle classes and only indirectly from the experience and organization of those who bear the brunt of neoliberalism's assaults on the rural.

CHAPTER 6

Contesting the Script

> It was like a wartime ward. Except that in Delhi there was no war other than the usual one—the war of the rich against the poor.
>
> —Arundhati Roy, *The Ministry of Utmost Happiness*[1]

> Anand Mehta felt again the thrill of having bet on that grandest of investments: A growing human being.
>
> —Aravind Adiga, *Selection Day*[2]

To observe the entanglements of contemporary fiction with the neoliberal script is not to argue that fiction is *merely* a means of shoring up capitalist ideology. Nor is it to deny the existence of overtly oppositional works, which are often used as a stand-in for literature from the global South writ large. This chapter turns to two such works—Arundhati Roy's *The Ministry of Utmost Happiness* (2017) and Aravind Adiga's *Selection Day* (2016), whose explicit, sardonic critiques of neoliberalism exemplify what Pankaj Mishra has described as "the growing literary assessment of the ideology and practice of … capitalism" within fiction from Rising Asia.[3] Both novels expose corporate and finance capital's tightening grip on social relations in India and examine its implications, particularly for the poor. The dispossessed protagonists of these texts fit Wendy Brown's description of subjects who are asked to "sacrifice" themselves to the demands of the prevailing political-economic and cultural order.[4] However, unlike Brown's class-neutral account of subject formation, the novels highlight stark differences in the experiences of rich and poor, and point to the role of not simply ideas but also economic exploitation and dispossession in the shaping of subjectivities.

The Ministry of Utmost Happiness attends to the vulnerability of groups that have suffered from longstanding patterns of political and economic violence

Beyond Alterity

and are now targeted by new forms of predatory capitalism. Meanwhile, *Selection Day* focuses specifically on the economic and psychic dominance of a parasitic financier class that finds investment opportunities in poor sportsmen. In both texts, the assessment of contemporary capitalism takes place partly through the subversion of narrative forms by which the neoliberal script has proliferated. *Ministry*, for instance, contests dominant, streamlined stories of personal and national emergence through its strategies of expansion and layering on the one hand and fragmentation on the other. Relative to *Ministry*'s idiosyncratic and undisciplined mode of storytelling, *Selection Day* features a relatively predictable *Bildung* plot which on the surface resembles that of the generic cricket novel, or "crick lit," in which cricket functions as an arena for catalyzing the upward mobility of talented subjects. However, the ever-present possibility of failure in Adiga's novel contributes to its contestation of crick lit's promise of impending transformation. In the end, Roy's and Adiga's narratives self-consciously unpack and confront the familiar fictional modes used to animate the neoliberal script.

Emily Johansen and Alissa Karl define the "neoliberal novel" as "particularly attuned to the economic rationalities of its time," and as evidence of how the novel as a genre has undergone formal and thematic changes that "speak to the epistemic changes under capital in its current incarnation."[5] Jeffrey Williams also uses the term "neoliberal novel"—to reference US bestsellers like Brett Easton Ellis's *American Psycho* (1991), Jonathan Franzen's *Freedom* (2010), and Jennifer Egan's *A Visit from the Goon Squad* (2010), which have "foreground[ed] the economic and political consequences of the past thirty years" and exposed class tension in a society long dominated by the fiction of classlessness. Contesting Walter Benn Michaels's claim that contemporary US representations subordinate class to questions of identity, Williams asserts that, on the contrary, neoliberal novels "echo the fiction of a century before, such as Frank Norris's *The Octopus* (1901) and *The Pit* (1903) and Theodore Dreiser's *The Financier* (1912) and *Titan* (1914), which chronicle the massive accumulation of capital in their time." The contemporary US fiction of Ellis, Franzen, and Egan "similarly represent our own gilded age," Williams claims, even if their "signature feeling is chagrin or numbness rather than outrage, and they are less oppositional than the previous generation's political fictions, which excoriated coterie power."[6]

Like Williams, Pankaj Mishra maps the relationship between heightened inequality and capitalist depredation in fiction of prior and present eras. His area of focus, though, is not exclusively US fiction but also novels from contemporary Asia like Adiga's Booker Prize-winning *The White Tiger* (2008), Mohsin Hamid's *How to Get Filthy Rich in Rising Asia* (2013), Tash Aw's *Five Star Billionaire* (2013), and Randy Boyagoda's *Beggar's Feast* (2013), which, he argues, enact a "kind of moral reckoning [with capitalism] that happened at another time in the West," when "Writers—from Dickens to Balzac and Zola and Dreiser—regarded with appalled fascination … the sudden respectability of selfishness and greed, which had been stigmatized for centuries by traditional religions and philosophies."[7] In what follows I show how, in attuning to the "economic rationalities of [our] time," as well as its particular political and cultural manifestations, *Ministry* and *Selection Day* adopt the sort of oppositional stance that Williams associates with US fiction of the first Gilded Age.[8] In other words, if these are neoliberal novels, it is because they are not simply *attuned* to the workings of neoliberal capitalism but are also overt *critiques* of the "war of the rich against the poor," as Roy puts it, that this capitalism has heightened. It is their explicit oppositionality—on the level of both form and content—that enables them to provide a "literary vision of capitalism red in tooth and claw."[9]

I end this discussion of the neoliberal novel with the recent Netflix television series based on *Selection Day*, which exemplifies a new phase in the commodification of literary fiction. Moreover, the series—made for consumption by India's middle classes as well as foreign audiences—evinces the sticky hold of the neoliberal script on the popular imagination, both within post-liberalization India and beyond. If Adiga's novel contests the notion that capitalism simply needs to be made more ethical and socially responsible, then the adaptation holds up precisely this sort of mythified capitalism as its hope for "new" India. Its production and distribution contexts, as well as ideological contradictions, raise important questions, about both the meaning of literature and the work of (postcolonial) literary criticism in the present.

Undisciplined Storytelling in *The Ministry of Utmost Happiness*

The Ministry of Utmost Happiness parallels the stories of Anjum, a poor Muslim *hijra* or transgender woman from Old Delhi, and Tilo, a middle-class New Delhi woman who witnesses horrific state violence in Indian-occupied Kashmir and who functions as an ally of Kashmiri separatists.[10] Beyond illuminating the travails of these central figures, the narrative wanders into the lives of their friends and fellow survivors of dispossession including Saddam Hussein—a Dalit refugee of caste violence who changes his name on arriving in Delhi from rural Haryana—as well as minor personages such as the hunger-striking revolutionary Dr. Azad Bharatiya. The novel begins with Anjum, formerly Aftab, who since her teenage years has been a resident of an Old Delhi community of *hijras* known as the Khwabgah or "house of dreams." After barely surviving the 2002 anti-Muslim pogrom in Gujarat, a traumatized Anjum leaves the Khwabhah at the age of 46 and begins squatting in a Delhi graveyard. To cope with her trauma she builds a guesthouse in the graveyard that she calls Jannat, or paradise. Eventually this graveyard guest house comes to function as a refuge for not just Anjum but also her newfound friends, like Saddam Hussein and Tilo.

While the opening chapters, narrated in the third person, are closely aligned with Anjum's perspective, the rest of the novel treats her as one

135

amongst many characters, as it expands to include Tilo, Saddam, and also Biplab Dasgupta, whose first-person narration channels the government's stance on Kashmir and recounts the triangulated intimacies that bind him to Tilo and their mutual friends, Naga and Musa. Biplab's first- person account interrupts the focalization of Anjum's perspective, and is in turn followed by third-person narration, this time aligned with Tilo, who eventually becomes a resident of Jannat guest house and co-parent with Anjum and Saddam of abandoned orphan Udaya Jebeen. The novel ends in 2014 with Musa being killed in Kashmir, Biplab and Naga wrecked internally from decades of service as government stooges, the far-right Hindu nationalist government of Gujarat ka Lalla (or "Gujarat's Beloved," aka Narendra Modi) being voted into office, and the orphaned baby—a child of state-sanctioned rape—being doted on by her new family at the Jannat guest house. *Ministry*'s many-layered and somewhat untraditional network narrative weaves together the stories of characters that represent some of India's most violated and marginalized citizens. Connecting these characters' stories are the actions of a state whose turn to militant Hindu nationalism, the novel suggests, has been solidified in a global climate of post-9/11 Islamophobia.

The author and *New York Times* critic Michiko Kakutani laments what she describes as the novel's various "detours" and "digressions."[11] After expressing some surprise that "years of writing often didactic nonfiction—on subjects like nuclear tests, political corruption and Hindu extremism—have not damaged [Roy's] gift for poetic description," Kakutani complains that when the Indian novelist turns from the "specifics of her characters' lives" to generalize about the plight of the nation, the prose grows "labored and portentous." As an instance of this labored prose she quotes the following lines from *Ministry*:

> Normality in our part of the world is a bit like a boiled egg: its humdrum surface conceals at its heart a yolk of egregious violence. It is our constant anxiety about that violence, our memory of its past labors and our dread of its future manifestations, that lays down the rules for how a people as complex and as diverse as we continue to coexist—continue to live together, tolerate each other and, from time to time, murder one another. (155)

Kakutani's use of these lines as proof of Roy's labored and portentous generalizations lays bare the source of her misreading of the novel, for here she confuses a *character*'s voice with the *author*'s. The voice that speaks in these lines and claims to represent India's hybrid society is not the omniscient third-person narrator—who can reasonably be taken as a stand-in for the authorial voice—but rather the first-person perspective of Biplab Dasgupta, a bureaucrat and self-declared "servant of the Government of India" who speaks in a self-ironizing, but ultimately self-justifying, manner about his role in enabling the government's longstanding military occupation of Kashmir. Dasgupta's perspective provides an inside view of a state that alternates between strategies of militarism and ideological cooptation in order to undermine the movement for self-determination in Kashmir.

Before he introduces the metaphor of a boiled egg with a "yolk of egregious violence," Dasgupta describes his equanimity on witnessing the mass murder of Sikhs by ordinary civilians in 1984. Had Kakutani contextualized the passage, it would become clear that the bureaucrat uses such horrific stories to make generalizations about the violent essence of the Indian population and thereby make a case for why the state *needs* to play a policing role in places like Kashmir—to keep the "yolk of egregious violence" committed by separatists and civilians from running. While his deliberate use of metaphor can at first make his voice appear indistinguishable from that of the third-person narrator (who often playfully indulges in exaggeration), over time this voice reveals a numbness in the face of brutality, a cynicism about ordinary people, and strong faith in the government's policing role—all of which sets it apart and establishes it as a perspective that the novel is not simply channeling but also critiquing.

Kakutani's is neither a surprising nor exceptional misreading, though, considering how frequently Roy continues to be portrayed first and foremost as the author of Booker Prize-winning *The God of Small Things* (1997). By describing the 1997 novel as being primarily about "the personal and the private," Kakutani erases its political commentary. In fact, her way of reading the novel provides one explanation for how, despite its critique of the postcolonial nation-state, *The God of Small Things* and its award-winning author came to be regarded as emblematic of a liberalizing, yet enduringly exotic, India.[12] Kakutani builds on the reception of this first novel and its author, in order to assert that, "Roy's gift is not for the epic but for the personal." Furthermore, contrasting Roy's "gift" with Salman Rushdie's, she claims that *Ministry*, with its various political detours and digressions, fails to rise to the level of a "transporting parable about modern India"—unlike epic political fiction such as *Midnight's Children*.

By invoking Rushdie, Kakutani repeats an often-made comparison between the two writers on the assumption that they write in the style of magical realism.[13] Magical realism—which depicts "reality as naturally interposed by magic and by phenomena that ordinary common sense cannot explain"—has often been perceived as "a faculty of artists (inherited from a romantic lineage that conceives the poet as seer)" and, moreover, as "a postcolonial universal," or "a narrative mode that carries the particular postcolonial experience of the underdeveloped world."[14] Roy's Booker Prize led to her consecration in the global literary marketplace as a postcolonial writer,[15] and specifically a writer who uses magical realism to poetic ends (a characterization she herself has resisted).[16] Kakutani's condescending containment of Roy as a "personal" author of magical realism evidences some of the core attitudes guiding the critical reception of contemporary fiction in general and of postcolonial fiction in particular. Within the context of the United States, Rachel Greenwald Smith describes this attitude as a "critical suspicion toward oppositionality" and preference for the "depoliticization of art."[17] Explicit political engagement and "oppositionality" in art is considered to be a risk, something that—except in rare instances like Rushdie's magical realism—can potentially "damage" a writer's capacity to convey inner experience, which, in turn, is assumed to be the purview of artistic expression.

But the "digressions" and "detours" of *Ministry* that Kakutani dismisses in fact perform several important functions within the novel. To begin with, they are key components of its response to the mythologization of New India as "a nuclear power and an emerging destination for international finance" (42). In one digressive moment, the third-person narrator lists the dimensions of an elaborate myth-making machinery that has repeatedly sold the nation "on TV shows, on music videos [sic], in foreign newspapers and magazines, at business conferences and weapons fairs, at economic conclaves and environmental summits, at book festivals and beauty contests. *India! India! India!*" (100). Meanwhile, "The newly dispossessed, who lived in the cracks and fissures" of Delhi tried to make a living selling knickknacks and also "pirated management books" with titles like *How to Make Your First Million, What Young India Really Wants*, or "quick-fix spiritual manuals" like "*You are Responsible for Your Own Happiness ...* or *How to Be Your Own Best Friend*" (104). This juxtaposition between the dispossessed vendors and the books they sell by "swarm[ing] around the sleek, climate-controlled cars" brings into stark relief what neoliberalization has meant for the relatively affluent versus the poor. For the middle classes and elites it has meant immersion in capitalist propaganda, directed especially at a "Young India" that is being schooled in personal responsibility and in how and what to desire. On the other hand, for poor rural migrants to the city, neoliberalization has meant being displaced from their homes and being forced to survive by selling cultural products that, ironically, reinforce these migrants' social marginality and invisibility.

Beyond digression and direct narrative intervention, the text's strategy of weaving in multiple strands of economic and political reality in India contributes to complicating the omnipresent and streamlined stories of the individual entrepreneur's rise and, relatedly, that of the entrepreneurial nation. The text's capacious form encapsulates its alternative approach to storytelling, where the emphasis is not on tracking the forward trajectory of enterprising protagonists but rather on tracing the connections that bind social beings to one another and to their environments. This approach is a response to and reaction against the ways in which, as Sujatha Fernandes notes, storytelling is "reconfigured" in the neoliberal era "on the model of the market to produce entrepreneurial, upwardly mobile subjects and is leveraged toward strategic and measurable goals drive by philanthropic foundations." Fernandes characterizes the dominant, market-mediated mode of storytelling as "instrumental" or "utilitarian," and as consisting mainly of "Curated personal stories [that] shift the focus away from structurally defined axes of oppression and help to defuse the confrontational politics of social movements." Deployed within human rights activism, for instance, this utilitarian approach "reduce[s] experiences and histories to easily digestible soundbites in service of limited goals."[18] Although it is guided by a belief in the power of personal testimony and by the impetus of "giv[ing] a voice to those who are marginal, powerless, and silent," this storytelling tends to "ampli[fy] some voices at the expense of others. Those who are able to make their personal experiences legible to the mainstream through drawing on dominant narratives and devices are given a platform while other voices are silenced." In other words, those who conform to a "universal model of conflict-driven stories" or those who process their experiences according to dominant narrative models such as "conversion narratives, epic narratives, or narratives of uplift," as well as tropes such as "deserving immigrants," "caring masters," and individual victims"[19] are able to find an audience, especially within "human rights service markets."[20]

Ministry comments on and complicates this market-enabled reconfiguration—indeed disciplining—of storytelling. In an extended "detour" that takes the reader through a gathering of protestors in Delhi's Jantar Mantar, the central characters move into the background while a mobile camera-like third-person narrator glides through space, tracking the various activist groups gathered. Embodying the capaciousness of the cinematic long take, the mobile narrative perspective explores the segregated landscape of Delhi, exposing its ongoing class war and the relationship between this war and the various political struggles taking place all over the country. Thus the reader/viewer of the scene is prompted to look at the "frame" in its entirety—including the figures in the foreground as well as the background—and to slowly, even if briefly, occupy the positions of various personages and players (human and nonhuman) that enter and leave the frame.

In one moment we are led by the undisciplined, mobile narrator to the Association of Mothers of the Disappeared "whose sons had gone missing, in their thousands, in the war for freedom in Kashmir" and whose plight is paralleled with that of those living the aftereffects of the 1984 Union Carbide gas leak in Bhopal. "Some of the Mothers," we learn, "like some of the Bhopal gas leak victims, had become a little jaded. They had told their stories at endless meetings and tribunals in the international supermarkets of grief, along with other victims of other wars in other countries" (118–119). With "supermarkets of grief," Roy satirizes the various human rights tribunals and truth commissions that have become venues for what Fernandes calls "curated" storytelling, and which reduce felt experience to standardized commodities, or what Joseph Slaughter refers to as the "singularized spectacular suffering of an individual victim."[21] Owing to their awareness of the problems with storytelling in human rights tribunals, when we are later introduced to the Kashmiri separatists we learn that they view the journalist Naga "not [as] a fellow traveler by any means, but [as] someone who could be useful—a member of the 'human right-wing,' as some militants jokingly called Indian journalists who wrote even-handedly and equally conscientiously about the excesses committed by the security forces as well as the militants" (230–231). Here dominant narratives of human rights connote a defanged politics—a politics of even-handedness that, even if unwittingly, ends up being in service of the government-as-occupier, that uses propaganda to disavow its violence against the people of Kashmir.

As opposed to the "supermarkets of grief" and Naga's "even-handed" human rights narratives is Tilo's fragmented storytelling from the Kashmiri perspective. Her creation of *The Reader's Digest Book of English Grammar and Comprehension for Very Young Children* features a series of minor, irony-filled short stories about various facets of daily life under military occupation. These stories, a far cry from the regular fare promoted by Reader's Digest in India,[22] focus on the lived experience of military occupation in Kashmir, where, for instance, ordinary people can become so inured to gun violence that being photographed with an AK-47 might become someone's "greatest desire," or where Kashmiri school children are targeted by state-sponsored propaganda and taken on "Sadbhavana" or goodwill tours to "keenly observe the progress made by other [Indian] states" and to thereby disidentify with the resistance movement around them. Such juxtaposition of disparate fragments and anecdotes serves to transcend the ideological limits of narrowly personalized forms of storytelling and to lay bare the role of both the repressive and ideological state apparatus[23] in enabling one of the most violent military occupations in the world.

The Private and the Common

The story of the rural migrant Saddam Hussein features prominently in the novel's capacious and undisciplined storytelling. Saddam, originally known as Dayachand, comes to the city to escape caste violence in the villages. Although a Hindu, he adopts the Muslim name Saddam Hussein after watching a video of the hanging of the Iraqi leader and finding himself "impressed by the courage and dignity of that man in the face of death." When Anjum protests that "Saddam Hussein was a bastard" who killed many people (94), Saddam/Dayachand argues that he would "like to be this kind of bastard ... I want to do what I have to do and then, if I have to pay a price, I want to pay it like that" (95). We learn that along with many other rural migrants who are employed as security guards at a Delhi museum, Saddam works 12 hours a day and six days a week. Sangeeta Madam, his labor contractor, is "among the better paymasters," but she charges a commission that is "60 percent of [the workers'] salary, which left them with barely enough for food and a roof over their heads" (78). Through Saddam's story, the reader is introduced to the normalized exploitation of the poorest of Delhi's poor—"the trainloads of desperate villagers freshly arrived in the city" (78), who guard the "homes, schools, farmhouses, banks, ATMs, stores, malls, cinema halls, gated housing communities, hotels, restaurants and the embassies and high commissions of poorer countries" (79).

Saddam's job at the National Gallery of Modern Art in Delhi also reveals the imbrication of the art world in the exploitation of rural migrant labor.

In one episode, "*Art First*, a cutting-edge contemporary art magazine owned by a leading steel magnate," sponsors an art show in the museum (80), where artworks are sold "for the price of a two-bedroom LIG (Lower Income Group) flat" (79). The juxtaposition of the value of the artwork with that of a low-income housing flat conveys a view of the museum world from the perspective of Delhi's poor, including new migrants like Saddam Hussein who, while personally incapable of affording low-income housing that sells at prices equivalent to museum exhibits, are employed to guard these exhibits. The exhibits, meanwhile, feature fetishized "everyday artifacts made of stainless steel—steel cisterns, steel motorcycles, steel weighing scales with steel fruit on one side and steel weights on the other, steel cupboards full of steel clothes, a steel dining table with steel plates and steel food, a steel taxi with steel luggage on its steel luggage rack—extraordinary for their verisimilitude, … [and] beautifully lit and displayed in the many rooms of the gallery" (79). The narrator's repetition of "steel" in the descriptions of the various museumized artifacts calls attention to the corporate sector's control over artistic production. An exhibited stainless steel banyan tree also prompts the reader to think back to the living banyan tree in the graveyard where Anjum finds refuge. The living banyan tree is a hub of relations—a host to various birds (including the "friendly" vultures who were once its visitors before they were poisoned to death) as well as to Anjum, who begins to have intimate knowledge of the birds' patterns and to model her identity as a host on the tree. By contrast, the stainless steel tree seems to freeze an entire ecology of relations. Its form merely reflects harsh sunlight that ends up burning Saddam's eyes, leaving him unemployed. Having already been displaced by caste violence in his village, he is thus further dispossessed of his job of safeguarding the private property status of expensive art exhibits.

In contrast to fetishized art, the Jannat guest house, built within the space of the graveyard, emerges as a microcosm for the commons. The guest house is built illegally, and the municipal authorities threaten Anjum "that any unauthorized construction would be demolished within a week" (71). She nevertheless manages to reach an arrangement with the municipal workers, promising "a not-inconsiderable sum of money to be paid to them, along with a non-vegetarian meal, on Diwali as well as Eid" (71–72). This agreement enables her to "enclose the graves of her relatives and build rooms around them" as well as to steal electricity "from the mortuary, where the corpses required round-the-clock refrigeration" (72–73). Anjum then offers the space to friends like "Imam Ziauddin, who was being unkindly treated by his son and daughter-in-law" (72), and to *hijras* "who, for one reason or another, had fallen out of, or been expelled from, the tightly administered grid of Hijra Gharanas" (73). Although she charges rent in some cases, as with Saddam Hussein, it is at "a rock-bottom price—less than it would have cost him to rent [a room] in the old city" (76–77). Ultimately, Anjum's illegal operations yield also "a People's Pool, a People's Zoo and a People's School" (406) within the space of the graveyard. The graveyard thus becomes an oasis—where schools and zoos and swimming

Beyond Alterity

pools exist for common rather than merely private consumption, in a city that is being transformed by the government and corporate sector into the "supercapital of the world's favourite new superpower" (100).

This illegal construction of a commons exemplifies the novel's use of irony to contest neoliberal mythologies that place on poor and dispossessed individuals the responsibility of explaining and accounting for their attempts to survive under highly unequal and unjust social structures. Anjum, with her acts of enclosing and stealing, is far from the idealized entrepreneurial subject—as is Saddam, who once he becomes jobless begins to hustle by duping sick poor people and selling stale pigeon feed. However, this un-idealized picture of the entrepreneurialism of the poor is not subjected to moral judgment within the novel. Of Saddam's various jobs and hustles, the narrator states, with characteristic irony, "All of it—short-changing pigeons and exploiting sick people's relatives—was tiring work, especially in summer, and the income was uncertain" (82). The reader is thereby prompted to tolerate the contradictions that accompany a life of precarity. Similarly, Anjum's squatting in the graveyard and stealing electricity is not treated as a moral problem that has to be explained and justified for the middle-class reader. Instead, it is used to expose the bizarre irony that the poor are able to afford the luxury of air conditioning only as dead bodies.

Relatedly, Roy's narration of Anjum's trauma from surviving the anti-Muslim pogrom in Gujarat invokes, but also significantly transforms, stories of private trauma that circulate via human rights markets. On returning to the Khwabgah, Anjum shows all the classic signs of being traumatized—by her witnessing of mass killings, including the death of her friend, Zakir Mian, and by having been forced to re-inhabit a gender identity that she had chosen many years ago to leave behind. Her recurring memories of Zakir Mian's killing, and her persistent guilt about being spared, recalls trauma theorist Cathy Caruth's notion of trauma's inherent belatedness, "its refusal to be simply located, in its insistent appearance outside the boundaries of any single place or time."[24] The image of Zakir Mian's neatly folded dead body is an "insistent appearance" that refuses to go away, as is her guilt over being "Butcher's Luck" (67), which leads her to retreat from the world into the graveyard that she eventually makes her home. But whereas in the standard trauma narrative there is a tendency to "restrict the moral focus to the singularized spectacular suffering of an individual victim,"[25] and to hint at recovery through the acts of remembering and confessing trauma, here the "tide of grief and fear" simply "subsides" over time and the "Fort of Desolation scale[s] down into a dwelling of manageable proportions" (70). What causes the subsiding of grief is not public sharing of private trauma but simply acts of kindness by several of Anjum's friends and relatives. In the end, building the graveyard guest house and playing host to others who have suffered dispossession becomes Anjum's chief method of coping with privately experienced trauma.

Thus, it is not personal confession at all but, ironically, Anjum's trauma-induced silence and retreat to the graveyard that catalyzes her healing, by pushing her to leave behind the compromised existence of her life *prior* to trauma—a "lifetime of spurious happiness" (61) owing to structural constraints to which she had simply adjusted herself. Squatting in the graveyard allows Anjum to find companionship among the dead (especially those who suffered social marginalization), the birds, and ultimately the other dispossessed people who gather there once she builds the guest house. By communing with these various beings she becomes, as she puts it, a *mehfil* or "a gathering. Of everybody and nobody, of everything and nothing" (8). In other words, the process of grieving that is narrated here is not one that moves energetically forward from recovery of traumatic memory to personal confession and private reconciliation. If grief made Anjum retreat and disconnect from "the Duniya," or world, she is ultimately reconnected to it through the kindness of others and through her hosting of others at the illegally constructed guest house. Roy's novel offers a decidedly social model of narrating personal trauma as well as dispossession—one that moves beyond the confines of dominant, commodified narratives of private suffering.

Pure Dark Muscle: Reframing "Human Capital" in *Selection Day*

The plight of the dispossessed haunts the fiction of Aravind Adiga as well. His 2016 novel *Selection Day*—published exactly 25 years after the implementation of structural adjustment—satirizes the commodification of human beings in neoliberal India and thereby complicates the concept of "human capital" first popularized by neoliberals like Gary Becker and then critiqued by Michel Foucault and Wendy Brown. The rapidly commercializing arena of Indian cricket serves as the novel's vehicle for exploring the culture produced by neoliberalization, in which—as Jodi Dean puts it—"the number of poor people isn't [perceived as] a social problem, it's an investment opportunity."[26]

Selection Day deploys some of the conventions of "crick lit"[27]—a genre that, as Claire Westall's notes, typically uses cricket "to examine late capital and manage the anxieties neoliberalism brings."[28] Referring to cricket novels published in 2008—including Chetan Bhagat's *The 3 Mistakes of My Life* and American writer Joseph O'Neill's *Netherland*—Westall argues that contemporary cricket fiction contends with, but also tends to deny the consequences of the global financial crisis of 2008–2009.[29] *Selection Day* activates the striver figure that recurs through much of crick lit. But rather than trace this figure's journey from poverty to wealth, it instead uses satirical inversion and an anti-climactic plot to bring into relief the exploitation and predation that is intrinsic to the profit-driven world of professional sports. On the whole, rather than "manage" the anxieties attending neoliberalization, Adiga uses satire to expose these anxieties' economic determinants and to locate their effects on subjectivity—thereby, like Roy, weaving the personal back into a web of structured social relations.

Beyond Alterity

The novel garnered positive reviews, including in the US, where cricket is in no way a popular sport.[30] Subsequently, the Indian branch of the global streaming giant Netflix began production of a television series based on the novel[31]—testifying to the ways in which the Indian novel in English has found increased marketability, in part for its complication of official narratives of India's professed emergence as an economic power. Adiga, in particular, has come to symbolize the political potential of the anglophone novel from "new" India. Since the success of his Booker Prize-winning *The White Tiger* (2008)—also a satire of "new" India—Adiga has been celebrated regularly for his "gritty urban realism,[32] "sinewy, compact prose," and his ability to "dissect" social reality in order to lay bare its underlying truths.[33] Over the last decade, Adiga's fiction has become emblematic of cultural production that exposes truths about the economic emergence of Southern nations that cannot be discerned through official and government narratives.[34]

Selection Day's plot revolves around the development of Manju Kumar, a 14-year-old boy who along with his older brother, Radha, is being molded by their disciplinarian father to become a cricket prodigy with the potential to lift the family out of poverty. On moving to Mumbai, the boys' father, Mohan Kumar, finds a sponsor for his sons in Anand Mehta, a traditionally wealthy, America-returned investor who identifies with Nietzsche's philosophy of the "superman" and draws inspiration from the highly lucrative US sponsorship system for college athletes. Eventually the Kumar brothers grow to not just resent their father but also fail to become star cricketers. Adiga uses their failure in the hyper-competitive business of cricket to highlight the oppressiveness of the prevailing capitalist system and its shaping of poor athletes as "human capital." The novel explicitly invokes both US slavery and contemporary college football in its exploration of coercive capitalist dynamics in post-liberalization India, implying links between the vulnerabilities experienced by aspiring cricketers in India and by racialized and socially marginalized college athletes in the United States who are "compelled to perform unpaid athletic labor."[35]

The novel thus points to continuities between modes of exploitation in professional sports across the North and South. The introduction in 2008 of the Indian Premier League (IPL) has fueled a culture of commercialization within Indian cricket that is modeled on North American professional sports. With teams in major Indian cities attracting some of the best players from around the world, the IPL has transformed cricket from a sport that did not pay very well to one in which top players can become millionaires. As in the case of American football, IPL cricket matches are spectacular, revenue-generating events featuring Western cheerleaders, attended by Indian movie stars, politicians, and businessmen, and leading to televised "bidding wars" in which players are "auctioned" and "traded." The IPL has, moreover, been the source of much controversy over match fixing and politically backed betting, helping to explain why the word "cricket" is all too often linked to "corruption" in popular discourse,[36] and why some reviews of *Selection Day* describe it as a novel about "cricket and corruption."[37]

Contesting the Script

The novel's US-educated venture capitalist, Anand Mehta, is emblematic of this brave new world of Indian cricket and its affinities with US sports. The investor figure, however, does not act alone; rather, he is shown as operating in concert with the longstanding disciplinary apparatuses of the school and family. In its attunement to the discipline imposed by the family and school, Adiga's text joins a number of popular culture narratives in India that attest to the increasing pressure that family members and educators exert on young people to fashion themselves as strivers and competitors in the national and global marketplace.[38] But, unlike the optimism of most of these popular narratives, *Selection Day* reveals how familial and school discipline ultimately serves the interests of capital and, moreover, disproportionately targets the poor. Manju Kumar, like his older brother, struggles to perform the role of prodigy and "investment opportunity." His attraction to Javed—a wealthier cricketer who can afford to break free of the disciplinary apparatus of corporatized cricket—prompts Manju to confront his alienation from both the predatory world of professional cricket and the heteronormative and patriarchal world of the Indian family. In the end Adiga suggests that poor athletes like Manju are "human capital" not because—as Wendy Brown would argue—they are "*constrained* to self-invest," but rather because they *cannot* self-invest, given that they are at the mercy of (finance) capital, which can withdraw its investment at any point.

Many moments in Adiga's satire resonate with Brown's thesis on the subordination of all aspects of life to market forces. For instance, Anand Mehta's blatant references to the Kumar brothers as his "investment" are evidence of the "economization" that, according to Brown, reconfigures subjectivity as human capital. His elaborate calculations of the players' monetary value highlight how bodies become "assets" under what Brown refers to as "the market metrics of our time."[39] The money Mehta spends on the boys is part of the accounting ledger alongside their bodily attributes, including height and weight. Both are quantifiable and must be tracked closely—as "value" that can appreciate or depreciate. Ultimately the boys are, as a result of their father's contract with Mehta, dispossessed of a third of their earnings, and their bodies are reduced to "pure dark muscle." Over the course of the narrative, their movements and media performances are highly monitored, as all these elements determine the "value" of Mehta's "assets." Later in the novel, the financier invites other speculators to become shareholders in his "investment."

But at the same time that the novel's satirical voice affirms Brown's observations about the "economization" and marketization of humans, it also complicates the classless character of her account of the shaping of subjectivities. The rhetoric of fairness in Anand Mehta's contract with Mohan Kumar makes it seem mutually beneficial. What becomes clear, however, is that power lies only with the investor. Mehta thinks of the contract as Mohan Kumar "selling" his sons (57) to him, and he considers the boys to be his assets, with Manju being the "Younger Asset" (59). The contract renders

Beyond Alterity

the boys un-free on a number of levels: they cannot fully enjoy the supposed profits generated from their skills and talents, or "human capital." Far from being entrepreneurs of themselves, Manju and his brother have a status recalling that of indentured labor. As in the case of indentured labor, the boys' exploitation takes place through a contract. They are legally bound to Anand Mehta, given that they depend on him materially and that a third of all their future earnings is his "legal property."

In other words, the novel implies that subjectivity in the case of the Kumar brothers is being shaped through relations of overt domination and coercive subordination rather than simply through an internalized compulsion to "self-invest." Whereas Brown argues that "interest" no longer defines subjectivities in the present, the precarious and impoverished subjects of Adiga's novel are very much interest-driven. Yet once they enter into a contract with Mehta, Manju's and Radha's laboring bodies are literally speculative capital for the parasitic financier. If this is the "age of human capital," as Gary Becker would argue,[40] then Adiga suggests it is only so because a large number of people are compelled to become the "investments" of predatory capitalists in order to survive.

The trope of slavery is a recurring one in the novel. Manju's friend and love interest, Javed, frequently tells him not to be a "slave" to his father and to Anand Mehta, not realizing that the Kumar family is economically dependent on the investor, and that Mohan Kumar's use of his son as capital makes Manju perceive his body as not his to own but rather as the property of others. Despite Manju's interest in science and forensics, Manju's father and Anand Mehta deny him an education, perceiving this education to be an impediment to the honing of his more commodifiable (i.e. cricketing) skills. Although the wealthier Javed is also vulnerable to pressures from his father to become the captain of the cricket team, his relative privilege means that he is unbound to a sponsor and hence better positioned than Manju to leave cricket and to "self-invest" by pursuing his interest in poetry. The novel's various references to slavery also prompt consideration of the compatibility between liberal democratic societies based on so-called free labor and illiberal economic systems of forced or indentured labor.

At first glance, Anand Mehta resembles the recurring figure of the usurious moneylender from an earlier era of Indian fiction.[41] Unlike this traditional moneylender, however, Mehta's predation is based on legitimate alliances with local as well as transnational elites. Throughout the novel, the narrator refers to the investor as "Anand Mehta" (never calling him by just his first or last name), thereby prompting the reader to view him from a critical distance. Of all the characters in the novel, this investor figure appears closest to the idealized subject of neoliberal reason: he is quite free to "self-invest" and to create and re-create his identity like a malleable work of art.[42] Except that, far from being the mythicized self-made man, Mehta, we learn, inherited his wealth from his stockbroker father. It is this inherited wealth that allows him to travel abroad and to experiment with taking on multiple identities:

Contesting the Script

> Anand Mehta had been a Communist for a semester and a half; but then, changing his politics, he had read Kahlil Gibran and Friedrich Nietzsche; had gone to New York to study business and have a love affair with a black New Yorker, had enjoyed life in that meritocratic metropolis, a coliseum of competing nationalities and races (but of all these pulsating ethnicities, one stood out: driven, Anglophone, numerate, and freed by postcolonial entitlement from almost all forms of liberal guilt or introspection—and of this privileged group, Anand Mehta intended to be the most privileged, because he was the one Indian financial analyst who had read Nietzsche). (54)

This concise survey of the young Anand Mehta's ideological shifts exemplifies how the novel's satire works—by simultaneously channeling and ironically commenting on the character's view of the world. The reference to New York as "meritocratic metropolis, a coliseum of competing nationalities and races" reflects Mehta's internalization of uncritical celebrations of this global center of financial power. Mehta belongs to a "privileged group" or class of educated, cosmopolitan Indians that performs liberal attitudes towards race, gender, and postcoloniality—but this is a liberalism that masks their economic and ideological ties to predatory US finance capitalism. Even when he returns to India, Mehta appears frequently next to American financiers like the investment banker who jokes with him, "I like my prose paratactic, my women flexible, and my government libertarian" (96). Mehta shares this man's sexist joke, as well his confidence in the rationality of "free" and "flexible" markets.

The references in the above passage to Nietzsche also satirize Mehta's aspiration to fashion himself as a lone intellectual in the world of financial analysts. Other references in the novel to Nietzsche's imagination of the self-willed, responsible, and self-sacrificing *übermensch* or "superman" suggest that Mehta finds in Nietzsche a justification for his economic power. Mehta fancies himself as someone set apart from the masses by his willingness to sacrifice wealth for the upward mobility of the Kumar family—so that they, too, can join the league of "supermen." He therefore paternalistically describes Manju to an Indian-American businesswoman he meets in Mumbai as "his fully sponsored little superman" (240).

The attractiveness of Nietzsche's ideas to men like Anand Mehta might in part be connected to the German philosopher's professed anxiety about the emergence of liberal democracies and the resulting decline of aristocracy. Tracing the resonance between Nietzsche's ideas and Austrian economist Friedrich Hayek's neoliberalism, Corey Robin points out that just as Nietzsche worried about how modern democracy "elevates the worker and the slave," Hayek expressed anxiety about socialism's challenge to the status of the "wealthy and well-born as an avant-garde of taste, [and] as makers of new horizons of value from which the rest of humanity took its bearings."[43] Anand Mehta's attraction to Nietzsche appears linked to his desire to see himself as a naturally endowed "legislator of value" in a world that he sees as requiring intervention by a noble and intellectual elite. Indeed, Mehta is not merely

Beyond Alterity

concerned with making profits from his investments; his focus lies *also* in proving to himself and to the world that his investment in the teenaged cricketers is an act of beneficence—designed to create value by delivering freedom and opportunity to the poor.

Thus, Mehta's character is designed to reflect the faith that many in the upper echelons of society have in the neoliberal script. But underlying this faith, the novel suggests, is a fear of the poor (much like Nietzsche's fear of the elevation of workers under liberal democracy) and a desire to control them. In Mehta's imagination, the poor are a potentially dangerous, lumpen lot—vestiges of a prior postcolonial and (in his mind) socialist economy—that needs to be managed through appropriate "investment" by private capital. At one point Mehta sees in Mohan Kumar's eyes what he thinks of as "a 'pre-liberalization stare,' an intensity of gaze common in people of the lower class before 1991, when the old socialist economy was in place, and which you found these days only in Communists, terrorists, and Naxalites" (59). If in the neoliberal present the poor have been discursively rendered entrepreneurs of themselves, and thereby made safe for India's upper classes, the "pre-liberalization" poor, for Mehta, are those that have not yet been disciplined by market forces into obeisance and that hence remain eminently interchangeable with communists, terrorists, and Naxalites. In investing in Manju and Radha, Mehta believes he is evolving the poor out of this dangerous "pre-liberalization" mindset. When Manju receives funding to travel to England, Mehta feels a "thrill of having bet on that grandest of investments: A growing human being ... One minute, slum; next minute, *Angleterre*" (149). It is the familiar narrative of the poor boy's ascent—and its channeling of the neoliberal script—that excites the financier. Further, the novel suggests that it is men like Mehta who construct an ideological opposition between the pre- and post-liberalization poor. They imagine that liberalization has meant liberation of the poor from a backward "socialist" economy; but this discourse of the poor's liberation is only a way of justifying their own implication within predatory capitalism.

On occasion, Mehta is capable of noting the contradictions that underlie his work and his thinking. When he witnesses a gathering in Mumbai of foreign "social entrepreneurs" who aim to "both do well and do good in India," (240) Mehta thinks of himself as "living inside a paradoxography, surrounded by a bestiary of financial analysts, brokers, and bankers who had been transformed, from the waist down, into Mother Teresa." In perceiving the gathering as a "bestiary," Mehta exhibits an awareness of the predatory character of the financial sector in which he operates; further, by seeing himself as "living inside a paradoxography," he acknowledges the irreconcilability between doing well (i.e. serving only oneself by making personal profit) and doing good (i.e. benefiting society through acts of altruism). He is, therefore, well aware of the irony of a Lehman banker running a corporate social responsibility consultancy, or a man working in junk bonds turning to windmills (239). But while not blind to the contradictions of such entrepreneurship, he nonetheless remains committed to rationalizing his own pursuit of profit as socially necessary. Thus, reflecting on his investment in Manju, he says to himself, "In Bombay I have set a man free" (266). Ultimately, Mehta's awareness of the paradox of social entrepreneurship does not weaken his conviction that his "investment" in the Kumar brothers is for their own good—to set them free.

No matter what Mehta believes he is doing, the novel makes clear that his wealth is based on exploitation. In a paternalistic exchange with Mohan Kumar, he presents his personal justification for engaging in predatory capitalism:

> Entrepreneurship. Most of what we hear about it in the media is absolute bullshit, Mr. Mohan. Don't invest in a new business in India. That's some shit we feed the Yanks and Japs. Real money is in turning around old businesses, because the heartland of this country is a Disneyland of industrial disasters: thousands of socialist factories, sick, or semi-sick, or partially shut down. (89)

In blatantly embracing the opportunities inherent in India's "Disneyland of industrial disasters," the America-returned Mehta displays his comfort with becoming rich off investments not just in poor cricketers but also "sick" industries and cities in ruin. He later describes Mumbai as a city that is "finished" and whose "future is in distressed assets." His entrepreneurialism, in other words, entails getting rich at the expense of a dispossessed working class, while producing nothing of social value. When he speaks of old industrial plants in Dhanbad (literally, "city of wealth") that he wants to turn around, his investment is not for the purpose of making things—which would at least require hiring workers and responding to social needs. Distressed industries are, for him, simply cheaply purchasable assets—akin to young cricketers from Mumbai slums. Recognizing the predatory nature of his finance capitalism, the scout, Tommy Sir, connects Mehta to a crab that he spots in the sewage "hunting for its food—emerald-backed, slime-coated, iridescent, with many moving red arms, many moving plans" (126).

The biggest irony is that not only is Mehta *not* a self-made man, he is also shown repeatedly to be a failure as an investor. If he survives after "speculating, and squandering his family's money" (55), it is only because of his class background and inherited wealth—thereby giving a lie to utopian neoliberal narratives that celebrate businessmen as "entrepreneurs of themselves" and exemplars of private capital's greater efficiency and profitability relative to state-run and public-sector initiatives. By channeling Mehta's hubristic voice, and by tracking his mental maneuvers as well as his failed endeavors, the narration of *Selection Day* provides insight into the socio-psychological character and global scope of neoliberalism's class project.

Beyond Alterity

Hard and Soft Power

The boys' school is born out of collaboration between Indian and American capital—"run in partnership with the Joseph P Weinberg Memorial Institute of Lafayette, Mississippi"—and "known for its headline-capturing cricket team, into which boys [are] recruited, with financial aid, if necessary, and from deep within the slums, if necessary" (130). Like US colleges that give financial aid to promising athletes from marginalized communities, the school depends on poor athletes like Manju and Radha for its good reputation and sustained ability to recruit students. Also like American colleges, the school depends on violent processes of gentrification for its geographical expansion within the city, thereby contributing to what the narrative voice, referring to Joseph Schumpeter's idea of "creative destruction," describes as "equal parts creation and destruction, that happens sooner or later to every suburb in Mumbai" (129).

But in conjunction with the school, the patriarchal family, another key site of social reproduction, aligns the boys' subjectivities and sexuality with the interests of capitalism, thereby ensuring that neoliberal ideas take root, as Brown puts it, in "subjects and in language, in ordinary practices and in consciousness." Adiga's construction of an almost entirely male domestic universe—in which not only women's work but women themselves are invisible—exposes the role of patriarchal authority in reconciling (male) subjects with what Brown refers to as the disavowed, "socially male and masculinist" character of neoliberalism.[44] Cricket is socially sanctioned because it is deemed masculine, commodifiable, and hence instrumental for his family's survival. Manju learns early to distinguish between the kind of "play" that is socially allowed and the kind that needs to be repressed. What gets repressed is a kind of sensuous and imaginative engagement with the world that he enjoys only in private (1).

Denied a maternal figure to tame the excesses of patriarchal discipline and to soften the blow of economic deprivation, the Kumar brothers experience no relief from their father's numerous and arbitrary rules that Radha thinks of as "prison bars" framing the world around him (27). When Radha is five years old, Mohan makes him grow his hair and hold his bat like the great Indian batsman, Sachin Tendulkar—thereby preparing the boy, via imitation, to internalize the identity of a budding male cricket star. The boys grow up with stories about how "Sachin had been taken to sit at the great Achrekar's feet to learn the science of batsmanship" (50)—thereby being taught to venerate "scientific" cricketing skills but also the genuflection to prior "gods" of cricket like Achrekar. Having convinced himself that his sons can become great batsmen, Mohan then moves them to a Mumbai slum, begins his life as a chutney seller, and micro-manages his sons' development into "Young Lions" and "geniuses of will power" (37).

When Radha Krishna breaks a world record for the number of runs recorded by a batsman under 16, Anand Mehta "talk[s] superman-to-superman with

Mohan Kumar" (89), interpellating the latter in his own brand of predatory capitalist jargon. They then team up to "dissect" and assess Radha's media performance and to shame him for it.

Alongside these paternal figures, Tommy Sir—the cricket scout who writes a popular newspaper column—plays a crucial role in disseminating neoliberal values through "soft power." Hyperbolically titled "Some Boys Rise, Some Boys Fall: Legends of Bombay Cricket and My Role in Shaping Them" (142), Tommy's column deploys all the classic tropes of a neoliberal discourse that claims to transform the lives of poor boys through tapping into their ingeniousness and individual talent. When Manju enjoys a winning streak, Tommy speaks of the boy as a "legend" with "mighty forearms" who was "discovered ... in a slum in Dahisar"—"proof of the magical power of cricket to uplift lives in today's India" (192). But when Manju's record is beaten by a new player, the newcomer is in turn referred to as "a teenage human skyscraper" (177), an instance of hyperbole that unites key figures of India's aspirational culture, the teenage athletic prodigy and the skyscraper.

At the end of the novel we learn that Radha Kumar is disabled in an accident and rendered physically unable to compete. Meanwhile Manju becomes an example of one of those boy legends/teenage skyscrapers that "falls." Although he manages to secure a contract, it is eventually terminated—evidence of how cricket ultimately churns out more "losers" than the "legends" and "supermen" that Tommy and the other parental and authority figures in the novel dream about. The adult Manju with whom the novel leaves us resembles in crucial ways the father he detests. Unable to escape the structural constraints acting on him, he becomes someone whose battle with the unjust world is redirected inwards—into a battle within himself.

Shortly before his contract with Anand Mehta is drawn up, the narrator comments on Mohan Kumar's palpable anger at the rich by asserting, "Revenge is the capitalism of the poor" (41). As the brothers grow up to confront their own constraints, they are in turn described as budding "entrepreneurs of revenge" (51). If neoliberals like Becker suggest that our insides are a set of traits and talents that can be "capitalized" on to make us all entrepreneurs of ourselves, then the desire for revenge, the narrator proposes, is equally part of our "human capital." Our insides, in other words, are complex—not just traits and talents but also affects and desires produced by conditions on the outside such as poverty, as well as the "terror" of coercive power relations that require alienation from one's labor and from one's inner experience.

Like his father, who represses his rage at the injustices committed by the rich and powerful, Manju, too, comes to repress his anger, along with his sexual desire, and resemble the responsibilized subject that Wendy Brown describes. Rather than choose to be with his love, Manju instead succumbs to the internalized obligation to provide for his family; he therefore remains in the cutthroat world of corporate cricket. His youthful rage at his father and investor abates over time, as Manju is compelled by his circumstances to realize that his material interests and responsibilities are wedded to

Beyond Alterity

the world of professional cricket. By the end of the narrative, having long severed his connection with Javed, and finding himself compelled to take on the job of cricket scout, Manju is left completely alienated—from his labor and also from his body and his deep desires. Manju's internalization of his oppression, his brother's coerced resignation to his condition, and their father's longstanding suppression of his anger all attest powerfully to the subjective effects of the same economic system that acts on the dispossessed of *The Ministry of Utmost Happiness*—and that Brown describes in an especially vivid moment in *Undoing the Demos* as "vampire-like, exploitative, alienating, inegalitarian, duplicitous, profit-driven, compulsively expanding, fetishistic, and desacralizing of every precious value, relation and endeavor."[45] Manju and his brother stand in for the neoliberal subject who has been "sacrificed" to this vampiric, desacralizing system.

Serializing Adiga's Novel in the Age of Netflix

Interestingly, Netflix's serialized adaptation of *Selection Day* (created by Marston Bloom, 2018–2019) significantly blunts the literary text's critique of the coercive laws of capital. In fact, the series—which translates the novel for a domestic as well as international audience—depends, ironically, on the potency of the same neoliberal script that the novel explicitly contests. Simran Sethi, director of international originals at Netflix, describes the series as a "joyous and emotional coming of age story" to be shared "with India and the world."[46] Thus, Adiga's anti-*Bildungsroman* is consciously returned to the more familiar form of the *Bildungsroman* to ensure its palatability to a transnational audience consisting of readers and non-readers alike.

Mumbai appears in the series relatively cleansed of extreme poverty, and the city's seething class antagonism seems also to have been tamed. Within this context, cricket in general and the persona of Sachin Tendulkar in particular stand as uncontroversial and readily recognizable symbols of upward mobility—so much so that the star cricketer came out on Twitter to publicly celebrate the series and also to help promote its second season.[47] Netflix India promoted the series by releasing behind-the-scenes videos of the actors playing with Tendulkar, as well as inspirational messages to youth about following your dream and committing to your vision.[48] If there is a problem with Indian cricket, then, the series and its accompanying promotional content suggests this problem arises largely from the sport's continued control by an older, corrupt form of capitalism—as opposed to the new, talent-based neoliberal capitalism that has made Tendulkar a legend, and that carries the potential to do the same for poor prodigies like Manju and Radha Kumar.

Perhaps most significant is the series's papering over of class conflict by presenting the possibility of a benevolent elite that is aligned with an earnest, entrepreneurial poor. In a clear departure from the novel, the series positions corporate and finance capital as minor antagonists. Anand Mehta is rewritten as a condescending and corrupt, but ultimately toothless figure. More powerful than him is the corrupt urban mafia, represented by the underworld don—a recurring villain in post-liberalization Hindi cinema. For all his flaws, Mehta nevertheless arranges for the Kumar family to move into better accommodation and to attain a degree of upward mobility. The underworld don, by contrast, is purely evil and sadistic. The fair-skinned and light-eyed actor who plays Anand Mehta, and who speaks English like India's elite, suggests a new, attractive face of Indian capitalism that is duplicitous but still weaker and less predatory than an older, blatantly unethical version of Indian capitalism represented by the notably dark-skinned underworld don, whose English is heavily inflected by vernacular languages, and who makes overt threats of violence. These casting choices make the underworld don an easily legible antagonist who must be defeated to make way for a more honest "free-market" capitalism to take hold in India.

This superior form of capitalism is also exemplified by *female* entrepreneurs—Anand Mehta's wealthy and charitable girlfriend who works in the corporate sector, Mohan Kumar's lower middle-class love interest who is full of ideas for honest street hustles, and the well-meaning school principal who takes an active interest in nurturing her students' talents. These women represent a softer, more ethical, and progressive capitalism that promises relief from the old-fashioned patriarchal coercion represented by Mehta, Kumar, and the underworld don. Although apparently in opposition, the male and female characters together secure the illusion that the problem lies not with capitalism *per se*—nor with the class war it inevitably produces—but only with a particular, *corrupt* form of capitalism that needs to be replaced with free markets and honest entrepreneurialism.

In keeping with the series's taming of the novel's critique is its rewriting of the character of the cricket coach, Tommy Sir. In the novel he is part of a soulless media and corporate establishment that is trying to profit off poor cricket prodigies. In the series he is a gentle, well-meaning, and inspiring coach who has the boys' best interest at heart and who spends a great deal of his time training them, whilst also caring for his ailing wife. His character suggests the possibility of not just a more earnest and honest capitalism, but also a more benign, rather than rigidly authoritarian, *patriarchal* order in "new" India. Similarly, the opportunistic school authority figures in the novel are replaced in the series with the character of the encouraging and maternal school principal. As a result, the novel's critique of gendered social reproduction within the context of neoliberal capitalism is contained primarily within the figure of the overtly abusive patriarch, Mohan Kumar. On the whole, the series replaces a structural critique of the disciplining of poor youth in contemporary India with a moral critique of bad capitalists and rigid patriarchs.

Towards the end of season two, Anand Mehta is killed by the Mumbai underworld after he fails to deliver on his pact with them. The series ends,

Beyond Alterity

not—as in the novel—with an adult Manju compelled to withdraw from professional cricket because his contract is not renewed, but rather with a young Manju, who makes it successfully through Selection Day only to find out that his investor is no longer Anand Mehta but instead the underworld don. With the elimination of Anand Mehta, the audience is left with the suggestion that the *real* danger for a rising Manju Kumar comes from the underworld's old-fashioned thuggery. In the process, the popular rhetorical opposition between a new, private sector-led India and an older, more feudal and corrupt nation is implicitly invoked and reactivated. Manju's innocence stands in for an "emerging" India that is striving to succeed and to overcome outdated, coercive elements of this society such as the underworld don, and the abusive and rigidly patriarchal Mohan Kumar. Ultimately, through the still-young Manju Kumar, as well as the budding female entrepreneurial figures, neoliberal India appears, despite its flaws, as charged with potential—as a prototypical "emerging" economy. Thus, Adiga's critique of "new" India becomes, ironically, the basis for a reassertion of the neoliberal script. The gap between Adiga's novel and the series testifies to the enduring potency of myths of neoliberal capitalism in not just the Indian context but also the global public sphere.

***

The serialized adaptation of *Selection Day* raises larger questions about what it means to "read" world literature in a moment in which digital streaming services like Netflix, Hulu, and Amazon have acquired an undeniable centrality—both as avenues through which to access audiovisual material and as forces that are influencing the publication of books and thereby shifting prevailing conceptions of literature globally. The relationship between digital streaming and book publishing has increasingly elicited discussion, given the important role of fiction and nonfiction books in supplying the "content" that fuels streaming platforms' constantly changing archives of films and televisual series. Literary adaptations have emerged as "big business" because of their capacity to generate profitable audiovisual entertainment while simultaneously driving up book sales.[49] Thus, novels appear frequently as money-making "properties" and "irreplaceable resource[s]" in the lexicon of streaming company executives who sound like modern-day prospectors in constant pursuit of "new voices," "literary talent," diverse forms of "original content," and "opportunit[ies] for worldbuilding." Typically, literary texts with a past record of publishing success, and especially those associated with reputed authors, are viewed as strong candidates for audiovisual adaptation. These texts minimize risk for streaming companies that tend to be risk-averse and to target audiences or "taste communities" with tailor-made entertainment. But new works are also heavily pursued, especially those belonging to genres for which markets can easily be anticipated in advance of production. All of this decision-making unfolds through executives from companies like Netflix—the world's largest streaming service—going on "book acquisition sprees," conducting "book-scouting efforts," and attending literary rights events at international book fairs.[50]

In the calculations of prominent—largely American—streaming companies like Netflix, nations of the global South like India represent both untapped markets for audiovisual consumption and sources for diversifying their "content." (Streaming company executives speak, for instance, of "expanding into the African continent" because "There's a lot of great literature there.")[51] With India viewed as a "big potential subscriber growth opportunity," the Indian English novel is much sought after as a source of "sweeping complex narratives" with the potential to reach simultaneously local, diasporic, and global audiences.[52] While genres like crime "thrillers and mysteries are [deemed] best suited for binge" entertainment[53]—which partly explains why Vikram Chandra's *Sacred Games* became the first Netflix original series in India—"literary" works like Adiga's *Selection Day* are also being pursued by "content teams" as potent raw material that can be "repurposed" into series or films. Moreover, an increasing openness to producing literary content in languages other than English means that an English-language novel like *Sacred Games* can be produced in Hindi and directed by prominent Hindi film directors (Vikramaditya Motwane and Anurag Kashyap). The choice to film in Hindi and other vernacular languages is seen as lending "authenticity" to the production and as potentially expanding the viewership to non-anglophone Indian audiences, as well as foreign audiences who can watch with subtitles. While sales for particular Indian novels have gone up after the introduction of series and feature film versions, typically it is not book sales *per se* but rather the selling of filming rights that is deemed especially lucrative. As Indian English-language writer Krishna Udayasankar observes, "the money is not in (selling) the books, but in selling the screen rights." In turn, because screen rights are emerging as "a serious source of revenue," Indian publishers "are now going for titles that have the potential to get adapted."[54]

In other words, in India, as elsewhere, authors are being asked to reckon with the adaptability of their writing, and publishers are being led to make decisions about what fiction to publish on the basis of whether or not its world-building might be translatable into audiovisual "content." With books in general and fictional works in particular functioning as streamable content—influencing what gets published, but also how books are read, received, and engaged with—the category of "literature" is in a state of flux. Moreover, with the web-streamed series in particular emerging as a close cousin to the novel—more amenable than feature-length film to conveying the depth and density of the novel form, the slow development of character, the detailed exposition of plot, and the cultivation of a world that unfolds over time—it is increasingly difficult to think of imaginative writing as a category that exists as distinct from the world of audiovisual production.

In some ways, this book's attention to literature's incorporation and animation of official forms of mythmaking and storytelling reveals how

Beyond Alterity

already-existing scripts that pervade public discourse and consciousness might underwrite to some extent the "original" work of imaginative and creative genius. The above-described developments in the terrain of cultural commodification further complicate the fetishized originality of literary works, as well as their elite status and supposed uniqueness relative to other forms of cultural production. Far from being unique, owing to their mystified creative process, literary works are now clearly embedded in and integral to the workings of the film and television industry's profit-making machinery. Subsequent studies of neoliberalism and literature would do well to attend closely to the implications of this rapidly transforming field of cultural production. Within this changing global field of literary and cultural commodification, moreover, literature from the South cannot be assumed to be necessarily resistant or simply on the margins. As the serialized adaptation of *Selection Day* suggests, "world literature" from places like India is increasingly being consumed by a much wider audience—composed of readers and non-readers alike—and calculations for appealing to this audience often entail tapping into culturally dominant scripts, even when those scripts may be challenged by the original literary work. To rethink our perspective on literature from the South within this rapidly evolving field of cultural commodification is not to simply reinstate facile notions of globalism, akin to those circulating amidst the post-Cold War triumphalism of the 1990s, when the world was assumed to have been flattened by US-led corporate globalization. Rather, it is to attune carefully to capital's similar ways of molding experience and representation across distinct geographical and cultural contexts. The current conjuncture necessitates that we move beyond assumptions of absolute opposition between North and South and invest instead in confronting the converging forms and fates produced by neoliberal capitalism.

Notes

Introduction

1 Pankaj Mishra, *Age of Anger: A History of the Present* (New York: Farrar, Straus and Giroux, 2017; Kindle edition), 346.
2 The notion of postcolonial literatures "writing back" to the West was made popular by Bill Ashcroft, Gareth Griffiths, and Helen Tiffin's *The Empire Writes Back: Theory and Practice in Post Colonial* (London/New York: Routledge, 1989). Perhaps the most influential framing of postcolonial literatures as existing in opposition to Western individualism can be found in Fredric Jameson's "Third World Literature in the Era of Multinational Capitalism," *Social Text* 15 (1986), 65–88.
3 For more on the entanglement of postcolonial*ism* with postcoloniali*ty*—of the academic anti-colonial project with the metropolitan commodification and exoticization of literatures from the formerly colonialized world—see Graham Huggan's *The Postcolonial Exotic: Marketing the Margins* (London/New York: Routledge, 2001).
4 Wendy Brown, *Undoing the Demos: Neoliberalism's Stealth Revolution* (Brooklyn: Zone Books, 2015).
5 Jameson, "Third World Literature," 70.
6 Ibid., 65, 71.
7 Ibid., 69, 72, 69.
8 Aijaz Ahmad, "Jameson's Rhetoric of Otherness and the 'National Allegory,'" *In Theory* (New Delhi: Oxford University Press, 1992), 95–122.
9 Pascale Casanova, *The World Republic of Letters* (Cambridge: Harvard University Press, 2005), 83.
10 Franco Moretti, "Conjectures on World Literature," *New Left Review* 1 (Jan.–Feb. 2000), 58.
11 Efrain Kristal, "'Considering coldly …': A Response to Franco Moretti," *New Left Review* 15 (May 2002), 69–70.
12 Warwick Research Collective, *Combined and Uneven Development: Towards a New Theory of World Literature* (Liverpool: Liverpool University Press, 2015), 57.

Notes

13 Ibid., 62.
14 Ibid., 68 (emphasis mine).
15 Gabriele Lazzari, "The Semi-Peripheral Novel: Narrating the Neoliberal Present from Southern India and Southern Italy," *Cambridge Journey of Postcolonial Literary Inquiry* 8.1 (Jan. 2021), 39–59.
16 Pierre Bourdieu, *The Rules of Art: Genesis and Structure of the Literary Field* (Stanford: Stanford University Press, 1996).
17 Ibid., 205.
18 Sarah Brouillette, "Neoliberalism and the Demise of the Literary," *Neoliberalism and Contemporary Literary Cultures*, ed. Mitchum Huehls and Rachel Greenwald Smith (Baltimore: Johns Hopkins University Press, 2017), 281.
19 Sharae Deckard and Stephen Shapiro, eds., *World Literature, Neoliberalism, and the Culture of Discontent* (Cham: Palgrave Macmillan, 2019), 29.
20 For key Marxist accounts of neoliberalism see: David Harvey, *A Brief History of Neoliberalism* (New York: Oxford University Press, 2005); Jamie Peck, *Constructions of Neoliberal Reason* (Oxford: Oxford University Press, 2010); Robert Brenner, *The Economics of Global Turbulence* (New York: Verso, 2006); Giovanni Arrighi, *Adam Smith in Beijing: Lineages of the Twenty-First Century* (London: Verso, 2007); Silvia Federici, *Re-enchanting the World: Feminism and the Politics of the Commons* (Oakland: PM Press, 2018). For the rise of neoliberalism as an ideological dominant see Philip Mirowski and Dieter Plehwe, eds., *The Road from Mont Pèlerin: The Making of the Neoliberal Thought Collective* (Cambridge, MA: Harvard University Press, 2009) and Quinn Slobodian, *Globalists* (Cambridge, MA: Harvard University Press, 2018).
21 For Foucauldian accounts of neoliberal subjectivity see Wendy Brown's *Undoing the Demos* (2015) and *In the Ruins of Neoliberalism* (New York: Columbia University Press, 2019); Aihwa Ong, *Neoliberalism as Exception: Mutations in Citizenship and Sovereignty* (Durham, NC: Duke University Press, 2006); Nikolas Rose, *Governing the Soul: The Shaping of the Private Self* (London: Routledge, 1989); Lisa Rofel, *Desiring China: Experiments in Neoliberalism, Sexuality, and Public Culture* (Durham, NC: Duke University Press, 2007); Michael Feher, "Self-Appreciation; or, the Aspirations of Human Capital," trans. Ivan Ascher, *Public Culture* 21.1 (2009), 21–41; Vanessa Lemm and Miguel Vatter, eds., *The Government of Life: Foucault, Biopolitics, and Neoliberalism* (New York: Fordham University Press, 2014).
22 For an overview of recent trends in scholarship on neoliberalism in anthropology and American cultural studies, respectively, see Tejaswini Ganti, "Neoliberalism," *Annual Review of Anthropology* 43 (2014), 89–104; and Lisa Duggan, "Neoliberalism," *Keywords for American Cultural Studies*, ed. Bruce Burgett and Glenn Hendler (New York: NYU Press, 2020), 182–185. For media and cultural studies perspectives on neoliberalism, see Julie Wilson, *Neoliberalism: Key Ideas in Media and Cultural Studies* (New York: Routledge, 2018).
23 See the editors' introductions to these special issues: Jane Elliott and Gillian Harkins, "Introduction: Genres of Neoliberalism," *Social Text* 31.2 (2013), 1–17; Jeremy Gilbert, "What Kind of Thing Is 'Neoliberalism'?", *New Formations* 80–81 (2013), 7–22; Emily Johansen and Alissa G. Karl, "Introduction: Writing the Economic Present," *Textual Practice* 29.2 (2015), 201–214.
24 For more on the Euro-American "neoliberal novel," see Walter Benn Michaels, "Going Boom," *Bookforum* (Feb.–Mar. 2009) and "Model Minorities and the Minority Model—The Neoliberal Novel," *The Cambridge History of*

Notes

the American Novel, ed. Leonard Cassatu, Clare Virginia Eby, and Benjamin Reiss (Cambridge: Cambridge University Press, 2011), 1016–1030; Jeffrey Williams, "The Plutocratic Imagination," *Dissent* 60.1 (Winter 2013), https://www.dissentmagazine.org/article/the-plutocratic-imagination; Rachel Greenwald Smith, *Affect and American Literature in the Age of Neoliberalism* (New York: Cambridge University Press, 2015); Mitchum Huehls, *After Critique: Twenty-First-Century Fiction in a Neoliberal Age* (Oxford: Oxford University Press, 2016); Huehls and Greenwald Smith's edited volume, *Neoliberalism and Contemporary Literary Culture*; and Arne de Boever, "What Is the Neoliberal Novel? Neoliberalism, Finance, and Biopolitics," *New Approaches to the Twenty-First-Century Anglophone Novel*, ed. S. Baumbach and B. Newmann (Cham: Palgrave Macmillan, 2019). For works focused on neoliberalism and the world novel—including but not exclusively Euro-American fiction—see Emily Johansen and Alissa Karl, eds., *Neoliberalism and the Novel* (London: Routledge, 2017), Michael K. Walonen, *Contemporary World Narrative Fiction and the Spaces of Neoliberalism* (Cham: Palgrave Macmillan, 2016); Deckard and Shapiro, *World Literature*; and Nivedita Majumdar, "The Novel in a Time of Neoliberalism," *BRICS and the New American Imperialism*, ed. Vishwas Satgar (Johannesburg: Wits University Press, 2020).

25 Some of the most notable among these include: Sarah Brouillette's *Literature and the Creative Economy* (Stanford: Stanford University Press, 2014); Greenwald Smith, *Affect and American Literature*; Leigh Claire La Berge, *Scandals and Abstraction: Financial Fiction of the Long 1980s* (Oxford: Oxford University Press, 2015); and Annie McClanahan, *Dead Pledges: Debt, Crisis, and Twenty-First Century Culture* (Stanford: Stanford University Press, 2017).

26 See the editors' introductions to the following special issues, in which Trump's 2016 election serves as a point of departure: John Marx and Nancy Armstrong, "Introduction: How Do Novels Think about Neoliberalism," *Novel: A Forum on Fiction* 52.2 (2018), 157–165; and Michael J. Blouin, "Neoliberalism and Popular Culture," *The Journal of Popular Culture* 51.2 (2018), 277–279.

27 See, for instance, the much-cited collection of essays, *Neoliberalism and Contemporary Literature*, edited by Huehls and Greenwald-Smith, where most of the contemporary texts discussed emanate from North America and Europe.

28 Wilson, *Neoliberalism*, 12.

29 Emily Johansen, "Neoliberalism and Contemporary Anglophone Fiction," *Oxford Research Encyclopedia of Literature*, Aug. 2017, Oxford University Press, http://literature.oxfordre.com/view/10.1093/acrefore/9780190201098.001.0001/acrefore9780190201098-e-185.

30 Gilbert, "What Kind of Thing Is 'Neoliberalism'?", 11.

31 Marx and Armstrong, "Introduction," 159.

32 Elliott and Harkins, "Introduction," 5.

33 Emily Davis, "The Betrayals of Neoliberalism in Shyam Selvadurai's *Funny Boy*," *Textual Practice* 29.2 (2015), 218, 227.

34 Anis Shivani, "We Are All Neoliberals Now: The New Genre of Plastic Realism in American Fiction," *Huffington Post* (Jun. 12, 2015), https://www.huffpost.com/entry/we-are-all-neoliberals-no_b_7546606.

35 This is Walter Benn Michaels's argument in "Model Minorities and the Minority Model—The Neoliberal Novel," *The Cambridge History of the American*

Notes

    Novel, ed. Leonard Cassuto, Clare Virginia Eby, and Benjamin Reiss (New York: Cambridge University Press, 2011), 1016–1030.

36 Mitchum Huehls and Rachel Greenwald-Smith, "Four Phases of Neoliberalism and Literature: An Introduction," *Neoliberalism and Contemporary Literature* (Baltimore: Johns Hopkins University Press, 2017), 8.

37 Matthew J. Christensen, "African Popular Crime Genres and the Genres of Neoliberalism," *Social Text* 31.2 (115) (Summer 2013), 106.

38 Elliott and Harkins, "Introduction," 14, 13.

39 Gabriel Giorgi, "Improper Selves: Cultures of Precarity," *Social Text* 31.2 (115) (Summer 2013), 78.

40 Jeanne-Marie Jackson, "Plurality in Question: Zimbabwe and the Agonistic African Novel," *Novel: A Forum on Fiction* 51.2 (2018), 339–361 (340).

41 Lily Saint, "From a Distance: Teju Cole, World Literature, and the Limits of Connection," *Novel: A Forum on Fiction* 51.2 (2018): 322–338 (323).

42 Brown, *Undoing the Demos*, 9.

43 Ong, *Neoliberalism as Exception*, 3.

44 David Harvey, *The New Imperialism* (New York: Oxford University Press, 2003), 137–182.

45 Peck, *Constructions of Neoliberal Reason*, xii.

46 Mark Tully, "Manmohan Singh: Architect of the New India," *The Sikh Times* (Nov. 14, 2005), http://www.sikhtimes.com/bios_111405a.html.

47 C.P. Chandrashekhar and Jayati Ghosh, *The Market that Failed: A Decade of Neoliberal Economic Reforms in India* (New Delhi: Leftword, 2006), 19–20.

48 Raewyn Connell and Nour Dados, "Where in the World Does Neoliberalism Come from?", *Theory and Society* 43 (2014), 123.

49 These coinages all come from *New York Times* columnist, Thomas Friedman, whose foreign affairs journalism in the 1990s positioned India as exemplary case of capitalist globalization's salutary effects. See Friedman's *The Lexus and the Olive Tree* (New York: Farrar, Straus, Giroux, 1999) and *The World Is Flat: A Brief History of the Twenty-first Century* (New York: Farrar, Straus, Giroux, 2005).

50 For more on how these discourses have operated in post-liberalization India, see Nandini Gooptu, ed., *Enterprise Culture in Neoliberal India: Studies in Youth, Class, Work and Media* (New York: Routledge, 2013), Ravinder Kaur, *Brand New Nation: Capitalist Dreams and Nationalist Designs in Twenty-First-Century India* (Stanford: Stanford University Press, 2020); and Meera Nanda, *The God Market: How Globalization is Making India more Hindu* (New York: Monthly Review Press, 2011).

51 For more on liberalization's impact on India's poor see Chandrashekhar and Ghosh, *The Market that Failed*; Dipankar Gupta, *The Caged Phoenix: Can India Fly?* (Stanford: Stanford University Press, 2010); and Jean Dreze and Amartya Sen, *An Uncertain Glory* (Princeton: Princeton University Press, 2013).

52 Dreze and Sen, *An Uncertain Glory*, 8.

53 Lucas Chancel and Thomas Piketty, "Indian Income Inequality, 1922–2015: From British Raj to Billionaire Raj? *World Inequality Database Working Paper Series* (July 2017), http://wordpress.wid.world/wp-content/uploads/2017/08/ChancelPiketty2017WIDworld.pdf.

54 Ruchir Sharma, "The Billionaire Boom: How the Super-Rich Soaked up Covid Cash," *Financial Times* (May 14, 2021), https://www.ft.com/content/747a76dd-f018-4d0d-a9f3-4069bf2f5a93.

55 See Thomas Piketty, *Capital in the Twenty-First Century*, trans. Arthur Goldhammer (Cambridge, MA: Harvard University Press, 2014).
56 According to Ruchir Sharma, "By 2015, ... [US] Billionaire wealth had surged to 15 per cent of GDP ... [In 2020] the sheer scale of US billionaire wealth mushroomed in the space of one year to nearly 20 per cent of GDP" ("The Billionaire Boom"). Between March and October 2020, India's richest man and CEO of Reliance Industries, Mukesh Ambani more than doubled his wealth. According to an Oxfam report, "During that period, the average increase in Ambani's wealth in just over four days represented more than the combined annual wages of all of Reliance Industries' 195,000 employees." Esmé Berkhout, Nick Galasso, Max Lawson, Pablo Andrés Rivero Morales, Anjela Taneja, and Diego Alejo Vázquez Pimentel, "The Inequality Virus," *Oxfam Briefing Paper* (Jan. 25, 2021), https://www.oxfam.org/en/research/inequality-virus.
57 Klaus Schwab, "We Must Move on from Neoliberalism in the Post-COVID Era," *World Economic Forum* (Oct. 12, 2020), https://www.weforum.org/agenda/2020/10/coronavirus-covid19-recovery-capitalism-environment-economics-equality/; Joseph Zeballos-Roig, "The IMF Says Governments Should Consider New Wealth Taxes to Raise Cash from the Rich as Coronavirus Slams the Global Economy," *Business Insider* (Apr. 21, 2020), https://www.businessinsider.com/governments-wealth-taxes-imf-new-source-revenue-coronavirus-economy-consider-2020-4; "Virus Lays Bare the Frailty of the Social Contract," *Financial Times* (Apr. 3, 2020), https://www.ft.com/content/7eff769a-74dd-11ea-95fe-fcd274e920ca.
58 Many thanks to Tim Brennan for prompting me to clarify how and why neoliberalism is more than simply a discourse of individualism.
59 William Callison and Zachary Manfredi, eds., *Mutant Neoliberalism: Market Rule and Political Rupture* (New York: Fordham University Press, 2019).
60 Huggan, *The Postcolonial Exotic*, vii, 13.
61 Donald Greenlees, "Investment Banker Becomes Best-Selling Author in India," *New York Times* (Mar. 14, 2008), https://www.nytimes.com/2008/03/14/world/asia/14iht-writer.1.11078431.html.
62 A Neilson book market report in 2015 described India's book market as the sixth largest in the world and the second largest for English-language books. See "Indians are Reading: Country's Book Market Will Be Worth Rs 739b by 2020," *The Hindu Business Line* (Jan. 22, 2018), https://www.thehindubusinessline.com/news/variety/indians-are-reading-countrys-book-market-will-be-worth-739b-by-2020/article7937712.ece.
63 Mark McGurl, *Everything and Less: The Novel in the Age of Amazon* (New York: Verso, 2021), Kindle Edition.
64 Suman Gupta, "Big Issues around a Small-Scale Phenomenon: Vernacular Pulp Fiction in English Translation for Indian Readers," *The Journal of Commonwealth Literature* 48.1 (2013), 164.
65 Sangita Gopal, "'Coming to a Multiplex Near You': Indian Fiction in English and the New Bollywood Cinema," *A History of the Indian Novel in English*, ed. Ulka Anjaria (Cambridge: Cambridge University Press, 2015).
66 Joseph Slaughter, *Human Rights Inc.: The World Novel, Narrative Form, and International Law* (New York: Fordham University Press, 2007).
67 For more on this concept see Gooptu, *Enterprise Culture in Neoliberal India*.

Notes

68 For more on this concept, and its origins in the work of Ramachandra Guha among others, see Rob Nixon, *Slow Violence and The Environmentalism of the Poor* (Cambridge, MA: Harvard University Press, 2011).
69 Sujatha Fernandes, *Curated Stories: The Uses and Misuses of Storytelling* (New York: Oxford University Press, 2017).

Chapter 1

1 Michel Foucault, *The Birth of Biopolitics: Lectures at the College de France*, trans. Graham Burchell (New York: Palgrave Macmillan, 2008), 226.
2 Philip Mirowski and Dieter Plehwe, eds., *The Road from Mont Pèlerin: The Making of the Neoliberal Thought Collective* (Cambridge, MA: Harvard University Press, 2009). Prominent neoliberals, Friedrich Hayek, Milton Friedman, and Gary Becker served at different points as presidents of the Mont Pèlerin Society: Hayek 1948–1960; Friedman 1970–1972; Becker 1990–1992.
3 Dieter Plehwe, "Introduction," *The Road from Mont Pèlerin: The Making of the Neoliberal Thought Collective*, ed. Philip Mirowski and Plehwe (Cambridge, MA: Harvard University Press, 2009), 13.
4 For alternative accounts of the historical rise of neoliberalism in the twentieth century, see David Harvey, *A Brief History of Neoliberalism* (Oxford: Oxford University Press, 2005); Jamie Peck, *Constructions of Neoliberal Reason* (Oxford: Oxford University Press, 2010); Angus Burgin, *The Great Persuasion* (Cambridge, MA: Harvard University Press, 2015); Quinn Slobodian, *Globalists* (Cambridge, MA: Harvard University Press, 2018). Slobodian's account, unlike the others, begins its genealogy not with the formation of the Mont Pèlerin Society but rather in the 1920s, with the fall of the Austrian empire. Unlike the Chicago School, the Austrian neoliberals did not reject the state but rather aimed to harness state power to the task of defending capital.
5 In his preface to the 1982 edition of *Capitalism and Freedom* (University of Chicago Press, 2002 [1962]), Milton Friedman argued, "Only a crisis—actual or perceived—produces real change. When that crisis occurs, the actions that are taken depend on the ideas that are lying around. That, I believe, is our basic function: to develop alternatives to existing policies, to keep them alive and available until the politically impossible becomes politically inevitable" (xiv).
6 Foucault, *The Birth of Biopolitics*, 131.
7 Ibid., 323.
8 See, for instance, Harvey, *A Brief History of Neoliberalism*; Peck, *Constructions of Neoliberal Reason*.
9 Aihwa Ong, *Neoliberalism as Exception: Mutations in Citizenship and Sovereignty* (Durham, NC: Duke University Press, 2006), 12.
10 Wendy Brown, *Undoing the Demos: Neoliberalism's Stealth Revolution* (Brooklyn: Zone Books, 2015), 27.
11 Ibid., 31.
12 Annie McClanahan, "Serious Crises: Rethinking the Neoliberal Subject," *Boundary 2* 46.1 (2019), 103–132.
13 Brown, *Undoing the Demos*, 35
14 Pierre Bourdieu and Loic Wacquant, "New Liberal Speak: Notes on the New Planetary Vulgate," *Radical Philosophy* 105 (Jan.–Feb. 2001), 3, 5.

Notes

15 Pankaj Mishra, *Age of Anger: A History of the Present* (New York: Farrar, Straus and Giroux, 2017; Kindle edition).
16 Aihwa Ong, "Neoliberalism as a Mobile Technology," *Transactions of the Institute of British Geographers*, New Series, 32.1 (Jan. 2007), 3–8 (4).
17 Ibid., 3.
18 Ibid., 4.
19 Ong, *Neoliberalism as Exception*, 1.
20 Ibid., 3.
21 Ibid., 12.
22 Ibid., 76, 78, 75.
23 Ibid., 79 (emphasis mine).
24 Ibid., 92.
25 Ibid., 93.
26 Ibid., 96.
27 Ibid., 228.
28 Ibid., 178.
29 Ibid., 4.
30 Ibid., 239.
31 Ibid., 228.
32 Ibid., 219, 239.
33 Ibid., 169.
34 Ibid., 164, 165.
35 Ibid., 166.
36 Ibid., 228.
37 Harvey, *A Brief History of Neoliberalism*, 76–77.
38 Foucault, *The Birth of Biopolitics*, 223.
39 Ibid., 226.
40 Ibid., 270.
41 Brown, *Undoing the Demos*, 70.
42 Ibid., 33.
43 Ibid., 83.
44 Ibid., 177.
45 Ibid., 83.
46 McClanahan, "Serious Crises," 117.
47 Gary S. Becker, "Introduction to the First Edition," *Human Capital: A Theoretical and Empirical Analysis, with Special Reference to Education*, 2nd ed. (Chicago: University of Chicago Press, 1975), 9, http://www.nber.org/books/beck75-1.
48 Gary S. Becker, "Human Capital Revisited," *Human Capital: A Theoretical and Empirical Analysis, with Special Reference to Education*, 3rd ed. (Chicago: University of Chicago Press, 1994), 21, http://www.nber.org/chapters/c11229.
49 F.A. Hayek frequently refers to the market agent as a "player" in a game. See *Law, Legislation, and Liberty*, vols. 1–3 (London: Routledge, 1998).
50 David Harvey, *Seventeen Contradictions and the End of Capitalism* (New York: Oxford University Press, 2014), 185. Harvey adds: "if what the worker truly possessed in bodily form was capital ... then he or she would be entitled to sit back and just live off the interest of his or her capital without doing a single day's work" (185–186).
51 Ibid., 186.
52 Brown, *Undoing the Demos*, 84.

Notes

53 Ibid., 22.
54 Ibid., 38.
55 Brown's recent work, *In the Ruins of Neoliberalism*, is far more attuned to the realities of inequality—and in this later work, Brown links growing inequality to the rise of a reactionary, nihilistic subject. But this work, too, is mostly silent on class struggle in the US, and its role in shaping subjectivities. See Wendy Brown, *In the Ruins of Neoliberalism: The Rise of Antidemocratic Politics in the West* (New York: Columbia University Press, 2019).
56 Brown, *Undoing the Demos*, 38.
57 Ibid., 36.
58 Jodi Dean, "Neoliberalism's Defeat of Democracy," *Critical Inquiry* (Oct. 27, 2015), https://criticalinquiry.uchicago.edu/neoliberalisms_defeat_of_democracy/.
59 Brown, *Undoing the Demos*, 48.
60 Ibid., 47.
61 Erin Hutton, *Coerced: Work under Threat of Punishment* (Berkeley: University of California Press, 2020), 19.
62 Ibid., 11.
63 Ibid., 13.
64 Ibid., 20.
65 For more on the effects of subprime lending, see US Department of Housing and Urban Development, "Unequal Burden: Income and Racial Disparities in Subprime Lending" (archived Jan. 20, 2009), https://archives.hud.gov/reports/subprime/subprime.cfm. For a longer view of racial discrimination and predation in the real estate and housing mortgage market, see Keeanga-Yamhatta Taylor, *Race for Profit: How Banks and the Real Estate Industry Undermined Black Homeownership* (Chapel Hill: University of North Carolina Press, 2019).
66 Sarah Burd-Sharps and Rebecca Rasch, "Impact of the US Housing Crisis on the Racial Wealth Gap across Generations," Social Science Research Council and American Civil Liberties Union (Jun. 2015), 2, 6, https://www.aclu.org/files/field_document/discrimlend_final.pdf.
67 Brown, *Undoing the Demos*, 35.
68 Ananya Roy, *Poverty Capital: Microfinance and the Making of Development* (New York: Routledge, 2010), 3.
69 Ibid., 5.
70 K. Kalpana, "Microcredit Wins Nobel: A Stocktaking," *EPW* 41.50 (Dec. 2006), 5110–5113.
71 Roy, *Poverty Capital*, 31.
72 Ibid., 32.
73 Michael Levien, *Dispossession without Development: Landgrabs in Neoliberal India* (New York: Oxford University Press, 2018), 4.
74 Ibid., 9.
75 See Vasanth Kannabiran, "Marketing Self-Help, Managing Poverty," *Economic and Political Weekly* 40.34 (Aug. 2005), 3716–3717, 3719; Tara S. Nair, "Commercial Microfinance and Social Responsibility: A Critique," *EPW* 45.31 (Jul.–Aug. 2010), 32–37.
76 Lamia Karim, *Microfinance and Its Discontents: Women in Debt in Bangladesh* (Minneapolis: University of Minnesota Press, 2011), 202.
77 Ibid., 199.
78 Ibid., 198.

79 Ibid., 195.
80 Of course, it is possible to internalize and identify with values of competitive individualism even if one is not likely to benefit from market competition; but it is quite likely that in the face of material insecurity these internalized values of competitive individualism might conflict with other impulses, including the impulse to collectively organize.
81 Peck, *Constructions of Neoliberal Reason*, xvii.
82 For more on Chile's neoliberal experiment, including the role of the Chicago School, see Juan Gabriel Valdes, *Pinochet's Economists: The Chicago School in Chile* (Cambridge: Cambridge University Press, 1995). See also: Raewyn Connell and Nour Dados, "Where in the World Does Neoliberalism Come from? The Market Agenda in Southern Perspective," *Theory and Society* 43 (2014), 117–138; Harvey, *A Brief History of Neoliberalism*. Harvey notes that Chile's violent neoliberal experiment later came to serve as an example both for regimes in the developing world and for Reagan's and Thatcher's governments that were turning aggressively towards neoliberalism by the 1980s (*Brief History*, 9).
83 Peck, *Constructions of Neoliberal Reason*, xii.
84 Vijay Prashad, *The Poorer Nations* (New York: Verso, 2014), 5–6.
85 Ibid., 89.
86 Ibid., 135.
87 C.P. Chandrashekhar, "From Dirigisme to Neoliberalism: Aspects of the Political Economy of the Transition in India," *Development and Society* 39.1 (Jun. 2010), 29–59; 40, 32. See also C.P. Chandrashekhar and Jayati Ghosh, *The Market that Failed: A Decade of Neoliberal Economic Reforms in India* (New Delhi: Leftword, 2006).
88 Ravinder Kaur, *Brand New Nation: Capitalist Dreams and Nationalist Designs in Twenty-First-Century India* (Stanford: Stanford University Press, 2020), 7–8.
89 Ibid., 11.
90 Ibid., 16.
91 Ibid., 46.
92 Nandini Gooptu, "Introduction," *Enterprise Culture in Neoliberal India: Studies in Youth, Class, Work and Media* (New York: Routledge, 2013), 7.
93 Ibid., 20.
94 Ibid., 10.
95 Ibid., 12.
96 Ibid., 13.
97 Kaur, *Brand New Nation*, 36.
98 Mishra, *Age of Anger*, 31.
99 Brown, *In the Ruins of Neoliberalism*, 7.
100 Mishra, *Age of Anger*, 14.
101 Ibid., 26.
102 Ibid., 328.
103 Ibid., 26.

Notes

Chapter 2

1 "Created Equal," *Free to Choose* (1980), vol. 5, Free to Choose Network, https://www.freetochoosenetwork.org/programs/free_to_choose/index_80.php?id=created_equal.
2 Government of India Budget Speech, 1991–1992. Transcript available at https://www.indiabudget.gov.in/doc/bspeech/bs199192.pdf.
3 Gurcharan Das, *India Unbound: A Personal Account of a Social and Economic Revolution From Independence to the Global Information Age* (New York: Knopf, 2001), 259–260.
4 Pierre Bourdieu, *Acts of Resistance: Against the Tyranny of the Market*, trans. Richard Nice (New York: Norton, 1998), 29.
5 Philip Mirowski and Dieter Plehwe, eds., *The Road from Mont Pèlerin: The Making of the Neoliberal Thought Collective* (Cambridge, MA: Harvard University Press, 2009), 26.
6 Bourdieu, *Acts of Resistance*, 31.
7 For analyses of social scripts, see, for instance, William Simon and John H. Gagnon, *Sexual Conduct: The Social Sources of Human Sexuality* (New York: Routledge, 1973), which develops "sexual scripting theory" and reads sexual behavior as not simply expressive of biological drives but rather learned in a social and cultural context. For a more recent study that uses scripts for the study of race, see historian Natalia Molina's *How Race Is Made in America: Immigration, Citizenship, and the Historical Power of Racial Scripts* (Berkeley: University of California Press, 2014), which describes how "racial scripts" are constructed through exclusionary laws and institutional practices. Within literary studies, Robin Bernstein's *Racial Innocence: Performing Childhood and Race from Slavery to Civil Rights* (New York: NYU Press, 2011) approaches nineteenth-century US children's literature as well as items of material culture as "scriptive things" that prompt—or script—children's behavior in accordance with racialized norms.
8 Angus Burgin, "Age of Certainty: Galbraith, Friedman, and the Public Life of Economic Ideas," *History of Political Economy* 45 (2013), 191–219 (193).
9 Nancy McLean, "How Milton Friedman Exploited White Supremacy to Privatize Education," Institute for New Economic Thinking, Working Paper no. 161 (Sept. 1, 2021), https://www.ineteconomics.org/research/research-papers/how-milton-friedman-exploited-white-supremacy-to-privatize-education.
10 Radhika Desai, "Neoliberalism and Cultural Nationalism: A *Danse Macabre*," *Neoliberal Hegemony: A Global Critique*, ed. Dieter Plehwe, Bernhard Walpen, and Gisella Neunhoffer (London: Routledge, 2006), 231.
11 Jamie Peck, *Constructions of Neoliberal Reason* (Oxford: Oxford University Press, 2010), 41.
12 Melinda Cooper, *Family Values: Between Neoliberalism and the New Social Conservatism* (New York: Zone Books, 2019), 19. Cooper adds that, "At various moments, [Friedman] could be found lending his hand to proposals to introduce a basic guaranteed income, informing central bank policy on inflation, and calling for the introduction of tuition fees in the University of California system" (19). Burgin notes that Friedman's ideas "helped inspire the reappraisal of welfare that led to the Earned Income Tax Credit programs that were first implemented in 1975, made permanent in 1978, and dramatically

Notes

expanded between 1986 and 1993, as well as the subsequent welfare-to-work programs implemented in the Personal Responsibility and Work Opportunity Reconciliation Act of 1996" (Angus Burgin, *The Great Persuasion* (Cambridge, MA: Harvard University Press, 2015), 181). For more on Friedman's role in the first nationwide neoliberal experiment precipitated by the 1973 coup in Chile, see Naomi Klein, *The Shock Doctrine* (New York: Picador, 2007).
13 Milton Friedman, "Neo-Liberalism and Its Prospects," *Farmand* (Feb. 17, 1951), 89–93.
14 Milton Friedman and Rose Friedman, *Two Lucky People: Memoirs* (Chicago: University of Chicago Press, 1997), 257.
15 Angus Burgin, "Age of Uncertainty: Galbraith, Friedman, and the Public Life of Economic Ideas," *History of Political Economy* 45 suppl. 1 (2013), 193–194.
16 For a full list of foundations and corporations funding the program, see Friedman and Friedman, *Two Lucky People*, 603. Burgin notes that "foundations and corporations proved enthusiastic about contributing to the enterprise, which allowed them to make a nonprofit donation to support the propagation of ideas they supported while receiving exposure among a wealthy public-television audience" ("Age of Uncertainty" 209).
17 Burgin, *The Great Persuasion*, 108.
18 Burgin, "Age of Uncertainty," 213.
19 Milton Friedman and Rose Friedman, *Free to Choose: A Personal Statement* (New York: Harcourt Brace Jovanovich, 1979), xii.
20 Transcript from "The Power of the Market," *Free to Choose* (1980), vol. 1, Free to Choose Network, https://www.freetochoosenetwork.org/programs/free_to_choose/index_80.php?id=the_power_of_the_market.
21 For more on narration in documentary, see Bill Nichols, "The Voice of Documentary," *Film Quarterly* 36.3 (Spring 1983), 17–30.
22 Katie Quan, "Memories of the 1982 ILGWU Strike in New York Chinatown." *Amerasia Journal* 35,1 (2009), 76.
23 "The Tyranny of Control," *Free to Choose* (1980), vol. 2, Free to Choose Network, https://www.freetochoosenetwork.org/programs/free_to_choose/index_80.php?id=the_tyranny_of_control.
24 Jean Dreze and Amartya Sen, *An Uncertain Glory* (Princeton: Princeton University Press, 2013), 3.
25 Mary Ann Doane, "Indexicality: Trace and Sign: Introduction," *differences: A Journal of Feminist Cultural Studies* 18.1 (2007): 3.
26 Ibid., 6.
27 C.P. Chandrashekhar and Jayati Ghosh, *The Market that Failed: A Decade of Neoliberal Economic Reforms in India* (New Delhi: Leftword, 2006), 1.
28 Friedman and Friedman, *Free to Choose*, 57.
29 Ibid., 58.
30 Utsa Patnaik and Prabhat Patnaik, "The Drain of Wealth: Colonialism before the First World War," *Monthly Review* (Feb 1, 2021), https://monthlyreview.org/2021/02/01/the-drain-of-wealth/.
31 "Created Equal," *Free to Choose* (1980), vol. 5. Free to Choose Network.
32 The Bombay Textile Strike began in January 1982 and has not yet been officially called off by the workers. A quarter of a million workers joined the strike, which was seriously weakened after about 16 months. It provided factory owners with a convenient way of laying off workers without compensation

Notes

and eventually profitably selling off their already declining businesses. Nearly 60,000 workers lost their jobs during or in the aftermath of the strike. For more on the textile workers' strike, including its connections with the UK mineworkers' strike, see H. van Wersch, *The Bombay Textile Strike 1982–83* (Bombay: Oxford University Press, 1992) and Darryl D'Monte, *Ripping the Fabric* (New Delhi: Oxford University Press, 2005). For more on the significance of the air traffic controllers' strike in the story of US neoliberalism, see David Harvey, *A Brief History of Neoliberalism* (Oxford: Oxford University Press, 2005).

33 "From Cradle to Grave," *Free to Choose* (1980), vol. 4, Free to Choose Network, https://www.freetochoosenetwork.org/programs/free_to_choose/index_80.php?id=from_cradle_to_grave.

34 The transcript of this speech is available at https://www.indiabudget.gov.in/doc/bspeech/bs199192.pdf.

35 Vijay Prashad, *The Poorer Nations* (New York: Verso, 2014), 135.

36 Mark Tully, "Manmohan Singh: Architect of the New India," *The Sikh Times* (Nov. 14, 2005).

37 For Singh's role in the South Commission, see Prashad's *The Poorer Nations*.

38 Tully, "Manmohan Singh."

39 Whether or not India had a choice in accepting structural adjustment has been a point of controversy. Economists C.P. Chandrashekhar and Jayati Ghosh argue that "In fact … the option of a loan under the Structural Adjustment Facility was not the only one available to the government in 1991. India could have combined a smaller volume of non-conditional borrowing from the IMF with some import controls to tide over the problem created by foreign reserves and retained for itself the right to fashion an appropriate response to its growing balance of payments difficulties" (*The Market that Failed*, 31).

40 Michael Levien, *Dispossession without Development: Landgrabs in Neoliberal India* (New York: Oxford University Press, 2018), 1.

41 "P.M's Speech at the Function to Mark the Centenary of Tata Steel," Former Prime Minister of India, Dr. Manmohan Singh, Government of India, Apr. 22, 2008, https://archivepmo.nic.in/drmanmohansingh/speech-details.php?nodeid=650.

42 Shashi Tharoor is a novelist and politician who wrote *India: From Midnight to the Millennium and Beyond* (New York: Arcade, 1997); *Imagining India: The Idea of a Renewed Nation* (Haryana: Penguin India, 2008) is the work of Nandan Nilekani, head of Infosys, India's leading IT company. Nilekani, along with Viral Shah, later wrote *Rebooting India: Realizing a Billion Aspirations* (Haryana: Penguin India, 2015). Western journalists have also contributed to the national biography trend; see, for instance, Patrick French, *India, A Portrait: An Intimate Biography of 1.2 Billion People* (New York: Knopf, 2011).

43 Sahana Udupa, "Aam Aadmi: Decoding the Media Logics," *EPW* 49.7 (Feb. 15, 2014), 13–15. For more on the expansion of economic journalism and financial media in India and elsewhere, see Paula Chakravartty and Dan Schiller, "Neoliberal Newspeak and Digital Capitalism in Crisis," *International Journal of Communication* 4 (2010), 670–692.

44 Amartya Sen's review appears on Das's personal website: http://gurcharandas.org/dobg-amartya-sen.

45 Das, *India Unbound*, x.

46 Das's philosophical bent leads Meera Nanda to refer to him as "India's most

Notes

erudite neoliberal." Meera Nanda, *The God Market: How Globalization is Making India more Hindu* (New York: Monthly Review Press, 2011), 37.
47 Das, *India Unbound*, 222.
48 Ibid., 79.
49 Ibid., 77.
50 Ibid., 78.
51 Deepak Lal's *The Poverty of "Development Economics"* (1983) helped launch a critique of postwar developmentalism. For more on Lal, see Jennifer Bair, "Taking Aim at the New International Economic Order," *The Road from Mont Pèlerin: The Making of the Neoliberal Thought Collective*, ed. Philip Mirowski and Dieter Plehwe (Cambridge, MA: Harvard University Press, 2009), 347–385.
52 Ibid., x–xi.
53 Ryan Szpiech, *Conversion and Narrative: Reading and Religious Authority in Medieval Polemic* (Philadelphia: University of Pennsylvania Press, 2012), 217.
54 Ibid., 216.
55 Das, *India Unbound*, 83.
56 Ibid., 107.
57 Ibid., 108.
58 Joseph Schumpeter, *Capitalism, Socialism & Democracy* (New York: Routledge, 1976; eBook, 2003), 84.
59 Ibid., 83 (emphasis in original).
60 Das, *India Unbound*, ix, xii.
61 Ibid., 67.
62 Ibid., 86.
63 Ibid., 174.
64 Ibid., 168.
65 Ibid., 169.
66 Ibid., 187.
67 Das is not the only one to tell Dhirubhai's story in this manner. A number of commercially successful versions of his story have appeared in recent years, including most notably the Hindi film *Guru* (dir. Mani Ratnam, 2007). Another national biography, Anand Giridhardas's *India Calling: An Intimate Portrait of a Nation's Remaking* (New York: Times Books, 2011) features a chapter on Mukesh Ambani, Dhirubhai's son. Of India's major industrialists, the Ambanis, and Dhirubhai in particular, figure frequently as emblems of "new" India.
68 Das, *India Unbound*, 193.
69 Ibid., 194.
70 Ibid, 233.
71 Ibid., 347.
72 Ibid., 259.
73 Ibid., 150.
74 Ibid., 153.
75 Ibid., 145.
76 Gurcharan Das, *India Grows at Night: A Liberal Case for a Strong State* (New Delhi: Allen Lane/Penguin, 2012), 3.
77 Ibid., 5.
78 Ibid., 9.
79 Ibid., 252.
80 Ibid., 6.

Notes

81. Ibid., 21.
82. Ibid., 22.
83. Ibid., 24.
84. Ibid., 40.
85. Ibid., 12.
86. Ibid., 160.
87. But, as Achin Vanaik observes, "it would be largely meaningless to talk of any *Indian* civilization [or culture], let alone one existing through millenniums [sic]. There have only been civilizations [and cultures] *in* India, where India is not any 'natural' territorial entity, but simply an extrapolation backwards in time of the geographical space that came to be defined by British colonial rule" (Part II, chapter 3, "Civilization and Culture" section, para 4). Achin Vanaik, *The Rise of Hindu Authoritarianism: Secular Claims, Communal Realities* (New York: Verso, 2017; Kindle edition).
88. Nanda, *The God Market*, xxiv. Nanda makes the case that there has been an increasing Hinduization of the public sphere since economic liberalization. As she puts it, "Hindusim has become the de facto religion of the 'secular' Indian state which is constitutionally bound to have no official religion" (3).
89. Ibid., 7.
90. Das, *India Unbound*, 71.
91. Nanda, *The God Market*, 59.
92. Das, *India Unbound*, xiii.
93. Ibid., xiv.
94. Ibid., xv.
95. Prabhat Patnaik, "Why Neoliberalism Needs Neofascists," *The Boston Review* (Jul. 19, 2021).

Chapter 3

1. F.A. Hayek, *Law, Legislation, and Liberty*, Vol. 2: *The Mirage of Social Justice* (London: Routledge, 1998), 112.
2. Chetan Bhagat, *The 3 Mistakes of My Life* (New Delhi: Rupa, 2008; Kindle edition), 97. Subsequent citations from this novel are in the main text.
3. Parinda Joshi, *Made in China* (New Delhi: HarperCollins India, 2019; Kindle edition), ch. 3.
4. Shiv Khera, *You Can Win: A Step-by-Step Tool for Top Achievers* (New Delhi: Bloomsbury India, 1998); A.P.J. Abdul Kalam, *Wings of Fire: An Autobiography* (Hyderabad: Universities Press, 1999).
5. In the early to mid-2000s Bhagat's bestselling novels were selling for Rs. 95, the price of a movie ticket. Bhagat wanted his novels to appear in supermarkets "next to jeans and bread." Robert McCrum, "Chetan Bhagat: The Paperback King of India," *Guardian* (Jan. 23, 2010), https://www.theguardian.com/books/2010/jan/24/chetan-bhagat-robert-mccrum.
6. Meghna Majumdar, "Why Is It Not Considered Cool to Read Tamil Books, Questions Chetan Bhagat," *The Hindu* (Mar. 25, 2019), https://www.thehindu.com/books/books-authors/a-love-story-in-any-language/article26633597.ece.
7. Manisha Basu, *The Rhetoric of Hindu India: Language and Urban Nationalism* (Delhi: Cambridge University Press, 2017), 168.

8 "Most Creative People 2011: Chetan Bhagat," *Fast Company* (May 18, 2011), https://www.fastcompany.com/3018453/47-chetan-bhagat.
9 John Frow, Melissa Hardue, and Vanessa Smith, "Introduction," *Textual Practice* 34.12, special issue: "The Bildungsroman: Forms and Transformations" (2020), 1905–1910 (1905).
10 Joseph Slaughter, *Human Rights Inc.: The World Novel, Narrative Form, and International Law* (New York: Fordham University Press, 2007), 109.
11 Ibid., 114, 115.
12 Ibid., 111.
13 Quoted in Frow, Hardie, and Smith, "Introduction," 1907.
14 Ibid., 1906.
15 For more on the construction of middle-class identity in post-liberalization India, see Leela Fernandes, *India's New Middle Class* (Minneapolis: University of Minnesota Press, 2006).
16 Ibid., 208.
17 Mark McGurl, "Introduction: Retail Therapy," *Everything and Less: The Novel in the Age of Amazon* (New York: Verso, 2021; Kindle edition). McGurl argues that in the age of Amazon, the writer is asked to see himself as an entrepreneur and service provider for the "reader-customer."
18 Like Bhagat, other commercially successful English-language writers such as Amish Tripathi and Ashwin Sanghi have also penned self-help books. See Somak Ghoshal, "How to Win at Self-Help," *Mint Lounge* (Apr. 4, 2018), https://lifestyle.livemint.com/health/wellness/how-to-win-at-self-help-111644475238605.html.
19 The back cover of *Making India Awesome* (New Delhi: Rupa, 2015) describes the book as offering "inspired solutions to the country's most intractable problems—poverty, unemployment, corruption, violence against women, communal violence, religious fundamentalism, illiteracy and more."
20 Ghoshal, "How to Win at Self-Help."
21 Manisha Basu, *The Rhetoric of Hindu India*, 168.
22 Rachel Lopez, "How Amish Tripathi Changed Indian Publishing," *Hindustan Times* (Apr. 27, 2013), www.hindustantimes.com/brunch/cover-story-how-amish-tripathi-changed-indian-publishing/story-6sLX57GQfixzLO5Nw2ZLNO.html.
23 For more on this boom in India's domestic publishing industry, see, for instance, Jaya Bhattacharji Rose, "English-Language Fiction Publishing in India," *Logos* 22.2 (2011), 26–36.
24 Sarah Brouillette, "Neoliberalism and the Demise of the Literary," *Neoliberalism and Contemporary Literary Cultures*, ed. Mitchum Huehls and Rachel Greenwald Smith (Baltimore: Johns Hopkins University Press, 2017), 281.
25 According to the 2016 Nielson India book market report, "Whilst reading for pleasure is an important component of the market and the audience for general trade books (fiction, nonfiction and noneducational children's) looks set to grow, school books account for the bulk of the country's overall book market. In fact, purchases of K-12 school books are estimated to account for some 71% of the market, with higher education books accounting for an additional 22%." See "Read All about It: India's Book Market Is Poised for Growth," Nielson.com (Mar. 22, 2016), https://www.nielsen.com/us/en/insights/article/2016/read-all-about-it-indias-book-market-is-poised-for-growth/.
26 Saudamini Jain, "The Reading Conundrum: Is the Books Business Booming or Dying?", *Hindustan Times* (Nov. 23, 2015), https://www.hindustantimes.com/

Notes

brunch/the-reading-conundrum-is-the-books-business-booming-or-dying/story-hvCX4vW9oX1xa0sllz8zzK.html.
27 Suman Gupta, "Indian 'Commercial' Fiction in English, the Publishing Industry, and Youth Culture," *Economic and Political Weekly* 46.5 (2012), 52.
28 Bhagat's *Five Point Someone* (2004), *One Night @ the Call Center* (2005), *2 States: The Story of My Marriage* (2009), and *Half Girlfriend* (2014) have all been adapted into film and released respectively as *3 Idiots* (dir. Rajkumar Hirani, 2009), *Hello* (dir. Atul Agnihotri, 2008), *2 States* (dir. Abhishek Varman, 2014), and *Half Girlfriend* (dir. Mohit Suri, 2017).
29 Sangita Gopal, "'Coming to a Multiplex Near You': Indian Fiction in English and the New Bollywood Cinema," *A History of the Indian Novel in English*, ed. Ulka Anjari (Cambridge: Cambridge University Press, 2015), 360.
30 Gupta, "Indian 'Commercial' Fiction in English," 52.
31 The Indian novel in general and the Indian English novel in particular emerged in the second half of the nineteenth century. As Meenakshi Mukherjee puts it, "This was roughly a generation after Macaulay's 'Minute' decreed English as the language of higher education, exposing an entire class of urban Indian men to British narrative models." See Mukherjee, "The Beginnings of the Indian Novel," *A History of Indian Literature in English*, ed. A.K. Mehrotra (New York: Columbia, 2003), 94.
32 Rashmi Sadana, *English Heart, Hindi Heartland: The Political Life of Literature in India* (Berkeley: University of California Press, 2012), 15.
33 Priyamvada Gopal, *The Indian English Novel: Nation, History, Narration* (Oxford: Oxford University Press, 2009), 6.
34 Prominent examples include Mulk Raj Anand's *The Untouchable* (1935), R.K. Narayan's *Swami and Friends* (1935), and Raja Rao's *Kanthapura* (1938).
35 According to Jon Mee, "The appearance of *Midnight's Children* in 1981 brought about a renaissance in Indian writing in English which has outdone that of the 1930s." See Mee, "After Midnight: The Novel in the 1980s and 1990s," *A History of Indian Literature in English*, ed. A.K. Mehrotra (New York: Columbia University Press, 2003), 318.
36 Priya Joshi, *In Another Country* (New York: Columbia University Press, 2002): 260.
37 Ibid., 261.
38 Graham Huggan, *The Postcolonial Exotic: Marketing the Margins* (New York: Routledge, 2001), vii.
39 Ronit Frenkel, "The Politics of Loss: Post-Colonial Pathos and Current Booker Prize-Nominated Texts from India and South Africa," *Scrutiny* 213.2 (2008), 78.
40 Ibid., 79.
41 Sadana, *English Heart*, 143.
42 Roanne Kantor, "A Case of Exploding Markets: Latin American and South Asian Literary 'Booms,'" *Comparative Literature* 70.4 (2018), 469.
43 The book publishing industry is said to be booming with an annual growth rate of about 30 per cent. And this boom is attributed to "rising literacy rates, a youthful population and an expanding economy" ("Indian Book Publishing Industry Booming: Purohit," *United News of India* (May 31, 2019), http://www.uniindia.com/indian-book-publishing-industry-booming-purohit/south/news/1616601.html. See also, Amit Roy, "A Book Market Boom," *Telegraph* (Oct. 28, 2019), https://www.telegraphindia.com/opinion/a-book-market-boom/cid/1687314.

Notes

44 Amardeep Singh, "The Indian Novel in the 21st Century," *Oxford Research Encyclopedia of Literature* (2018), https://oxfordre.com/literature/display/10.1093/acrefore/9780190201098.001.0001/acrefore-9780190201098-e-414.
45 Manisha Basu, *The Rhetoric of Hindu India*, 170.
46 Tripathi's bestselling *Shiva Trilogy* was released with an original soundtrack album. "Shiva Trilogy Becomes Fastest Selling Book Series in the History of Indian Publishing," *India Times* (Apr. 30, 2010), https://web.archive.org/web/20130501041030/http://www.indiatimes.com/lifestyle/work-and-life/shiva-trilogy-becomes-fastest-selling-book-series-in-the-history-of-indian-publishing-74920.html.
47 Priya Joshi, "Chetan Bhagat: Remaking the Novel in India," *A History of the Indian Novel in English*, ed. Ulka Anjari (Cambridge: Cambridge University Press, 2015), 312.
48 Chetan Bhagat quoted in Nupur Sharma, "I Write, Therefore I Am ...," *The Hindu* (Jul. 14, 2011), https://www.thehindu.com/features/metroplus/i-write-therefore-i-am/article2224553.ece.
49 Bhagat, "Acknowledgements," *The 3 Mistakes of My Life*.
50 Jonathan Shapiro Anjaria and Ulka Anjaria, "The Fractured Spaces of Entrepreneurialism in Post-Liberalization India," *Enterprise Culture in Neoliberal India: Studies in Youth, Class, Work and Media*, ed. Nandini Gooptu (New York: Routledge, 2013), 200.
51 Paroma Chakravarti, "Fantasies of Transformation: Education, Neoliberal Self-Making, and Bollywood," *Enterprise Culture in Neoliberal India: Studies in Youth, Class, Work and Media* (New York: Routledge, 2013), 49.
52 Mahmood Mamdani, *Good Muslim, Bad Muslim: America, the Cold War, and the Roots of Terror* (New York: Doubleday, 2005).
53 Evelyn Alsultany, *Arabs and Muslims in the Media: Race and Representation after 9/11* (New York: NYU Press, 2012), 128.
54 These are the words of an editor from HarperCollins India, and they appear on Parinda Joshi's webpage: https://www.parindajoshi.com/.
55 Parinda Joshi, "Author's Note," *Made in China*.
56 Ibid., ch. 3.
57 Ibid., ch. 5.
58 Ibid., ch. 18.
59 Ibid., ch. 17.
60 Ibid., ch. 11.
61 Ibid., ch. 7.
62 Sangita Gopal, "'Coming to a Multiplex Near You': Indian Fiction in English and the New Bollywood Cinema," *A History of the Indian Novel in English*, ed. Ulka Anjaria (Cambridge: Cambridge University Press, 2015), 361.
63 This article appears on Parinda Joshi's website: https://www.parindajoshi.com/post/the-entrepreneurial-gene.
64 Manisha Basu, *The Rhetoric of Hindu India*, 193. Like Bhagat, author Amish Tripathi has in recent years channeled the Hindu right's civilizational discourse about Hindutva, and spoken of secularism as a "Western import." See Sravasti Dasgupta, "Ram Mandir Bhoomi Pujan a 'Civilizational Moment' for India, Author Amish Tripathi Says," *The Print* (Aug. 11, 2020), https://theprint.in/theprint-otc/ram-mandir-bhoomi-pujan-a-civilisational-moment-for-india-author-amish-tripathi-says/479223/.

Notes

65 Bhagat, who often critiques the elitism of the publishing industry, has been a strong advocate of selling his work in regional Indian languages. See, for instance, Meghna Majumdar,, "Why Is it Not Considered Cool to Read Tamil Books." Similarly Amish Tripathi—whose mythological fiction has been translated even more widely than Bhagat's and whose sales have set new records—has strongly supported the selling of his fiction in translation. See "'Regional Languages Are the Key to Reaching the Masses,'" domain-b.com (Mar. 23, 2016), https://www.domain-b.com/people/interviews/20160323_amish_tripathi.html.

Chapter 4

1 Vikas Swarup, *Q&A: A Novel* (New York: Scribner, 2005), 133. Subsequent citations from this edition are in the main text.
2 Paulo Lins, *City of God: A Novel*, trans. Alison Entrekin (New York: Black Cat, 2006; Kindle edition), 429. Subsequent citations from this edition are in the main text.
3 See for instance Ajay Gehlawat, "Introduction: The *Slumdog* Phenomenon," *The Slumdog Phenomenon: A Critical Anthology*, ed. Ajay Gehlawat (London/New York: Anthem Press, 2013), xv–xxiii; Mitu Sengupta, "A Million Dollar Exit from the Slum-World: *Slumdog Millionaire*'s Troubling Formula," *The Slumdog Phenomenon: A Critical Anthology*, ed. Ajay Gehlawat (London/New York: Anthem Press, 2013), 69–89; Georgia Christinidis, "Slumdog Millionaire and the Knowledge-Based Economy: Poverty as Ontology," *Cultural Critique* 89 (2015), 38–60; Jigna Desai, "Pulp Frictions," *Re-Orientalism and South Asian Identity Politics: the Oriental Other Within*, ed. Lisa Lau and Ana Christina Mendes (New York: Routledge, 2011), 72–88; Nivedita Menon, "Reading Swarup, Watching Boyle," *Outlook* (Jan. 28, 2009), https://www.outlookindia.com/website/story/reading-swarup-watching-boyle/239578.
4 Ana Christina Mendes and Lisa Lau, "India through Re-Orientalist Lenses," *Interventions: International Journal of Postcolonial Studies* 17.5 (2015), 706–727. For other critical engagements with Swarup's novel, and not just its film adaptation, see Snehal Shinghavi, "Slumdogs and Millionaires: Facts and Fictions of Indian (Under)Development, *The Slumdog Phenomenon*, ed. Ajay Gehlawat (London/New York: Anthem Press, 2013), 91–105; Chinmoy Banerjee, "Vikas Swarup: Writing India in a Global Time," *Postliberalization Indian Novels in English*, ed. Aysha Iqbal Viswamohan (London/New York: Anthem Press, 2013): 31–40; Barbara Korte, "Can the Indigent Speak? Poverty Studies, the Postcolonial and Global Appeal of Q&A and *The White Tiger*," *Connotations* 20.2–3 (2010–2011), 293–312; Menon, "Reading Swarup, Watching Boyle."
5 Mendes and Lau, "India through Re-Orientalist Lenses," 712.
6 Ibid., 716.
7 Katherine Boo, *Behind the Beautiful Forevers: Life, Death and Hope in a Mumbai Undercity* (Gurgaon: Penguin India, 2012).
8 Mike Davis, *Planet of Slums* (New York: Verso, 2006), 2. Davis predicts that, "cities will account for virtually all future world population growth, which is expected to peak at about 10 billion in 2050"—and that with the unprecedented scale and velocity of Third-World urbanization, "Ninety-five percent

Notes

of this final buildout of humanity will occur in the urban areas of developing countries" (2).

9 For the history of rural-urban migration in India and its role particularly in Bombay, see Rajnarayan Chandavarkar, *The Origins of Industrial Capitalism in India: Business Strategies and the Working Classes in Bombay, 1900–1940* (Cambridge: Cambridge University Press, 1994). For a documentary portrait of the conditions of rural migrants in Bombay during the 1980s, see *Our City* (dir. Anand Patwardhan, 1984).

10 Davis, *Planet of Slums*, 14–15.

11 For more on the structures producing urban poverty in Brazil, see Janet Perlman, *The Myth of Marginality: Urban Poverty and Politics in Rio de Janeiro* (Berkeley: University of California Press, 1976); Janet Perlman, "The Metamorphosis of Marginality: Four Generations in the Favelas of Rio de Janeiro," *The Annals of the American Academy of Political and Social Science* 606 (Jul. 2006), 154–177; Edmund Amann and Werner Baer, "Neoliberalism and Its Consequences in Brazil," *Journal of Latin American Studies* 34.4 (Nov. 2022), 945–959; and Marta Peixoto, "Rio's Favelas in Recent Fiction and Film: Commonplaces of Urban Segregation," *PMLA* 122.1 (2007), 170–178.

12 This language informs the following World Bank report on South Asian urbanization: Peter Ellis and Mark Roberts, "Leveraging Urbanization in South Asia: Managing Spatial Transformation for Prosperity and Livability," World Bank Group (2016). A full copy of the report can be found at https://openknowledge.worldbank.org/handle/10986/22549

13 Elmo Gonzaga, "The Cinematographic Unconscious of Slum Voyeurism," *Cinema Journal* 56.4 (Summer 2017), 104.

14 Swapna Banerjee-Guha notes that the term "world-class cities" has come to replace the concept of "livable" cities within the lexicon of urban planning. See Swapna Banerjee-Guha, "Neoliberalising the 'Urban': New Geographies of Power and Injustice in Indian Cities," *Economic and Political Weekly* 44.22 (May 30–Jun. 5, 2009), 97.

15 Perlman, "The Metamorphosis of Marginality," 158.

16 Peixoto, "Rio's Favelas," 171.

17 Claire Williams, "Ghettourism and Voyeurism, or Challenging Stereotypes and Raising Consciousness? Literary and Non-Literary Forays into the Favelas of Rio de Janeiro," *Bulletin of Latin American Research* 27.4 (2008), 487.

18 Michael Niblett, "The Long 1970s: Neoliberalism, Narrative Form, and Hegemonic Crisis in the Work of Marlon James and Paulo Lins," *World Literature, Neoliberalism, and the Culture of Discontent*, ed. Sharae Deckard and Stephen Shapiro (Cham: Palgrave Macmillan, 2019), 54.

19 Ibid., 54.

20 Ibid., 63.

21 Lins, *City of God*.

22 Alex Bellos, "Postcard from Hell," *Guardian* (Jul. 15, 2006), https://www.theguardian.com/books/2006/jul/15/featuresreviews.guardianreview17.

23 Meirelles speaks consciously of his "middle-class point of view": see Ed Gonzalez, "Interview: Fernando Meirelles on the Making of *City of God*," *Slant* (Aug. 27, 2003), https://www.slantmagazine.com/film/city-of-gods-an-interview-with-fernando-meirelles/.

24 Peixoto, "Rio's Favelas," 173.

Notes

25 Gonzaga, "The Cinematographic Unconscious," 104.
26 Sophia A. McClennen, "From the Aesthetics of Hunger to the Cosmetics of Hunger in Brazilian Cinema: Meirelles' *City of God*," *symploke* 19.1–2 (2011), 100–101.
27 Ibid., 104.
28 Peixoto, "Rio's Favelas," 174.
29 Rob Nixon, *Slow Violence and the Environmentalism of the Poor* (Cambridge, MA: Harvard University Press, 2011), 56.
30 James Dawes, *The Novel of Human Rights* (Cambridge: Harvard University Press, 2018), 153. For more on the picaresque as genre, see Giancarlo Maiorino, ed., *The Picaresque: Tradition and Displacement* (Minneapolis: University of Minnesota Press, 1996). For more on the picaresque in contemporary postcolonial fiction see Stacey Balkan, "Chris Abani's Graceland and the Petro-Picaresque," *The Global South* 9.2 (Fall 2015), 18–37.
31 Nixon, *Slow Violence*, 56.
32 Ibid., 55.
33 Ibid., 66. Nixon uses this phrase to refer to the speech of Animal, the protagonist of *Animal's People*, Indra Sinha's response to the legacies of the 1984 Bhopal Union Carbide disaster, and a novel that, according to Nixon, inaugurates the genre of the "environmental picaresque" (*Slow Violence*, 46).
34 Nixon, *Slow Violence*, 56.
35 Caren Irr, "Neoliberal Childhoods: The Orphan as Entrepreneur in Contemporary Anglophone Fiction," *Neoliberalism and Contemporary Literary Culture*, ed. Rachel Greenwald Smith and Mitchum Huehls (Baltimore: Johns Hopkins Press, 2017), 229.
36 The end of the Colonel Taylor episode somewhat complicates this presentation of the "good" servant, for it is Ram who gives away his master as a spy. Yet he remains honest, unlike the other servants; and whereas they are ultimately exposed as thieves, he is also clever enough to avoid getting caught as an informant.
37 Banerjee, "Vikas Swarup," 33.
38 Shinghavi, "Slumdogs and Millionaires," 98.
39 The framing of slums as sites of moral degradation and criminality is not new. In *Planet of Slums* Mike Davis describes how " For nineteenth-century liberals ... the slum was first and above all envisioned as a place where an incorrigible and feral social 'residuum' rots in immoral and often riotous splendor; indeed, a vast literature titillated the Victorian middle classes with lurid tales from the dark side of town." Similarly, in late nineteenth-century America the slum was seen as "inhabited by a squalid and criminal population" (22).
40 Other widely read fictional works categorized as Bombay Noir include the bestselling novels *Shantaram* (New York: Macmillan, 2003)—also adapted into a TV series—and *The Mountain Shadow* (London: Little, Brown, 2015), both by Australian novelist, Gregory David Roberts. Popular Hindi films in this category include *Satya* (dir. Ram Gopal Varma, 1998), *Company* (dir. Ram Gopal Varma, 2002), and *Black Friday* (dir. Anurag Kashyap), which focus on the criminal underworld and have been cited by Danny Boyle as influences on *Slumdog*. See Amitava Kumar, "Slumdog Millionaire's Bollywood Ancestors," *Vanity Fair* (Dec. 23, 2008), https://www.vanityfair.com/hollywood/2008/12/slumdog-millionaires-bollywood-ancestors.

Notes

41 Danny Boyle has said in interviews that Mehta's *Maximum City* was his "bible," that he would carry it around with him when he was filming *Slumdog*. He also bought the rights to Mehta's book. See "New Film by Slumdog Director Danny Boyle," *Marie Claire* (Mar. 6, 2009), https://www.marieclaire.co.uk/news/new-film-by-slumdog-director-danny-boyle-191125.

42 For the film's reception in India, see Ananya Roy, "Slumdog Cities: Rethinking Subaltern Urbanism," *International Journal of Urban and Regional Research* 35.2 (Mar. 2011), 223–238.

43 Tanushree Ghosh, "'Yet we believe his triumph might surely be ours': The Dickensian Liberalism of *Slumdog Millionaire*," *Neo-Victorian Studies* 8.1 (2015), 87.

44 Ibid., 77.

45 Roy, "Slumdog Cities," 224.

46 Nandini Chandra, "Slumdog Aesthetics and the Question of Indian Poverty," *The Slumdog Phenomenon: A Critical Anthology*, ed. Ajay Gehlawat (London/New York: Anthem Press, 2013), 36.

47 Jonathan Cavallero, "Transnational Adaptation: *Q&A*, *Slumdog Millionaire*, and Aesthetic and Economic Relationships between Bollywood and Hollywood," *The Journal of Popular Culture* 50.4 (2017), 843–844.

48 Christinidis, 40.

49 Evan Watkins, *Throwaways: Work Culture and Consumer Education* (Stanford: Stanford University Press, 1993), 3.

50 Ibid., 7.

51 Ellis and Roberts, "Leveraging Urbanization," 8.

52 Mumbai First advertises itself as a public-private partnership that is invested in "making Mumbai a better place to live, work, and invest in." See Mumbai First's website: https://mumbaifirst.org/. For the proposal, see *Vision Mumbai: Transforming Mumbai into a World-Class City*, a Bombay First-McKinsey Report (2003), available in full on Mumbai First's website: https://mumbaifirst.org/vision-mumbai-40-year-concept-plan-for-mmr/.

53 For more on the lack of involvement of slum dwellers in the redevelopment project, see Sheela Patel and Jockin Arputham, "An Offer of Partnership or a Promise of Conflict in Dharavi, Mumbai?" *Environment and Urbanization* 19.2 (2007), 501–508. Patel and Arputham also point to the regulations that make large numbers of Dharavi residents ineligible for free housing. For more on the Dharavi Bachao Andolan, or Save Dharavi Committee, see Banerjee-Guha, "Neoliberalising the 'Urban'." For redevelopment plans in Dharavi, see Sujit Mahamulkar, "Dharavi to Be Redeveloped as a Whole with 80% Private Stake," *Times of India* (Oct. 17, 2018).

Chapter 5

1 Zakes Mda, "Acceptance Speech for the Oliver Schreiner Prize," *English Academy Review* 14 (1997), 281.

2 Amitav Ghosh in Alessandro Vescovi, "Amitav Ghosh in Conversation," *ARIEL: A Review of International English Literature* 40.4 (2009), 140.

3 Isabel Hofmeyer and Michelle Williams, "South-Africa-India: Connections and Comparisons," *Journal of Asian and African Studies*, 44.1 (2009), 12.

4 In India, the top 0.1 percent of earners captured a higher share of total incomes than the bottom 50 percent in the 1980–2015 period—at 12 percent

Notes

(Lucas Chancel and Thomas Piketty, "Indian Income Inequality, 1922–2015: From British Raj to Billionaire Raj?", *World Inequality Database Working Paper Series* (July 2017), http://wordpress.wid.world/wp-content/uploads/2017/08/ChancelPiketty2017WIDworld.pdf). In South Africa, "the poorest half of all South Africans earned just 9.7 percent of national income, down from 11.4 percent in 1995" (Patrick Bond, "South Africa Tackles Global Apartheid," *South Atlantic Quarterly* 103.4 (2004), 819).

5 Patrick Jagoda, *Network Aesthetics* (Chicago: University of Chicago Press, 2016), 13–14. Caroline Levine observes, through the example of Charles Dickens's *Bleak House*, that there is nothing new about network narratives. Yet, as Jagoda notes, a "network imaginary" and "network aesthetics" gained currency in the late twentieth century, in conjunction with neoliberalism. Jagoda also points out that a "network imaginary remains adaptable to myriad ends" (18)—from naïve celebrations of economic globalization to attempts at opposing centralized power. For Levine's commentary, see "Narrative Networks: *Bleak House* and the Affordances of Form," *Novel: A Forum on Fiction* 42.3 (2009), 517–523.

6 Rita Barnard, "Fictions of the Global," *Novel* 42.2 (2009), 212.

7 The Sundarbans National Park—a UNESCO-designated World Heritage Site—spreads across India and Bangladesh. Annu Jalais notes that, "Apart from providing home to an important number of rare and endangered flora and fauna, it is the only mangrove forest in the world inhabited by tigers." Jalais, "The Sundarbans: Whose World Heritage Site?", *Conservation and Society* 5.3 (2007), 2

8 David Bordwell, *The Way Hollywood Tells It* (Berkeley: University of California Press, 2006). Film critic Bordwell uses the term "event frame" to refer to strategies deployed in cinematic network narratives to justify the convergence of multiple protagonists and stories. These strategies include "a common fate or significant occasion," such as "a celebration and a weekend holiday" or even a disaster event (97), that has the potential to bring characters together in a "multi-protagonist plot." In their choice of "event frame," Ghosh's and Mda's novels resemble other celebrated works of anglophone fiction from the early 2000s. In Michael Ondaatje's *Anil's Ghost* (2001), the America-returned Anil's arrival in Sri Lanka sets off the narrative's chain of events. In Gillian Slovo's *Red Dust* (2000), Sarah Barcant's return to South Africa after years of living in the US sets off the novel's plot of historical recovery. Antoinette Burton calls the female version of this diasporic subject "a stock character in [contemporary] postcolonial fiction: the Europe-or-America-returned professional woman struggling to maintain her hard-won status against all odds" (41). This stock character functions as an index of contemporary globalization—and the mobility it affords relatively privileged Western or Westernized subjects, in contrast to the vast majority in the global South. See Burton, "Archive of Bones: *Anil's Ghost* and the Ends of History." *Journal of Commonwealth Literature* 38.1 (2003), 39–56.

9 Warwick Research Collective, *Combined and Uneven Development: Towards a New Theory of World Literature* (Liverpool: Liverpool University Press, 2015), 11.

10 Ibid., 72.

11 Joshi, *In Another Country*.

12 Roshan G. Shahani, "Polyphonous Voices in the City: Bombay's Indian-English Fiction," *Bombay: Mosaic of Modern Culture*, ed. Sujata Patel and Alice Thorner (Bombay: Oxford University Press, 1995), 101, 107.

Notes

13 C.P. Chandrashekhar and Jayati Ghosh, *The Market that Failed: A Decade of Neoliberal Economic Reforms in India* (New Delhi: Leftword, 2006), 26.
14 Michael Levien describes the consequent "land grabs" in neoliberal India and also points to the grassroots struggles that have arisen in response to the dispossession of rural populations. He argues that India might possibly be the global epicenter of land grab protests (*Dispossession without Development: Landgrabs in Neoliberal India* (New York: Oxford University Press, 2018), 1). Whereas postcolonial regimes dispossessed rural populations for development purposes (e.g. dam building), the neoliberal era has been characterized by "dispossession without development," with the state acting as a broker for private capital.
15 Utsa Patnaik, "Neoliberalism and Rural Poverty in India," *EPW* 42.30 (2007), 3133.
16 One state with a consistently high number of suicides is Maharashtra, in which Mumbai—India's financial center—is located. In the nation as a whole, around 300,000 Indian farmers have committed suicide over the last 20 years. For more on farmer suicides, see Ajay Dandekar and Sreedeep Bhattacharya, "Lives in Debt: Narratives of Agrarian Distress and Farmer Suicides," *Economic & Political Weekly* (May 27, 2017); Arindam Banerjee, "Peasant Classes under Neoliberalism: A Class Analysis of Two States," *Economic and Political Weekly* (Apr. 11, 2009); P. Sainath, "A Long March of the Dispossessed to Delhi," *The Wire* (Jun. 23, 2018).
17 For more on this state-sanctioned massacre, see Annu Jalais, "Dwelling on Morichjhapi: When Tigers Become 'Citizens,' Refugees' Tiger Food'," *Economic and Political Weekly* (Apr. 23, 2005), 1757–1762; Ross Mallick, "Refugee Resettlement in Forest Reserves: West Bengal Policy Reversal and the Marichjhapi Massacre," *Journal of Asian Studies* 58.1 (1999), 104–125.
18 Amitav Ghosh, *The Hungry Tide* (New Delhi: HarperCollins India, 2006). All citations from this edition are in the main text.
19 Susie O'Brien, "Back to the World: Reading Ecocriticism in a Postcolonial Context." *Five Emus to the King of Siam*, ed. Helen Tiffin (New York: Rodopi, 2007), 182.
20 Through Nirmal's journal entries the reader learns about the tide patterns that remake the islands on a daily basis; the Morichjhapi settlers' utopian vision and uprising against state power; the various versions of the legend of Bon Bibi; and so on. Especially in its attention to the inhabitants' relationship with Bon Bibi, *The Hungry Tide* is in conversation with anthropological approaches to Sundarbans culture, including works like Annu Jalais's *Forest of Tigers: People, Politics and Environment in the Sundarbans* (New York: Routledge, 2010).
21 Patrick Jagoda, *Network Aesthetics* (Chicago: University of Chicago Press, 2016), 8.
22 These debates between representatives of the "local" and "global" are a recurring feature of both the novels discussed in this chapter—and indeed of other anglophone fiction featuring the return of a diasporic protagonist, e.g. Ondaatje's *Anil's Ghost* (2001) and Slovo's *Red Dust* (2000). In all these narratives, the debates between global and local perspectives are, moreover, underwritten with sexual tension between male and female characters.
23 Many have criticized the ending of *The Hungry Tide*. In a review for *The Nation*, Freudenberger argues that a "tendency to be overly neat is most jarring in the book's epilogue, where Ghosh can't help tying up every loose end. The dead

Notes

are memorialized, the characters are reunited and Kanai's wonderfully prickly Aunt Nilima offers a final observation worthy of Walt Disney" (27). Li points to the troubling political implications of this "overly neat" ending: "Both Kusum and Fokir, as 'authentic' subalterns who resist and remain heterogenous to hegemonic modernity, die so that their stories can be recounted and memorialized by literate, modern characters like Nirmal, Kanai and Piya" (291). See Nell Freudenberger, "Words Apart," *The Nation* (Jun. 13, 2005), 24–28; Victor Li, "Necroidealism, or the Subaltern's Sacrificial Death," *Interventions: International Journal of Postcolonial Studies* 11.3 (2009), 275–292.

24 Neil Lazarus, *The Postcolonial Unconscious* (New York: Cambridge University Press, 2011), 149.

25 Ashley Dawson, "Another Country: The Postcolonial State, Environmentality, and Landless People's Movements," *Democracy, States, and the Struggle for Global Justice*, ed. Heather Gautney, Omar Dahbour, Dawson, and Neil Smith (New York: Routledge, 2009), 248.

26 Dipankar Gupta, "Whither the Indian Village? Culture and Agriculture in 'Rural' India," *EPW* (Feb. 19, 2005), 751–758. Gupta notes that there continues to be resistance, even among intellectuals, to "accepting the fact that the Indian village is undergoing major changes, not just economically, but culturally as well" (751). Some of the clearest illustrations of this resistance can be found in the popular Hindi cinema of the post-liberalization period. The enormously successful *Dilwale Dulhaniya Le Jayenge* (dir. Aditya Chopra, 1995) represents rural India as unchanged, idyllic, and pastoral. But the closest parallel to Ghosh's novel in contemporary Hindi cinema is *Swades* (dir. Ashutosh Gowariker), released in 2004—the same year as *The Hungry Tide*. Like Piya, the protagonist of *Swades* is an urban and America-returned scientist, formerly employed at NASA, who encounters an Indian village. As with the metropolitans in Ghosh's novel, the male protagonist in *Swades* is morally transformed by his exchanges with locals, and his debates with his lover in particular lead him to realize that his scientific work ought to serve the needs of India's rural populations. The film's ending is not tragic, however: the protagonist succeeds in deploying his scientific training to procure clean drinking water for the village community that becomes his home. Both *The Hungry Tide* and *Swades* register distrust of the state's capacity to provide solutions to rural problems, and seem to find solutions to rural problems through the initiative of metropolitans.

27 Fokir's treatment in *The Hungry Tide* resonates with the representation of Velutha, an "untouchable" with whom the relatively privileged Ammu has an affair in Arundhati Roy's Booker Prize-winning novel, *The God of Small Things*. Like Fokir, Velutha possesses a special connection to the river that runs through the village of Ayemenem where the novel is set. If Fokir is presented as having the "river in his veins" and the unique capacity to see "right into the river's heart," then Velutha is described as moving with a special ease through the water, mud, trees, fish, and stars (333–334). Velutha's perceived grounding in his environment becomes especially significant given how the river changes over time, eventually smelling of "shit and pesticides bought with World Bank loans" (13). In the end, Velutha is killed at the hands of a violent and casteist police. Although Fokir's death is caused by a natural disaster, these characters' tragic deaths make both of them symbols of a lost

way of life. In *The God of Small Things*, Velutha is positioned within the context of Ayemenem's increasing destruction by the tourism industry—as a symbol of lost wholeness. See Arundhati Roy, *The God of Small Things* (New York: Random House, 1997).

28 Ramachandra Guha, "Radical American Environmentalism and Wilderness Preservation: A Third World Critique," *Environmental Ethics* 11.1 (1989), 77.

29 Rob Nixon, *Slow Violence and The Environmentalism of the Poor* (Cambridge, MA: Harvard University Press, 2011), 19.

30 Victor Li, "Necroidealism," 288.

31 For more on Mda's work as well as post-apartheid South African fiction see Rita Barnard, *Apartheid and Beyond* (New York: Oxford University Press, 2007) and Shane Graham, *South African Literature after the Truth Commission: Mapping Loss* (New York: Palgrave Macmillan, 2009).

32 David Bell, "Embedded in History: Camagu's amaXhosa Identity in Zakes Mda's *The Heart of Redness*," *Moderna språk* 2 (2009), 19.

33 For a detailed account of the history and afterlives of the Xhosa cattle killing, as well as its relation to other anti-colonial social and millenarian movements, see Jennifer Wenzel, *Bulletproof: Afterlives of Anticolonial Prophesy in South Africa and Beyond* (Chicago: University of Chicago Press, 2009).

34 Apartheid is in fact a system *premised* on the logic of accumulation by dispossession.

35 Patrick Bond, *Elite Transition: From Apartheid to Neoliberalism in South Africa* (London: Pluto, 2000), 23. Bond notes, "The IMF ceased lending [to the apartheid regime due to pressure from social justice groups], but during the 1980s sent in advisory teams each year to help the apartheid government switch to neoliberal economic policies" (159).

36 Memorable representations of the Truth and Reconciliation Commission in literature and film include Antjie Krog's memoir, *Country of My Skull* (2000), its cinematic adaptation, *In My Country* (dir. John Boorman), the documentary, *Long Night's Journey into Day* (dir. Deborah Hoffman and Frances Reid, 2000), Gillian Slovo's novel, *Red Dust* (2000), its cinematic adaptation, *Red Dust* (dir. Tom Hooper, 2004), and the fiction film, *Forgiveness* (dir. Ian Gabriel, 2004).

37 For more on the function of human rights discourse during South Africa's political transition, see Richard Wilson, *The Politics of Truth and Reconciliation in South Africa: Legitimizing the Post-Apartheid State* (Cambridge: Cambridge University Press, 2001). For more on marketed and commodified human rights narratives, see Joseph Slaughter, *Human Rights, Inc.: The World Novel, Narrative Form, and International Law* (New York: Fordham University Press, 2007); Kay Schaffer and Sidonie Smith, *Human Rights and Narrated Lives: The Ethics of Recognition* (New York: Palgrave Macmillan, 2004); and Graham, *South African Literature after the Truth Commission*.

38 See Ian Taylor, *Stuck in Middle GEAR: South Africa's Post-Apartheid Foreign Relations* (Westport, CT: Praeger, 2001). Taylor notes that the "ANC moved its politico-economic policies from a populist and vaguely socialist platform that held out a tacit promise for nationalising the means of production and which ... at least held out the potential for redressing the inequalities of the past, to that of a fiercely pro-capitalist framework...that sits well within the remit of the ongoing hegemonic order" (38). Patrick Bond adds that the new South Africa was the product of not just political compromise but also

Notes

a compromise between business and trade unions: several key members of the Congress of South African Trade Union (Cosatu) became managers of industrial policy and labor relations within the new government, and "big business began to find itself allied with the Democratic Movement on behalf of more rapid political and economic liberalization" (*Elite Transition*, 24).

39 For more on how the market logic in water and energy delivery has undermined states' development goals in both India and South Africa, see Sagie Narsiah and Waquar Ahmed, "The Neoliberalization of the Water and Energy Sectors in South Africa and India," *Journal of Asian and African Studies* 47.6 (2012), 679–694. For connections between anti-apartheid and post-apartheid struggles for the provision of electricity and basic infrastructural services, see Jennifer Wenzel, "Amandla! Awethu! Energy, Infrastructure, Rights, Services," *Interventions: International Journal of Postcolonial Studies* 18.6 (2016), 816–822.

40 For more on the downward pressure on wages, the rise in socio-economic inequality, and the work of social movements contesting the privatization of water and other public services in post-apartheid South Africa, see Ashwin Desai, "Neoliberalism and Resistance in South Africa," *Monthly Review* (Jan. 2003), 16–28.

41 Patrick Bond quotes a government report from October 2002 that shows the average income of black South African households as having "declined 19 percent from 1995 to 2000, while white household income was up 15 percent." Bond, "South Africa Tackles Global Apartheid," 819.

42 Zakes Mda, *The Heart of Redness* (New York: Picador, 2000). All citations from this edition are in the main text.

43 For more on mine workers, the Marikana Massacre (in which the government violently suppressed a 2012 wildcat strike at a Lonmin mine in Marikana), and past and present examples of rural resistance, see Lucy Graham, "Representing Marikana," *Interventions: International Journal of Postcolonial Studies* 18.6 (2016), 834–851.

44 Amitav Ghosh, "Folly in the Sundarbans: A Crocodile in the Swamplands,' Outlookindia.com (Oct. 18, 2004). In this essay, Ghosh calls out the folly of trying to build a beach resort in a region of mudflats and mangrove forests, and argues that it would be reinforcing the injustice of the Morichjhapi evictions. At the time Ghosh's essay was published in October 2004, the West Bengal state government was considering the Sahara Pariwar's proposal. Eventually the proposal was rejected, owing to pushback from grassroots groups.

45 In *UNESCO and the Fate of the Literary* (Stanford: Stanford University Press, 2019), Sarah Brouillette argues that the character Camagu in particular and the novel on the whole attests to Mda's own background in and commitment to cultural policy, which organizations like UNESCO have promoted in recent years as the key to redressing problems of uneven distribution of wealth and resources.

46 Harry Sewlall refers to Qukezwa as the "quintessential eco-feminist" (383) and argues that "Qukezwa's stance is vindicated by the present-day situation in South Africa where … According to a recent newspaper report, 'exotic plants and weeds are destroying our grazing and farming lands, forests, nature and game reserves'" (384). Sewlall, "'Portmanteau biota' and Ecofeminist Interventions in Zakes Mda's *The Heart of Redness*," *JLS/TLW* 23.4 (Dec. 2007), 374–389.

Notes

47 Pravina Pillay and Catherine Addison, "Organic Intellectuals in Zakes Mda's *The Heart of Redness*," *English in Africa* 42.3 (Dec. 2015), 89–110.
48 In *Bulletproof*, Jennifer Wenzel offers a rich reading of this final scene by drawing on Dipesh Chakrabarty's concept of "heterotemporality," which refers to the coexistence of a plurality of times. Wenzel argues that Qukezwa's singing "offers [the] fullest expression" of the novel's heterotemporality: "The two Qukezwas—and their different Nows—merge in her/their song of many voices, itself a figure for the novel's heterotemporality" (186). While I agree that Qukezwa's singing gives expression to the novel's investment in heterotemporality, I would argue that it also makes her time*less*, and frames her as an immortal mythic figure.
49 Vescovi, "Amitav Ghosh in Conversation," 140.
50 Mda, "Acceptance Speech," 281.
51 Meg Samuelson notes the contrast between the fates of Qukezwa and Xoliswa Ximiya: "the Unbelieving Xoliswa is childless; the womb of the Believing Qukezwa is the site of miraculous fertility" (237). In the end of the novel, while Qukezwa is a happy mother, Xoliswa wakes up one day to find that the "scars of history have erupted on her body." Although she "refuses to believe that they are part of an ancestral vengeance" (Mda 261), the narrative voice prompts us to think of the scars as a return-of-the-repressed—and as a reminder to the highly educated Xoliswa that the "redness" she rejects is in fact part of her being. This contrast between the punished childless woman and the celebrated childbearing one is a striking instance of the novel's conservative desire to frame Qukezwa as "natural." Meg Samuelson, "Nongqawuse, National Time and (Female) Authorship in *The Heart of Redness*," *Ways of Writing: Critical Essays on Zakes Mda* (Pietermaritzburg: University of KwaZulu-Natal Press, 2009).
52 Nixon, *Slow Violence*, 4. In India groups like the Save the Narmada Movement have since the 1980s protested the displacement of poor and indigenous inhabitants by dam building and private sector projects around the Narmada river. The post-liberalization period's pro-private sector policies have given rise to increased resistance, including militant tribal insurgencies against the state-sanctioned takeover of forestland by mining corporations. In recent years, coalition groups like the All India Farmers Organization have organized farmers and landless peasants in protests against land grabs and the privatization of agriculture. For more on some of these struggles, see Ashok Dhawale, "A Remarkable Struggle," *The Kisan Long March in Maharashtra*, ed. Vijay Prashad (New Delhi: LeftWord Books, 2018); Levien, *Dispossession without Development*; Sainath, "A Long March"; and Arundhati Roy, "Walking with the Comrades," Outlookindia.com (Mar. 29, 2010), https://www.outlookindia.com/magazine/story/walking-with-the-comrades/264738.

Chapter 6

1 Arundhati Roy, *The Ministry of Utmost Happiness* (New York: Alfred Knopf, 2017), 398. Subsequent citations from this edition are in the main text.
2 Aravind Adiga, *Selection Day* (New York: Scribner, 2016), 149. Subsequent citations from this edition are in the main text.

Notes

3 Pankaj Mishra, "Asia: 'The Explosive Transformation'," *The New York Review of Books* (Apr. 25, 2013), https://www.nybooks.com/articles/2013/04/25/asia-explosive-transformation/.
4 Wendy Brown, *Undoing the Demos: Neoliberalism's Stealth Revolution* (Brooklyn: Zone Books, 2015), 210–218. Brown refers in particular to the ubiquitous discourse of "shared sacrifice" that is used to justify austerity policies.
5 Emily Johansen and Alissa G. Karl, "Introduction: Writing the Economic Present," *Textual Practice* 29.2 (2015), 201, 204.
6 Jeffrey Williams, "The Plutocratic Imagination," *Dissent* 60.1 (Winter 2013), https://www.dissentmagazine.org/article/the-plutocratic-imagination.
7 Mishra, "Asia: 'The Explosive Transformation'."
8 The term Gilded Age has its roots in Mark Twain and Charles Dudley Warner's satirical novel, *The Gilded Age: A Tale of Today* (1873). For more on this novel, the era that it came to name, and the links between the early and new Gilded Age, see Daniel Shaviro, *Literature and Inequality: Nine Perspectives from the Napoleonic Era through the First Gilded Age* (London: Anthem, 2020).
9 This is Mishra's phrase, which builds on Tennyson. See "Asia: 'The Explosive Transformation'."
10 For more on the effects of India's military occupation of Kashmir, see Mohamad Junaid, "Death and Life under Military Occupation: Space, Violence, and Memory in Kashmir," *Everyday Occupations: Experiencing Militarism in South Asia and the Middle East*, ed. Kamala Visweswaran (Philadelphia: University of Pennsylvania Press, 2013), 158–190; and Hafsa Kanjwal, "Kashmiris Do Not Need to Prove Their Humanity. India Needs to Prove Its Own," *The Washington Post* (Jul. 12, 2017), https://www.washingtonpost.com/news/global-opinions/wp/2017/07/12/kashmiris-do-not-need-to-prove-their-humanity-india-needs-to-prove-its-own/. For Roy's nonfiction prose on Kashmir, see "Azadi: It's the Only Thing the Kashmiri Wants," *Outlook India* (Sept. 1, 2008), https://www.outlookindia.com/magazine/story/azadi/238272; and "Kashmir Is Potentially the Flashpoint for a Future Nuclear War," *Huffington Post* (Mar. 1, 2019), https://www.huffpost.com/entry/our-captured-wounded-hearts-arundhati-roy-on-balakot-kashmir-and-india_n_5c78d592e4b0de0c3fbf82bf.
11 Michiko Kakutani, "Arundhati Roy's Long-Awaited Novel Is an Ambitious Look at Turmoil in India," *New York Times* (Jun. 5, 2017), https://www.nytimes.com/2017/06/05/books/review-arundhati-roy-ministry-of-utmost-happiness.html.
12 On Roy's discursive construction as an exotic Indian author following the success of *The God of Small Things*, see, for instance, Graham Huggan, *The Postcolonial Exotic: Marketing the Margins* (New York: Routledge, 2001); Elleke Boehmer, "East Is East and South Is South: The Cases of Sarojini Naidu and Arundhati Roy," *Women: A Cultural Review*, 11.1–2 (2000), 61–70.
13 Joan Acocella's *New Yorker* review, for instance, also characterizes Roy as a magical realist writer, and compares her to Rushdie and Gabriel García Márquez, who use magical realism so as to not "induce tedium" when "reporting on political horror." There is the implication here that political content needs to be tamed in some manner, to soften its impact on the reader. See Acocella, "Arundhati Roy Returns to Fiction, in Fury," *New Yorker* (May 29, 2017), https://www.newyorker.com/magazine/2017/06/05/arundhati-roy-returns-to-fiction-in-fury.

Notes

14 Mariano Siskind, "Magical Realism," *The Cambridge History of Postcolonial Literature*, vol. II, ed. Ato Quayson (Cambridge: Cambridge University Press, 2011–2012), 834–835. Siskind argues that "The explicit coupling of magical realism and postcolonial discourse is a rather recent development" and that postcolonial theorists like Homi Bhabha and Gayatri Spivak have contributed to the characterization of magical realism as a unique postcolonial mode. For instance, Bhabha referred to it as "the literary language of the emergent postcolonial world" (833), and Spivak spoke of how "'magical realism', a style of Latin American provenance, has been used to great effect by some expatriate or diasporic subcontinentals writing in English." Siskind adds that "Both Bhabha and Spivak hinted towards this transition, this travel of magical realism, from Latin America in the 1960s to the postcolonial world at large since the end of the 1970s; from a restricted Latin American specificity, to a more universal form of particularism: magical realism as a postcolonial universal" (834).
15 For the cultural logic of literary prizes, see James English, *The Economy of Prestige: Prizes, Awards, and the Circulation of Cultural Value* (Cambridge, MA: Harvard University Press, 2005). Building on Bourdieu's work, English remarks that since the 1970s there has been a "feverish proliferation" (2) of literary awards—a "prize frenzy" whose "ritualized theater of gestures and countergestures" (5) have exposed the prize as a form of cultural capital and led to reinforcing a "mystical, essentially religious attitude toward culture" (7) and cultural icons.
16 See Viet Thanh Nguyen, "Delightful Listening: A Conversation Between Viet Thanh Nguyen with Arundhati Roy," *Los Angeles Review of Books* (Jul. 31, 2018), https://lareviewofbooks.org/article/delightful-listening-a-conversation-between-viet-thanh-nguyen-with-arundhati-roy/.
17 Rachel Greenwald Smith, "The Contemporary Novel and Postdemocratic Form," *Novel: A Forum on Fiction* 51.2 (2018), 298. Greenwald Smith frames this suspicion as part of what she calls "compromise aesthetics," which "envision[s] the artist as having the freedom of the entrepreneur" (293). For an extended version of this argument, see Rachel Greenwald Smith, *On Compromise: Art, Politics, and the Fate of an American Ideal* (Graywolf Press, 2021).
18 Sujatha Fernandes, *Curated Stories: The Uses and Misuses of Storytelling* (New York: Oxford University Press, 2017), 3.
19 Ibid., 5, 6.
20 Joseph Slaughter, "Hijacking Human Rights: Neoliberalism, the New Historiography, and the End of the Third World," *Human Rights Quarterly* 40.4 (2018), 768. Slaughter's use of this phrase draws on Upendra Baxi, *The Future of Human Rights* (New Delhi: Oxford University Press, 2002).
21 Slaughter, "Hijacking Human Rights," 768.
22 The audience of the Indian *Reader's Digest* consists of the middle- and upper middle-class English-speaking sections of society. Articles focus on topics such as food, mind, home, family, parenting, pets, gardening, and money. See https://www.readersdigest.in/.
23 Louis Althusser, "Ideology and Ideological State Apparatuses (Notes Towards an Investigation)," *In Lenin and Philosophy and Other Essays*, trans. Ben Brewster (New York/London: Monthly Review Press, 1971), 142–147, 166–176.
24 Cathy Caruth *Trauma: Explorations in Memory* (Baltimore: Johns Hopkins University Press, 1995), 9.

Notes

25 Slaughter, "Hijacking Human Rights," 768.
26 Jodi Dean, "Complexity as Capture—Neoliberalism and the Loop of Drive," *New Formations* 80–81 (2013), 144.
27 E. Dawson Varughese, *Reading New India: Post-Millennial Indian Fiction in English* (London: Bloomsbury, 2013), 17.
28 Claire Westall, "Cricket's Neoliberal Narratives: Or the World of Competitive Accumulation and Sporting Spirit in Contemporary Cricket Fiction," *World Literature, Neoliberalism, and the Culture of Discontent*, ed. Sharae Deckard and Stephen Shapiro (Cham: Palgrave Macmillan, 2019), 112.
29 Ibid., 113.
30 Reviews like Marcel Theroux's in the *New York Times* and Ron Charles's in the *Washington Post* make a case for why references to cricket in the novel would not detract from the US reader's pleasure. As Charles points out, the novel itself anticipates and addresses itself to the American reader in its ironic and self-reflexive Glossary of Cricketing Terms, where "Boring" is defined as, "What outsiders, especially Americans, find cricket" (Adiga, *Selection Day*, 288); Marcel Theroux, "Aravind Adiga's Novel Is about the Game of Cricket—and Sexual Awakening," *New York Times* (Jan. 27, 2017), https://www.nytimes.com/2017/01/27/books/review/selection-day-aravind-adiga.html; Ron Charles, "'Selection Day': Two Brothers and an Obsessed Dad Seek a Ticket out of Poverty," *Washington Post* (Dec. 30, 2016), https://www.washingtonpost.com/entertainment/books/selection-day-two-brothers-and-an-obsessed-dad-seek-a-ticket-out-of-poverty/2016/12/30/7e301824-cc79-11e6-a87f-b917067331bb_story.html.
31 "Netflix Announces Original Series *Selection Day*," *Netflix Media Center* (Oct. 8, 2018), https://about.netflix.com/en/news/netflix-announces-original-series-selection-day.
32 Sam Sacks, "A Novel about Cricket That Will Resonate with Americans," *Wall Street Journal* (Jan. 6, 2017), https://www.wsj.com/articles/a-novel-about-cricket-that-will-resonate-with-americans-1483734969.
33 Theroux, "Aravind Adiga's Novel Is about the Game of Cricket."
34 For instance, Adiga was interviewed and his 2011 novel *Last Man in Tower* featured in US National Public Radio series *BRICSion: Powerful Stories, Powerful Nations* on literature from the BRICS (Brazil, Russia, India, China, South Africa) nations. The host introduced the interview by saying, "We hear so much about the economic strategies driving growth in these countries, we thought it would be interesting to hear what fiction writers had to say." "Author Asks if Mumbai Money Can Flatten Tradition," *North Country Public Radio* (Aug. 15, 2012), https://www.northcountrypublicradio.org/news/npr/158870034/author-asks-if-mumbai-money-can-flatten-tradition.
35 Erin Hatton, *Coerced: Work under Threat of Punishment* (Oakland: University of California Press, 2020), 8.
36 For more on cricket and corruption, see James Astill, *The Great Tamasha: Cricket, Corruption, and the Spectacular Rise of Modern India* (New York: Bloomsbury, 2013). For a longer view of Indian cricket, see Ramachandra Guha, *A Corner of a Foreign Field: The Indian History of a British Sport* (London: Picador, 2003).
37 See, for instance, Kamila Shamsie, "*Selection Day* by Aravind Adiga—A Compelling Tale of Cricket and Corruption," *Guardian* (Sept. 10, 2016), https://www.theguardian.com/books/2016/sep/10/selection-day-by-aravind-adiga-review;

Annalisa Quinn, "Cricket and Difficult Choices in 'Selection Day,'" *National Public Radio* (Jan. 8, 2017), https://www.npr.org/2017/01/08/507162506/cricket-and-difficult-choices-in-selection-day.

38 Popular Hindi films of the last two decades have highlighted growing pressure on the young to succeed in an increasingly regimented and demanding educational system. For instance, in *Taare Zameen Par* (dir. Aamir Khan and Amole Gupte, 2007), the father is one of the chief culprits—resistant to seeing his son's learning disability for what it is, and instead demanding conformity to a neoliberal ethic of winning at all costs. A later film, *Dangal* (dir. Nitesh Tiwari, 2017), also highlights paternal discipline: a father and former wrestler lives vicariously through the successes of his daughters, whom he trains to become professional wrestlers. In this case, paternal discipline—though acknowledged as potentially restrictive of the children's freedom—is ultimately celebrated for its broad-mindedness, its ability to look past rigid gender norms, and its commitment to the uplift of girl children. Together, these films exemplify anxieties surrounding parental (especially paternal) discipline as well as pressures placed on the young in neoliberal India.

39 Brown, *Undoing the Demos*, 177.

40 Gary Becker, "The Age of Human Capital," *Education in the Twenty-First Century*, ed. Edward P. Lazear (Palo Alto: Hoover Institution Press, 2002).

41 A number of popular Indian films, for instance the landmark post-independence feature *Mother India* (dir. Mehboob Khan, 1957), deploy the trope of the usurious moneylender.

42 For more on this notion of the self as an art project and something to be worked on, see Sarah Brouillette's description and critique of the work of management gurus like Richard Florida: *Literature and the Creative Economy* (Stanford: Stanford University Press, 2014).

43 Corey Robin, "Nietzsche's Marginal Children: On Friedrich Hayek," *The Nation* (May 7, 2013), https://www.thenation.com/article/archive/nietzsches-marginal-children-friedrich-hayek/.

44 In conversation with social reproduction theory, Wendy Brown notes that a traditionally gendered division of labor within the family is crucial for enabling societies to survive the effects of neoliberal austerity. However, the discourse of neoliberalism disavows its indebtedness to patriarchal structures and also its construction of the so-called "generic individual" as "socially male and masculinist" (*Undoing the Demos*, 107).

45 Brown, *Undoing the Demos*, 111.

46 "Netflix Announces Original Series Selection Day," Netflix.com (Oct. 9, 2018), https://about.netflix.com/en/news/netflix-announces-original-series-selection-day.

47 See "Netflix Announces Selection Day Season 2. Sachin Tendulkar Eager to Know What Happens Next," *India Today* (Jan. 18, 2019), https://www.indiatoday.in/television/web-series/story/netflix-announces-selection-day-season-2-sachin-tendulkar-excited-1434056-2019-01-18.

48 See "The Cast of Selection Day Meets Sachin Tendulkar and Brian Lara," *Netflix India* (Apr. 18, 2019), https://www.youtube.com/watch?v=C2yGU45liGY.

49 Alexander Manshel, Laura B. McGrath, and J.D. Porter, "The Rise of Must-Read TV," *The Atlantic* (Jul. 16, 2021), https://www.theatlantic.com/culture/archive/2021/07/tv-adaptations-fiction/619442/.

Notes

50 Jason Boog, "The Netflix Literary Connection," *Publishers Weekly* (Apr. 12, 2019), https://www.publishersweekly.com/pw/by-topic/industry-news/page-to-screen/article/79793-the-netflix-literary-connection.html.
51 Ibid.
52 Suresh Mathew, "Erik Barmack on 'Sacred Games' and Netflix's Game Plan for India," *The Quint* (Jun. 29, 2018), https://www.thequint.com/entertainment/hot-on-web/sacred-games-netflix-india-erik-barmack-lust-stories-saif-ali-khan-nawazuddin-siddiqui#read-more.
53 Priyanka Agarwal, "Meet Sidharth Jain, on the Lookout for the Right Stories for India's Binge-Watching Audience," *India Times* (Jan. 21, 2020), https://www.indiatimes.com/news/india/sidharth-jain-bridging-the-gap-between-authors-and-filmmakers-504660.html.
54 Rohini Mohan, "Indian Novels Get Fresh Lease of Life as They Get Adapted into Movies, Web Series," *The Straits Times* (Oct. 27, 2019), https://www.straitstimes.com/lifestyle/entertainment/from-page-to-screen.

Index

Adiga, Aravind 13, 17, 73, 89
   Selection Day (novel) 17, 133–5, 143–55
   Selection Day (series) 17, 135, 152–6
Ahmad, Aijaz 3
Alsultany, Evelyn 78
alterity industry 13, 72, 73
Ambani, Dhirubhai 61–2, 68, 75, 85, 169n67
Anjaria, Jonathan Shapiro 75
Anjaria, Ulka 75
Arendt, Hannah 36
Armstrong, Nancy 7
austerity 2, 11, 54, 55
Aw, Tash 134

Balzac, Honoré de 134
Banerjee, Chinmoy 100
Basu, Manisha 69, 73, 86
Becker, Gary 26–8, 143, 146, 151
Bell, David 122
Bhagat, Chetan 13, 68, 69, 70
   The 3 Mistakes of My Life 14, 17, 67, 68, 70–1, 74–9, 81, 86–7, 143
   Kai Po Che! 70, 83–6, 87
Bildungsroman(e) 13–14, 68–9, 72, 73, 98, 103, 152
Bollywood 13, 68, 69, 70, 83, 102
   see also Hindi cinema
Bombay 59–60, 102, 105, 108, 149, 151
   Textile Strike 51, 167–8n32
   see also Mumbai
Bond, Patrick 123

Boo, Katherine 14, 90, 102
Booker Prize 16, 17, 72, 73, 134, 137, 144
Bourdieu, Pierre 5, 21, 39–40
Boyagoda, Randy 134
Boyle, Danny 73, 89, 102, 103, 106, 176n40, 177n41
   see also Slumdog Millionaire
Brazil 6, 34, 91, 93, 94, 96, 110
   see also City of God (film)
Britain
   colonialism 12, 41, 50, 51, 60, 72, 110, 122, 124–5, 127
   neoliberalism 1, 8, 12, 23, 52, 103
Brouillette, Sarah 6, 70, 187n42
Brown, Wendy 2, 6, 8–9, 36, 71, 133
   Undoing the Demos 20–32, 143, 145–6, 150, 152

capitalism
   class dynamics 6, 7, 8, 9, 20, 22, 27, 28, 29, 30
   free market perspective 14, 17, 39, 40, 43, 44–5, 49, 50–1, 54, 58, 62, 65, 103, 153
   Indian fiction's ways of imagining 14, 17, 71, 77, 79, 107, 153
   neoliberal era 2, 8, 15, 17, 31, 36, 37, 64, 69, 91, 123, 136, 152, 153, 154, 156
   see also developmentalism; Keynesianism
Caruth, Cathy 142

Index

Casanova, Pascale 4
caste 61, 62, 64, 71, 114, 127, 135, 140, 141
Cavallero, Jonathan 106
Chakravarti, Paroma 78
Chandra, Nandini 104
Chandra, Vikram 90, 155
Chandrashekhar, C.P. 34, 113
Chicago School of Economics 19, 20, 26, 33, 40, 52
China
  Communist era 45, 46
  neoliberal era 20, 25, 80, 81, 110
Chitester, Robert 43
City of God (film) 14–15, 90, 91, 94–7, 103, 105, 107
  see also Lins, Paulo, *City of God* (novel)
coercion
  economics and labor 22, 28, 30, 31
  patriarchy 153
Comaroff, Jean and John 22
Conrad, Joseph 127
core–periphery dynamics 4, 5
creative destruction 59, 60, 63, 64, 150
crick(et) lit 17, 74, 79, 134, 143

Das, Gurcharan 12, 40–2, 57, 68, 76
  India Grows at Night 62–4
  India Unbound 57–62, 64–5
Davis, Mike 91, 174–5n8, 176n39
Dawes, James 98
Dawson, Ashley 119
Dean, Jodi 29, 143
Deckard, Sharae 6
Delhi 13, 62, 63, 98, 118, 130, 133, 135, 138, 139–40, 141
developmentalism 10, 11, 57–8, 76
  state 9, 12, 41, 47, 58, 60, 62, 63
Dharavi 99, 100–1, 103, 108
Dickens, Charles 103, 134
Dreiser, Theodore 134
Dreze, Jean 10, 47
dystopia 12, 40, 46, 49

East Asia 9, 20, 21, 23–6
Egan, Jennifer 134
Ellis, Bret Easton 134
emergence
  India's 12, 16, 25, 54, 62, 144
  national 16, 17, 35, 109, 134

enterprise culture 10, 14, 35, 69, 75, 76, 84, 85
entrepreneurialism 31, 32, 35, 62, 75, 79, 86, 128, 142, 153
  subjectivity 17, 71, 111, 118, 142
environmentalism of the poor 16, 131

Fernandes, Sujatha 16, 138–9
Foucault, Michel 8, 20, 22, 23, 26–7, 29, 143
Franzen, Jonathan 134
free market *see* capitalism, free market perspective
Frenkel, Ronit 73
Friedman, Milton 19, 42–3, 62, 75
  Free to Choose 11–12, 40–2, 43–55, 59–61, 65
Friedman, Rose 11, 43
Fugard, Athol 90

Galbraith, John Kenneth 41, 43, 57–9
Gandhi (Mohandas) 55
Ghosh, Amitav 13, 14, 67, 69, 109, 113, 130
  The Hungry Tide 15–16, 109–22, 124–5, 127–8, 130–1
Ghosh, Jayati 34, 113
Gilbert, Jeremy 7
Gilded Age 134–5, 184n8
Gill, Stephen 22
global North *see* North, global
global South *see* South, global
Gonzaga, Elmo 92
Gooptu, Nandini 35
  see also enterprise culture
Gopal, Priyamvada 72
Gopal, Sangita 14, 70–1
Guha, Ramachandra 120, 129, 131
Gujarat 14, 56, 68, 75, 77, 79, 80, 82, 86, 100, 135, 136, 142
Gupta, Dipankar 119
Gupta, Suman 71

Hall, Stuart 22
Hamid, Mohsin 134
hard power 2, 21–2, 26, 29–32
  see also soft power
Harvey, David 6, 9, 22, 25, 28
Hayek, Friedrich 19, 28, 33, 42, 43, 57, 59, 63, 82, 147

190

Hindi cinema 13, 14, 70–1, 153
  see also Bollywood
Hindu right 12, 16, 64, 65
Hindutva 64, 65, 77, 86
  see also nationalism, Hindu
Hofmeyr, Isabel 109
homo oeconomicus 19, 20, 21, 26, 27
Hong Kong 20, 45–6, 48, 52, 59, 61
Huggan, Graham 13
  see also alterity industry
human capital 26–8, 71, 143–6, 151
Hutton, Erin 30

Indian English 13, 72, 73
  fiction 5–6, 13–14, 16, 68, 70, 72–4, 89, 113, 155, 172n31
Indian Institute of Technology (IIT) 69
Indian Premier League (IPL) 144
individualism 7–8, 9, 11, 22, 31–2, 33, 71
International Monetary Fund 7, 23, 40
internationalism 3, 17

Jagoda, Patrick 110, 117, 178n5
Jameson, Fredric 3–4, 6
Johansen, Emily 134
Joshi, Parinda 13, 70, 79–80, 86
  Made in China (film) 70, 83–5, 87
  Made in China (novel) 13–14, 67–8, 71, 79–82, 87
Joshi, Priya 72, 73–4, 113

Kakutani, Michiko 136–8
Kantor, Roanne 73
Karim, Lamia 32
Karl, Alissa 134
Kashmir 16, 135, 136, 137, 139, 140, 184n10
Kaur, Ravinder 34, 35
Keynesianism 10, 11, 19, 20

Lal, Deepak 57, 58
Lau, Lisa 89–90
Lazarus, Neil 119
Li, Victor 122
liberalization (economic) 9, 10, 14, 34, 39, 40, 41, 42, 54, 55, 56, 62, 63, 64, 65, 105, 113, 123, 148
License Raj 12, 41, 54, 58, 59, 60, 61

Lins, Paulo 92–3
  City of God (novel) 14–15, 89, 90, 91–4, 99, 103
  see also *City of God* (film)
Lund, Katia 14, 91, 94, 97
  see also *City of God* (film); Lins, Paulo; Meirelles, Fernando

McClanahan, Annie 21, 27
McClennen, Sophia 96
McGurl, Mark 13
Mamdani, Mahmood 78
Marx, Karl 57, 58, 59
Mda, Zakes 109, 122, 127, 131
  Heart of Redness 15–16, 109–13, 122–9, 131
Mee, Jon 72
Meirelles, Fernando 14, 91, 94, 97
  see also *City of God* (film); Lins, Paulo; Lund, Katia
Mendes, Ana Christina 89–90
Michaels, Walter Benn 134, 158–9n24
Mishra, Pankaj 1, 22, 36–7, 133, 134
Modi, Narendra 16, 17, 35, 42, 64–5, 86, 136
Moretti, Franco 4–5
Mulhern, Francis 69
Mumbai 13, 14, 15, 89, 90–2, 98, 99–105, 108, 147–50, 152, 153
  see also Bombay

nationalism 14, 17, 33, 77, 84
  cultural 11, 22, 35, 36, 42, 72, 86
  Hindu 2, 14, 35, 64, 84, 87, 136
  see also Hindutva
Nehru, Jawaharlal 58, 59, 61
neoliberal novel 134–5, 158–9n24
neoliberalism
  Foucauldian approaches 6, 8, 20, 22, 36, 158n21
  Marxist approaches 6, 8, 20, 22, 23, 158n20
  role of state 20, 22, 25, 29, 33
  subjectivity 7, 24, 27–8, 32, 152
  see also Brown, Wendy; capitalism, neoliberal era; Ong, Aihwa
Netflix 6, 17, 135, 144, 152, 154–5
network theory 116
  narrative form 15–16, 110, 114, 136

191

Index

New India 34, 57, 138
New York 44–6, 59, 102, 125, 147
Niblett, Michael 93
Nietzsche, Friedrich 36, 144, 147–8
Nixon, Rob 97, 121–2, 131
Norris, Frank 134
North, global 1, 4, 5, 8, 9, 20, 22, 31, 34
North–South divide 2, 5, 6, 9, 11, 15, 17, 21, 31, 32, 41

O'Neill, Joseph 143
Ong, Aihwa 6, 20, 21, 22
   Neoliberalism as Exception 8–9, 20–6, 32

Patnaik, Prabhat 50, 65
Patnaik, Utsa 50
Peck, Jamie 6, 9, 29, 33, 42
Peixoto, Marta 92, 97
periphery 4
   aesthetics of peripherality 5
   semi-periphery 5, 111
   (semi-)peripheral literature 5, 6, 111
   see also core–periphery dynamics
Philippines 24
picaresque, the 97–8, 102
Plehwe, Dieter 19
postcolonial studies 1, 8, 17, 90
Prashad, Vijay 33, 54
precarity 10, 18, 30, 36, 70, 101, 142
privatization (economic) 2, 11, 19, 21, 31, 33, 35, 40, 41, 42, 55, 57, 64, 110, 123

rationality (Foucauldian) 6, 8, 20, 23, 25, 36
Rawls, John 41, 57–8
Reader's Digest 43, 140
redistribution
   coercive 31
   popular and progressive 11, 41, 42, 114
   upward 10
Rio de Janeiro 91, 92, 94
Robin, Corey 147
Rose, Nicholas 22, 23
Roy, Ananya 31, 103
Roy, Arundhati 13, 16, 67, 73, 137
   The Ministry of Utmost Happiness 133–43
Rushdie, Salman 13, 14, 72, 137–8

Sadana, Rashmi 72, 73
Schumpeter, Joseph 57, 59, 60, 150
   see also creative destruction
self-help 31, 35, 67, 69, 79, 85
semi-periphery *see* periphery
Sen, Amartya 10, 47, 57
Seth, Vikram 13, 67, 69, 73
Shahani, Roshan 113
Shapiro, Stephen 6
Shinghavi, Snehal 100
Singapore 20, 24, 74, 75
Singh, Amardeep 73
Singh, Manmohan 9, 12, 35, 40, 41, 54–6, 64, 68
Sinha, Indra 89
Slaughter, Joseph 14, 68, 139
slum 90, 91, 92, 97, 99–108, 148, 150, 151
   see also City of God; undercity
Slumdog Millionaire 14–15, 64, 73, 89, 91, 92, 102–8
   see also Boyle, Danny
Smith, Adam 45, 65
Smith, Rachel Greenwald 137
soft power 2, 21–2, 26, 29–31, 34, 37, 150–1
   see also hard power
South Africa 6, 73, 111, 128
   Eastern Cape 16, 111, 122
   post-apartheid era 16, 34, 109–10, 112, 113, 122–4, 181–2n38
   Truth and Reconciliation Commission (TRC) 122, 181n36
   Xhosa Cattle killing 122, 127
South, global 1–2, 7, 17, 30, 31, 33, 37, 131, 155
   literature and culture from 3, 8, 15, 73, 90, 92, 109, 133
Sundarbans 15, 113, 114, 115, 118, 119, 122, 125, 130, 178n7, 182n44
Swarup, Vikas 89
   Q&A 14, 89–90, 97–103

Tata industries 56, 61
Tendulkar, Sachin 150, 152
Third World 15, 33, 34, 54, 103
   literature 3, 4, 6
   urbanization 91, 103, 105
Tripathi, Amish 69, 73, 171n18, 173n64, 174n65

Trotsky, Leon 111
Trump, Donald 7, 17

undercity 14, 15, 16, 90–1, 107, 108, 109
uneven development 5–6, 91, 97, 111–12, 121, 122, 124
United States (US)
  imperialism 17, 23
  inequality 10–11, 28
  migration to/from 79, 80, 111, 112, 122, 128, 130
  neoliberalization 6, 10, 22, 23, 29, 30, 39–40, 107, 137, 144
  see also Brown, Wendy, *Undoing the Demos*; Friedman, Milton, *Free to Choose*
utopia 12, 46, 49, 63, 76, 122, 149
  see also dystopia

Warwick Research Collective (WReC) 5–6, 111
Watkins, Evan 107
welfare (social) 12, 19, 30, 41, 52–4
welfare state 32, 33, 42, 52, 57, 61
Westall, Claire 143
Williams, Jeffrey 134–5
Williams, Michelle 109
World Bank 7, 9, 32, 33, 34, 108
world literature 4, 17, 111, 154, 156
World Trade Organization 7

Zola, Émile 134